Neither Here Nor There

Migration: Irish and Scots in Dumbarton and the Vale of Leven
1855 to 1900

C G Docherty

Published by Levenford

First printing: 2024

A CIP catalogue for this title is available from the British Library.

ISBN: 978-1-908898-60-9

In memory of my family and those others who lived and worked
in Dumbarton and the Vale of Leven

Foreword

The origins of this book lie in an undergraduate project completed nearly fifty years ago. It was an interesting time to examine the burgh of Dumbarton, as the new town centre and dual carriageway that ran from Glasgow Road to the Artizan Bridge, had obliterated the burgh's medieval street pattern. No buildings from that period had survived prior to the redevelopment, most were nineteenth or early twentieth century creations, but the plots and streets that had been laid down centuries ago were radically altered or swept away completely. In their place was a hollowed out town centre which at no time provided an adequate replacement for what was lost.

The Vale of Leven's settlements were younger, but they too were experiencing radical redevelopment. Alexandria was subjected to a similar fate as Dumbarton. Buildings were demolished to make way for new shops and houses in the town centre. It too, got an intrusive road running through its heart, leaving Alexandria's railway station effectively marooned in the middle of a large roundabout. Jamestown's terraced rows were demolished and replaced, through time, first by council, and then private housing. Bonhill also saw fundamental change with significant demolition around its core, including the removal of a distinctive row of shops and houses that had long faced the river. The biggest upheaval however, was the large scale expansion of council housing at Nobleston/Ladyton/O'Hare above Bonhill, with a new road running parallel to the old Bonhill Main Street. Renton had been experiencing a series of widespread clearances from the 1950s onwards. The area around Back Street, and large swathes of Main Street were cleared as houses, shops, pubs and people disappeared. New houses were built but, as in Dumbarton, local shopkeepers could ill afford to rent expensive, new premises (see valeofleven.org.uk).

The changes which were altering the character of the Vale and Dumbarton provided a stimulus for this book, as did my family who had been arriving in this area since the 1850s.

iii

I discovered that both my Irish great grandfathers lived in Dumbarton and worked in the shipyards, one was a hammerman, the other worked on a rivet squad. One of my grandfathers worked in Dennystown Forge and the other, aged eighteen, left his home in Renton to go to France in 1915 with the Argyll and Sutherland Highlanders. Severely wounded, he was discharged in 1917 and worked for a short time in Babcock and Wilcox before his early death at the age of thirty six. My grandmother, like so many other widows at this time, had to find work to support the family, and found employment in the British Silk Dying Company (known locally as the 'BSD' or the 'Silk Factory'). She worked there for many years as did my father who served his apprenticeship as a maintenance fitter. Two of his aunts, who lived in Westbridgend with their parents in the early twentieth century, were printworkers in the Vale of Leven. My mother worked in the accounts departments of Dumbarton Co-op and thereafter, Ballantine's Distillery.

The story of Irish immigration and Scots' migration from the Highlands and the parishes of the Central Lowlands to growing towns and cities is still being told. This book looks beyond a broad narrative. Objective census data, and other sources, have been used to shed some light on the history of the Leven Valley, and especially, its people.

Where had they come from?

Where did they live?

How did they make a living?

What living and working conditions did they experience?

Moreover, the focus in this book has not been confined entirely to the Vale of Leven and Dumbarton, comparisons have been made with reference to Scotland as a whole.

Finally, it is important to acknowledge and convey an appreciation of the remarkable mobility and resilience shown by those who moved to, from and within the Vale of Leven and Dumbarton in search of a better life.

List of graphs, maps and photographs

Neither Here nor There. Migration: Irish and Scots in Dumbarton and the Vale of Leven 1855-1900

Introduction, Context and Sources

The settlements of the Vale of Leven and the Burgh of Dumbarton are only a few miles apart, but their evolution was very different. The Vale's planned, or partly planned, villages were eighteenth century creations built to house those who had come to labour in the bleach, print and dye works. This was during the first wave of Scottish industrialisation, which was principally associated with textile manufacturing and processing. Dumbarton, a Royal Burgh since 1222, industrialised rapidly over the second half of the nineteenth century. Its prosperity lay in shipbuilding and heavy engineering during the later, and more durable, wave of industrialisation which transformed West Central Scotland.

Here, the migration of both Scots and Irish to the Vale and Dumbarton are examined alongside the growth of population, industry and townscapes. Consideration of employment, social status, health and housing help to distinguish the area within the context of Scotland in general and West Central Scotland in particular.

A Note on Sources

The principal sources employed in the writing of this book are the unpublished *census enumerators' books*[1] for Dumbarton and the Vale of Leven at the 1861, 1871, 1881 and 1891 censuses. These records are the 'raw materials' which are used to compile aggregated census data for the whole country.

Since 1801 the UK government has conducted a decennial census of population, (with the exception of 1941). The global covid pandemic delayed the planned 2021 Scottish Census by a year. Every 'head of household' is obliged to complete a census return, either online, by post or by return to the local enumerator.

In the nineteenth century, the job of enumerator, who was responsible for around 200 households per enumeration district, was to ensure that each household in the district was visited and that data was collected from each. In an era where transience was common, literacy levels were variable and even households themselves could be difficult to define, the job of the enumerator was rarely straightforward. The census data for each address revealed information on the name, sex, age, occupation, place of birth and relation to the head of household, of each inhabitant. The number of windowed rooms available to each 'family' (or more correctly, co-residing group) was also recorded. The aggregate data was collated and used by the government for planning purposes.

The sample upon which this book is based, consists of data from 3,800 households: 400 from Dumbarton and 400 from Vale of Leven in 1861 and 500 for each area for the years 1871, 1881 and 1891.[2]   This yields data on over 17,000 individuals. The sample was taken proportionately from each of the urban or 'townward' enumeration districts in Dumbarton and the Vale of Leven. All enumeration districts in the burgh of Dumbarton and the villages of the Vale of Leven were examined and a random sample based on the relative size of each district was taken.[3]

In effect, the data collection is akin to a large survey of the households of Dumbarton and the Vale of Leven at four consecutive census years in the second half of the nineteenth century. As it is a sample of the population, caution must be expressed over the interpretation of very small numbers, but the overall impression provided by large volumes of data gathered over four census points can be traced with a high degree of confidence.[4] Aggregate data is also lifted from the printed census reports and is used alongside the sample data. Indeed information from the printed census records largely confirm the veracity of the sample data.[5]

Nomenclature

As Dumbarton is situated on the Leven where it meets the Clyde, it could be regarded as part of the Vale of Leven, i.e. the Leven Valley. Here, to avoid ambiguity, the term 'the Vale of Leven' or 'the Vale' will be used only to refer to those settlements in the valley centred on

Alexandria and including Jamestown, Bonhill and Renton. Balloch, where Loch Lomond empties into the River Leven, is always referred to separately and was not included in the sampling of *cebs* data .

'Printworks' and 'printworkers' are the most commonly used terms for the bleach, print and dye works and those who worked in them.

'Immigration' and 'emigration', refer to the movement of people into or out of a country respectively. 'In-migration' and 'out-migration' refer to movements within a country.

Those born in Bonhill, Cardross and Dumbarton parishes are referred to as being 'local' or 'locally' born. 'Neighbouring Scots' or 'nearby' Scots' refer to those born in the rest of Dunbartonshire and its contiguous counties i.e Argyll, Stirling, Lanark (including Glasgow) and Renfrew, along with Ayr, which is part of the West Central Scotland 'region'. Scots from counties beyond this made up a small proportion of the residents and are referred to collectively as 'other Scots'.

Where the words 'under-represented' or 'over-represented' appear in parenthesis, this refers specifically to a statistical comparison of one group compared to the whole. For example, 'Irish males are "over-represented" among general labourers' means that compared to the total male working population, there are comparatively more Irish in this category than average.

The terms 'The Great Irish Famine', 'The Great Hunger' and 'An Gorta Mor', are all used in the book, but most often this catastrophe is referred to as 'the Famine'. This is for convenience only.

NOTES

[1] Hereafter *ceb or cebs* when appearing in footnotes.

[2] Because the populations of Dumbarton and the Vale of Leven were relatively small in 1861, the statistical accuracy of the sample was not significantly affected by drawing 400 rather than 500 household samples from either location in this instance.

[3] Only 'townward', or urban areas, were considered. 'Landward', or rural, districts were excluded. Where an enumeration district at the edge of a settlement contained both 'townward and 'landward' areas, only the 'townward' sections were sampled.

[4] The data was gathered for a PhD Thesis, C. Docherty, *Migration, ethnicity, occupation and residence in contrasting West of Scotland settlements: the case of the Vale of Leven and Dumbarton: 1861 -1891*, University of Glasgow. (1988). Hereafter referred to in footnotes as '*Thesis,*'.

Chapter 5 of the *Thesis* deals with 'the problems of sampling'. The figures quoted in this book are from the sample estimates unless otherwise noted. In this book figures from the sample are generally rounded to the nearest 0.5% for ease of comparison. Very small numbers or fine distinctions are treated with caution and are qualified.

[5] For example, the Irish population is recorded as being 15.2% of the total for the burgh in 1891 whereas the sample estimate is 15.1%; the percentage of males and females in the population are 51.1% and 48.9% respectively, whereas the sample yielded 50.8% and 49.2%; and, 38% of the population were under 15 years of age, but the sample recorded 37.5% in that category. Sample estimates will not always be as close to the 'real' figures as these, but no extravagant claims are made on their basis.

1 Urban beginnings: from Alt Clut to the New Statistical Account

Dumbarton

'If there is one fortified place where we can be certain both of its identification on the ground and of its military role it is Alt Clut... in modern times Castle Rock, Dumbarton.'[1]

Dumbarton Rock, at the confluence of Rivers Leven and Clyde was an important focal point for settlement in the Leven Valley after the end of the Roman era. There was a kingdom 'founded on Dumbarton Rock (Alt Clut) on the Clyde' which complemented the kingdom of Gododdin centred on Edinburgh. 'Beyond these fixed points there were other kingdoms... which are now lost'.[2] Alt Clut was 'the political centre of the northern Britons in the west'.[3] Several seventh century British Kings are explicitly identified as kings of 'Al Cluith' in Irish annalistic sources, and excavation at the Rock has produced artefacts of imports from both Mediterranean and Continental Europe. The demise of Alt Clut can be dated precisely to 870 AD when it was sacked by a large force of Dublin vikings who had laid siege to the Rock for four months before taking it.[4]

Archaeological and recorded Roman sources show that there were people living in the Leven Valley before this. An Iron Age fort has been located on Carman Hill and its 'overall character... suggests that it was a major settlement of the Damnonii' - one of four large British tribal groups that lived in an area centred between the two Roman walls - Hadrian's Wall in the south, begun in 122 AD, and Antonine's Wall in the north, built twenty years later, which has its western terminus on the Clyde at Old Kilpatrick. It has been suggested that Carman Fort 'may have been [the Damnonii's] chief centre of power in Pre-Roman times, eventually being eclipsed by Dumbarton in the late Roman period or shortly after'.[5] In the first century AD, 'Roman survey work' had identified Dumnonii (Damnonii) people living in this area, and in the second century AD, the writer Cassius Dio identified the Maiatai as living near 'the cross wall that cuts the island in half' (i.e. The Antonine Wall). It is possible that the Maiatai were a part of the tribal group that dominated the old 'Kingdom' of Damnonia 'as the second century came to a close'.[6]

Given the Romans' acute appreciation of strategic location and terrain, and the nearby Antonine Wall with its forts and camps, it is surprising that neither Carman Hill nor Dumbarton Rock have yielded any evidence of Roman occupation. Nevertheless while 'absence of evidence…is not evidence of absence' there is no trace of Roman settlement or use of these sites.[7]

By the fifth century, Dumbarton Rock, Alt Clut, had become an important fortress. James Fraser cites St Patrick who wrote an:

enraged letter to the warriors of Coroticos, apparently based at the stronghold at Clyde (now Dumbarton) Rock on the lower Clyde, (it) shows them to have been Christians with Irish links and, to Patrick's mind, his fellow citizens. The important 'citadel fort' atop Clyde Rock (Alt Clut) seems to have been established towards the end of the Roman Iron Age, and was probably not very old when Coroticos held it.[8]

Fraser suggests it is reasonable to suppose that in the late sixth and seventh centuries, the kingdom containing Alt Clut was the 'lineal successor' of a Roman Iron Age district, but that the 'Kingdom of Strathclyde' was a later entity centred on 'Clydesdale'.[9]

Tim Clarkson believes that 'many historians refer to the kingdom ruled from Dumbarton as Strathclyde' but this name more correctly belongs to 'the successor kingdom' which rose from the wreckage of Alt Clut and was centred near 'Govan where the Clyde could be crossed at low tide'. Its kings were no longer rulers of Alt Clut, the Rock of the Clyde, but Strath Clut, the strath or lower valley of the Clyde.[10] Simon Taylor, who has examined place name evidence in West Dunbartonshire, posits the following:

One casualty of the fall of the fortress of Al Clud (Dumbarton) was Arthgal king of the Britons…in 872 he was killed, presumably by the Dublin Norse… In the note on Arthgal's murder, which appears in one of the main sources for this period, the 'Annals of Ulster,' an important name change can be observed. He is referred to not as king of (the Britons of) Al Clud, but, for the first time, king of the Britons of Strathclyde (rex Britanorum Sratha Cluade). After this, the name Strathclyde completely ousts Al Clud (Dumbarton) as the name of the kingdom. This almost certainly reflects a shift in the centre of power within the north British kingdom southwards to the valley of the Clyde, centred around Cadzow (Hamilton) and Lanark.[11]

What all three authors agree on is that after the sacking of Alt Clut in 870 AD, it was no longer the centre of a British kingdom. The 'capital' of the Kingdom of Strathclyde was further up the Clyde valley, to the south east of Dumbarton and further away from the increasing incursions of Scots from the north and west.

By the eleventh century Scotland had become a weakly unified kingdom, and as the Gaelic language gained prominence, Alt Clut became known as Dun Breatann or 'fort of the Britons', from which the present name is derived. The influence of Gaelic speaking Scots had eclipsed that of the British speakers in an area then known as the Lennox.[12]

Dumbarton Rock's strategic location at the confluence of Rivers Leven and Clyde, attracted settlers and a royal burgh was erected nearby. The new burgh was given its charter in 1222 by King Alexander II.[13] In the following decade he appointed a sheriff, 'forcing the Earl of Lennox to give up his right to the castle rock'.[14] Alexander's motive for establishing the Royal Burgh of Dumbarton and his other burgh at Dingwall, was strategic, and not about trade, which earlier burghs had been founded to stimulate. Dumbarton Rock was an ideal vantage point for controlling traffic on the Clyde, and Alexander wanted 'to create frontier plantations at the forward edge of his expanding sphere of political control: both were founded in regions where he was militarily active in the 1220s'.[15] As tangible evidence of his incursions in the west of Scotland he 'left a castle at Tarbet on Kintyre, and on his road east founded a burgh at Dumbarton, as royal bases on the sea route to Argyll'.[16]

The Royal Burgh of Dumbarton was laid out in a similar way to other Scottish royal burghs such as Forres, Elgin and indeed, Edinburgh whose burgh plans consisted initially of long, wide (and topography permitting) relatively straight 'High Streets' leading from the castle gates. The wide main streets acted as market places. Long narrow strips of land (burgage plots) ran at right angles from their frontages on either side of the High Street and the other streets laid out in the Medieval period, and it was here that the burgesses had their houses and some land to cultivate crops and keep animals.[17] In Dumbarton's case the danger of flooding around the castle rock which was sometimes surrounded by water, meant that the burgh could not be built immediately adjacent to the castle but had to be planted about three quarters of a mile's walk to the north west where its High Street still follows the curve of the River Leven.[18] Kirk Vennel, (Church Street) and Cross Vennel (College Street) both running northwards from High Street, completed Dumbarton's early townscape.

Little is known of Dumbarton's early history, but it would appear from map evidence, reports from the Convention of Royal Burghs and other, secondary sources that up until the late eighteenth century, Dumbarton was in a moribund state. The small size of the burgh, its susceptibility to flooding and its lack of trade are in sharp contrast to the growing prominence of Glasgow fifteen miles further up the River Clyde. Glasgow and Dumbarton were involved in numerous trading and fishing disputes which arose from contradictions and ambiguities in successive burgh charters.[19]

Dumbarton possessed one distinct advantage over Glasgow in that larger sea going vessels could not progress further up the Clyde than Dumbuck where hard bedrock, not easily eroded by the river, created a 'shoal' that was only navigable by small and shallow draught vessels. In the sixteenth century when Dumbarton was one of Scotland's most important naval bases, the burghs of Dumbarton, Glasgow and Renfrew were unsuccessful in their attempts to deepen the river at Dumbuck. It was not until the 1770s that spectacular progress in opening up a channel to Glasgow was achieved.[20]

In the seventeenth century, the progressive burgesses of Glasgow had sought to circumvent the problem, making representation to those of Dumbarton regarding the setting up of a port there. Dumbarton's burgesses turned the Glaswegians down for no apparent reason other than pride, and subsequently Port Glasgow was built at Newark on the south bank of the Clyde.

Up until the nineteenth century, the officials of Dumbarton and Glasgow continued to squabble over dues and tolls levied to pay for the deepening and maintenance of the Clyde's navigable channel from the Dumbuck Ford to Glasgow Bridge.[21]

In the early decades of the eighteenth century, Dumbarton was in a group of 'small' towns requiring tax reductions from the Convention of Royal Burghs. Later in the century, lack of population and economic growth, meant that Dumbarton was unable to access funds to make significant improvements to the townscape.[22]

One episode illustrative of the burgh's inefficiencies is to be found in its attempts to bridge the River Leven. A decision was taken in 1682 to build a bridge on the site of the ford which crossed this fast flowing river, from the north end of the High Street to 'Levenford' in Cardross Parish. Stone was ordered for this purpose but it was sold off again in 1691. Work did not begin on a bridge until 1754 and it was finally completed in 1765: eighty three years after the idea was first seriously considered.

In 1715, the burgh had been involved in a more successful venture: supplying water to wells in the burgh via two springs on the west bank of the river near the old church of St Serf's.[23] In an early example of municipal enterprise, an engineer was commissioned to run a lead pipe underneath the river from the springs to feed three wells in the High Street.

A century before the bridge was first proposed, the burgh had suffered a catastrophic flood that 'drowned' land immediately to the north of its medieval core which at this time comprised the High Street and two streets running off to its north, Kirk Vennel which ran from the Parish Church, and Cross Vennel which ran from Dumbarton Cross. This left Dumbarton on a peninsula with the only land route out to the east. The inundation cut off a route which led from Cross Vennel to the north and on to Bonhill. Strathleven Road and its extension, Bonhill Road, ran off Church Street to the east and were constructed to skirt the drowned land. It took nearly three centuries and railway construction for this area to be reclaimed.[24]

The first factory of any note to set up in Dumbarton was the glassworks built by the Dixon family in 1777. Webster's Census in 1755, recorded 1,427 people in Dumbarton Parish, but by 1790, there were 2,000 people over the age of six living there, with 1,850 of these living in the burgh alone. *The Old Statistical Account*[25] attributes the increase in population not only to the building of the glassworks in the town but to the development of 'printfields'. The glassworks employed 130 men at that time and 'the extensive printfields in the neighbouring parishes employ(ed) about 86' Dumbarton residents.[26] The *Account* notes however, that the Burgh:

is by no means in a flourishing or increasing state owing to letters of deaconry preventing strangers from working at their trades without costly entries.[27]

Restrictive and protectionist practices by the burgh authorities discouraged growth and in-migration. Indeed, people were leaving the burgh to live and work in Renton, Bonhill and 'other new villages' to be nearer their employment.[28] Building was also taking place at 'Bridgend', on the western side of Dumbarton Bridge, opposite the burgh. (See the following paragraphs on the Vale of Leven).

At its peak, the glassworks employed around 300 people and was the single most important employer in the burgh. Shortly after the 1831 census had been taken, the glassworks ceased production. When it closed the effects were clear. High Street and Bridge Street became overgrown and rents dropped as landlords tried to retain tenants. The population of the parish including the rural (landward) areas dropped from 3,632 in 1831 to 3,106 in 1837 as a result of the closure, when many 'men were obliged to leave Dumbarton to seek employment in England and elsewhere.'[29] The glassworks reopened briefly towards the end of the decade before being closed for good.[30]

In 1839, 81 males were employed in 'manufacture'; 405 in 'retail trade or in handicraft'; 56 were 'wholesale merchants, professional persons etc' and there were 130 labourers employed in non agricultural work.[31] The *New Statistical Account* records that there was a brickfield and a 'small trade' in tanning and rope spinning. It also states that at the time of taking the 1831 census there were 'two large shipbuilding concerns in full operation', but that they too had closed and later resumed work 'but not to the same extent as formerly'.[32]

The burgh is described as consisting of 'one tolerably well built street (High Street) in the shape of a crescent and several other smaller streets' with houses 'generally very closely built together and many of them very ill-aired. The principal street is kept very clean and well paved and for some time has been lighted with gas.'[33]

Tourism had been established as early as the 1830s when Dumbarton was connected to Glasgow and Greenock by two steamers per day. On summer days, except Sundays, a horse drawn coach would leave from Dumbarton for Balloch with passengers for the Loch Lomond steam boat. It would return on time each evening to catch the steamer back to Glasgow.

'Two good inns' catered for those travelling to and from Loch Lomond and there were between 40 and 50 alehouses licensed annually (one for every 70 to 90 people in the burgh).

In addition to the Parish School, there were seven other, fee paying, schools. There was a public library where a fee or subscription was required for access, and both the Conservative and Liberal parties supported reading rooms in the burgh.

Dumbarton was a market town and the administrative centre of the County. It housed a Sheriff Court and was a 'post-town', i.e. the site of a district post office.

In 1839, the burgh was devoid of substantial industry and sat in marked contrast, not only to the busy villages of the Vale to its north, but to the thriving works in Kilpatrick Parish immediately to the east, which had 5,879 inhabitants in 1831 - nearly 2,500 more than twenty years earlier. Here, many were working in cotton spinning and power loom weaving mills located in Faifley, Duntocher, Milton and Hardgate where 1,000,000 pounds weight of cotton was being spun annually. Over 1,400 people were employed in these mills owned by William Dunn who also employed engineers, mechanics and iron and brass founders in Glasgow to produce and repair machinery for his factories. In Dalmuir, there was a paper mill and a 'soda works' producing sulphuric acid for use in the manufacture of bleaching powder. There were small shipyards and a distillery located in Bowling.[34]

Shipbuilding would transform the fabric of burgh life. There had been boatyards along the Leven for centuries, but it was only after the Clyde was deepened that Dumbarton began to benefit. In 1814, Archibald MacLachlan and William Denny, a carpenter to trade, launched two steam powered boats from Woodyard on the west bank of the Leven.

In 1818, David Napier made the engine and boiler for the steamer 'Rob Roy' which was constructed by his cousin William Denny. It plied the Greenock to Belfast route across the open waters of the Irish Sea.[35] These were notable accomplishments, but they were small scale. It would be thirty to forty years later before shipbuilding would begin to take firm root in the burgh

The Vale of Leven

The pre-industrial nucleus of the Vale of Leven was in Bonhill Parish. A church and then a school were located at the site of Bonhill village, although the name Bonhill, an earlier variation being 'Bonill', existed before the village, which grew up around a ferry crossing. In Roy's map of 1747 the settlement is described as 'Bonill boat' where the ferry crossing is evident alongside a small group of buildings. On the opposite bank is 'Towmartland Bonill and 'Millburn'.[36]

As late as 1755, when the population of Dumbarton burgh was 1,427, the remainder of the valley was predominantly rural in character with 901 people in the whole of Bonhill Parish.[37] Dumbarton's burgh status which embodied trading and fishing rights, may have retarded further urban growth nearby. Ross's map of the County of Dumbarton (1777) shows a number of estates, country houses and small farms, along with clusters of houses at Renton, Alexandria and Bonhill on the main roads running from Dumbarton northwards on either side of the Leven. Renton appears to be the largest settlement. Alexandria was beginning to develop around the junction between the main

'Dumbarton to Luss' road and the road to the ferry. Bonhill was growing along the Dumbarton to Stirling road by the Leven side close to the church and ferry.

Industry had established a foothold in the Vale in 1728 after 'The Board of Trustees for Improving Fisheries and Manufactures in Scotland' granted money for the purpose of setting up bleachfields.[38]

William Stirling bought the bleachfields at Dalquhurn, Renton, in Cardross Parish in the 1770s, and by1792 the adjoining Cordale printworks employed 876 people, nearly half of them children: 300 girls and 150 boys from 8 to 15 years old, worked as pencillers. The 'printfields of Dalquhurn and Cordale' are described in the *Old Statistical Account* for Cardross Parish written in 1796 as 'by far the most considerable and extensive of any in Scotland'.[39] The village of Renton had been founded in the previous decade, and 'opposite Dumbarton' a 'village is just now begun' … 'which it is probable when the present stagnation of business is over, will fast increase in population'.[40] This would be referred to as Bridgend in the *New Statistical Account,* (see below) and it became the site of Dennystown, but it always retained strong associations with Renton, two miles to the north.

By 1791 the population of Bonhill Parish had grown to 2,310. An appreciable increase had occurred since 1768 'when the first printfield had been erected', but the population had varied since then.[41]

…according to the briskness or dullness of manufactures; and therefore if the list of inhabitants had been taken during the summer the population would have been about 100 more.[42]

The *'Old Statistical Account'* records that the parish had three printfields employing 933 people of whom 67 were children under ten years of age. The numbers of male and female workers were 'almost equal'.[43] As the number of printfields in Scotland increased so did the demand for highly skilled journeymen who could now earn 18 shillings per week. Semi-skilled men

…those who had acquired any degree of skill in printing and dyeing may get about 7s weekly.[44]

15

Male printwork labourers could earn 6 shillings per week, and boys and girls around 6/8d a month. Women were poorly paid in comparison to men. At one time they had been paid 3 shillings per week, before 'piece work' rates were imposed upon them. Subsequently, they were paid per item they produced. 'They may be said to earn 14s at an average' per month, but that depended on how long and how hard the women were able to work. Employers found that 'piece work' was to their advantage: increasing output for less cost.[45] The general introduction of 'piece work' for 'operative manufacturers' had caused 'violent disputes' in the recent past and eventually workers came to an uneasy truce with their 'masters' who put in place regulations on work and pay - but not before workers were prosecuted and imprisoned for their protests.[46]

Even at this early stage, enduring features of the bleaching, printing and dyeing industry in the Vale of Leven were evident: the 'paternalistic' attitude of employers; employment of young children; the employment of many women, inevitably on low or 'piece work' rates; difficult employee/employer relationships; volatility of trade and the migration of workers in response to that volatility.

Bleaching was initially a small scale, seasonal activity that relied greatly on sunshine to bleach the cloth. It attracted temporary migrants who worked during the summer in open air bleachfields. Technical advances freed firstly bleaching, and then printing and dyeing, from reliance on sunshine and to an extent, seasonality. It was in the 1830s and 1840s that the industry became a burgeoning concern, attracting many 'permanent' settlers to the planned villages of Renton and Alexandria and to the growing village of Bonhill.

The owners of the bleach, print and dye works were drawn to the Vale by an inexhaustible supply of fresh, soft water from Loch Lomond via the Leven, and by their ability to pay lower wages than in Glasgow.[47] Water was needed to wash and rinse cloth and to dilute chemicals and, in the early days of the industry it was also used directly as a source of power. Water was channelled via narrow 'lades'[48] which led to water wheels. Later, direct water power was replaced by steam power. A large printworks could use as much as 400 million gallons of water annually[49] and the lack of a dependable water supply led to the failure of many bleach, print and dye works elsewhere. In nearby Duntocher, fast flowing burns provided direct power for cloth spinning via water wheels. When steam powered machines were installed the water supply was still adequate for the task, but the American Civil War caused a massive decline in the supply of raw cotton and the mills closed as a result (see Chapter 2) .

In the Vale, the Leven was also used as a sewer to dispense with pollutants, and its meanders both facilitated a diversion of water as well as the disposal of effluent. The lades were cut to divert fast flowing water into the works, initially to turn water wheels and later to provide water for steam powered machinery. The water was also used in the bleaching and dyeing processes and the polluted water was returned to the river. The Leven's outstanding locational advantages ensured the success of early operations and it was here in these new villages, that substantial factory industry was firmly established for the first time in the west of Dunbartonshire. The old burgh was partially, if temporarily, eclipsed by the thriving industrial colonies to the north.

The *New Statistical Account* for Cardross Parish written in 1839 comments on population growth in the parish which had grown by 491 between 1821 and 1831. This had 'taken place chiefly in the village of Renton and at 'Bridgend'' (i.e. 'Levenford' at the western end of Dumbarton Bridge).

Those in Renton and some in 'Bridgend', were employed in the printworks but the *New Statistical Account* states that although 'calico printing and bleaching carried on to a great extent along the river ... most works are situated in Bonhill'. In 1831, Renton had 185 houses, 349 families, and 1,860 people in total. The village was linked by a turnpike road to Dumbarton and there was a 'daily post' delivering mail to the burgh where it was sorted and dispatched.[50]

Bonhill in turn had experienced rapid population growth in the early decades of the nineteenth century, with 3,874 people recorded in the parish in 1831, just over 1,000 more than in 1821. Growth was directly attributed to 'the establishment of the bleachfields and printfields which now form [Bonhill's] chief trade and industry'.[51]

The *Account* lists eleven works including the small Millburn pyroligneous works which manufactured tars, spirits, creosote and 'a fine Prussian Blue' dye.

The print and dye works in Bonhill Parish ranged from Dalmonach which employed 900 people, used steam power and had eight printing machines each able to print up to six colours and produce 1,200 yards of printed material in an hour, to Levenfield which relied solely on water power. Most of the Bonhill works used steam power but also retained water wheels.[52]

It is notable that at this time the works employed more men than women as well as many young children. The Reverend William Gregor, author of the *New Statistical Account* for Bonhill Parish notes that 'about seven-eighths of the population inhabit the Vale of Leven and are employed at the public works, bleachfields and printfields'. He laments that 'to these works the children are sent, in too many cases, at and under seven years of age; and any learning they get afterwards is at the weekday evening and Sunday evening schools'. (Abstract Education Inquiry 1837).[53] A situation which was hardly conducive to meaningful learning.

As in Dumbarton, there were parish and private schools in both Cardross and Bonhill. There was a 'general subscription library' in Renton and a Mechanics' Institute serving the Vale which had been set up in 1834 but at the time of writing (July 1840) had still to find a permanent home. Like the Denny Institute founded later in Dumbarton, 'Mechanics' Institutes' were established in the 1820s, initially in Edinburgh, Glasgow, Liverpool, Manchester and London and were aimed at 'the respectable and aspiring working classes ... often supported by local industrialists with paternal and philanthropic inclinations. ... By the 1850s there were more than five hundred such Mechanics' Institutes spread across the towns and cities of the United Kingdom'.[54]

Here, in 1840, the Institute was struggling to make an impact. A course of 'around' 26 lectures was held 'mostly' on Saturday nights. Of the 1,176 male printworkers only 109 were members of the Institute. Overall, 170 people attended the lectures, but the Institute's committee struggled to provide a cohesive programme as lecturers chose their own subjects and their presentations were of variable quality.

Schools, libraries, sport and organised cultural and leisure activities were actively promoted in the Vale by printwork owners who were always keen to direct all aspects of community life.

As the nineteenth century progressed, there was a significant increase in population due to the rise of industry. The populations of Dumbarton Parish, Bonhill Parish (which included Alexandria and Bonhill village)[55] and Cardross Parish (which included Renton) grew slowly between 1801 and 1831. In 1831, Dumbarton and Bonhill parishes had similar sized populations (3,623 to 3,874 respectively), but over the next decade the eclipse of Dumbarton is clear as the population of Bonhill had grown by around 2,800, compared to Dumbarton's growth of around 770 (See figure 1:1). In the former, the rise is directly attributable to the consolidation of the textile finishing industries and especially the establishment of year round employment. In contrast, shipbuilding in Dumbarton was barely beginning to make its presence felt, and it was not until 1871 that the population of Dumbarton Parish exceeded that of Bonhill Parish.[56] In 1851 the relative importance of the industries is obvious, where the number of people employed in shipbuilding in Dunbarton County was under 300 while the number employed in cotton printing was ten times that.[57]

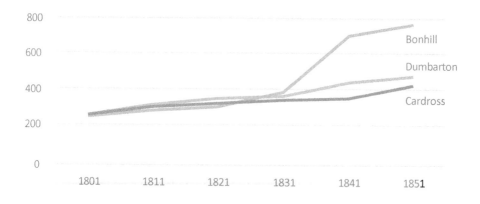

Figure 1:1 Parish Populations Dumbarton & the Vale of Leven 1801-1851

Figure 1:2 Dumbarton Burgh in 1832

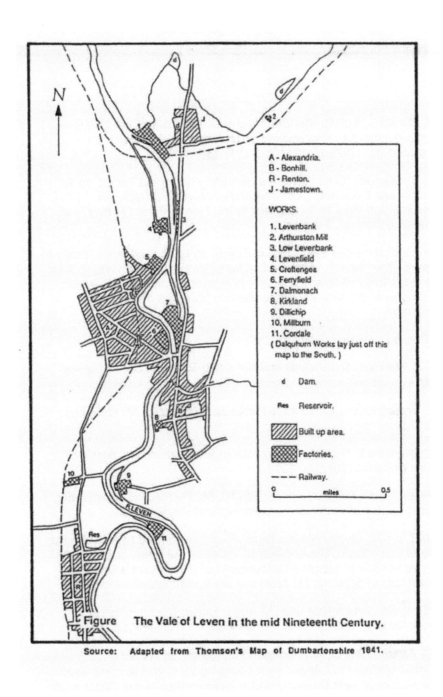

A - Alexandria.
B - Bonhill.
R - Renton.
J - Jamestown.

WORKS.

1. Levenbank
2. Arthurston Mill
3. Low Leverbank
4. Levenfield
5. Croftengea
6. Ferryfield
7. Dalmonach
8. Kirkland
9. Dillichip
10. Millburn
11. Cordale
(Dalquhurn Works lay just off this
map to the South.)

d   Dam.

Res   Reservoir.

[hatched] Built up area.

[crosshatched] Factories.

— — — Railway.

0   miles   0.5

Figure   The Vale of Leven in the mid Nineteenth Century.

Source: Adapted from Thomson's Map of Dumbartonshire 1841.

Figure 1:3 Map of the Vale of Leven in the mid-nineteenth century[58]

NOTES

[1] L. Alcock, 'A multi-disciplinary chronology for Alt Clut, Castle Rock, Dumbarton' *Proceedings of the Society of Antiquaries, Scotland 107* (1975-6) pp. 104-5

[2] S.T. Driscoll, 'Celtic Britain in the Early Historical Period' in J. Hunter and I. Ralston (eds) *The Archaeology of Britain, An introduction from earliest times to the Twenty-First Century*, 2nd Edition (2009) pp. 241-264

[3] It is also recorded as Al Clud, Al Cluith, Alclutha, and other, similar names. The name is from the Brythonic language which was spoken by the Britons of Strathclyde and is related to modern day Welsh. Brythonic and Gaelic comprise the two branches of the Celtic languages.

[4] Driscoll, 'Celtic Britain' p. 259

[5] T.J. Clarkson, *Strathclyde and the Anglo-Saxons in the Viking Age* (2014) p. 21

[6] J. Fraser, *From Caledonia to Pictland: Scotland to 795* (2009) pp. 16-9

[7] Quote from S. Forder, *The Romans in Scotland and the Battle of Mons Graupius* (2022) p. 101

[8] Fraser, *From Caledonia to Pictland* p. 89. Patrick was complaining about raiding of Christian settlements and slave taking.

[9] Ibid. p.136. Clydesdale is a term which can be used to describe the whole Clyde Basin, the immediate valley of the river, or the stretch between Lanark or Boswell according to F.H. Groome's *Ordnance Gazetteer of Scotland* (1882-4) *see www.visionofbritain.org.uk*

[10] Clarkson, *Strathclyde and the Anglo-Saxons* (Archaeological evidence of a 'palace' near Govan supports this view.) p. 47

[11] S.Taylor, 'The Early History and Languages of West Dunbartonshire' in I.Brown (ed) *Changing Identities Ancient Roots the history of west Dunbartonshire from earliest times* (2006) p. 25

[12] Ibid. p. 26

[13] R. Oram, *Alexander II, King of Scots 1214-1249* (2012) Specific reference to foundation of Dumbarton as a Royal Burgh p. 79

[14] M. Brown, *The Wars of Scotland 1214-1371* (2004) online version 2012 p. 30

[15] R.Oram, *Domination and Lordship: Scotland 1070 - 1230* (2011) p. 287

[16] Brown, *The Wars of Scotland* p. 75

[17] Burgesses were 'freemen' who usually owned land in the burgh and were craftsmen or merchants who had both rights and responsibilities. See I.H.Adams, *The Making of Urban Scotland* (1978) pp. 42-3

[18] 'In winter, sometimes when the tides are unusually high it (the Castle Rock) is entirely surrounded by water'. *New Statistical Account* (Hereafter *NSA*) Vol VIII. Dumbarton Parish. p. 1

[19] J.D. Marwick, *The River Clyde and the Clyde Burghs* (1909) describes numerous disputes between Glasgow and its nearby burghs.

[20] J.F. Riddell, *The Clyde. The Making of a River* (1979) p. 8

[21] Ibid. pp. 36-8. One of the main techniques used to deepen the river was to narrow its channel so that the river flowed more quickly and thus scoured out the river bed.

[22] B. Harris and C. McKean, *The Scottish Town in the Age of the Enlightenment 1740-1820* (2014) pp. 19-20 and p.128.

[23] Well sites at the mouth of the springs are signposted in Levengrove Park.

[24] See Chapter 2

[25] Hereafter referred to as in footnotes as *OSA*.

[26] *OSA* Dumbarton Parish. 1792. Vol IV. pp. 22-3

[27] Ibid.

[28] Ibid.

[29] *NSA* Vol VIII. 1845. Dumbarton Parish p. 9

[30] Ibid.

[31] Ibid. p. 10

[32] These 'large shipbuilding concerns' were modest when compared to the Dumbarton yards in operation a few decades later.

[33] *NSA* VIII p.11

[34] Ibid. pp. 23-9

[35] I.M.M. MacPhail, *Dumbarton through the Centuries* (1972) pp. 56-7

[36] *Roy Military Survey of Scotland 1747-1755* *https://maps.nls.uk* >roy

[37] *NSA* VIII p. 8 and p. 223

[38] H. Hamilton, *The Industrial Revolution in Scotland.* Reprint (1966) p. 102.

[39] *OSA* Cardross Parish. 1796. Vol XVII. pp. 214-5

[40] Ibid. pp. 216-217

[41] *OSA* Bonhill Parish. 1792. Vol. III. p. 445

[42] Ibid.

[43] Ibid.

[44] Ibid. p. 447

[45] Ibid.

[46] Ibid. p. 448

[47] A.Cooke, *The Rise and Fall of the Scottish Cotton Industry 1778 -1914* (2010) p. 23

[48] Lades are small canals. Here, they cut across a meander in the river, supplying water to the works and carrying effluent back into the river.

[49] K.L.Wallwork, 'The Calico Printing Industry of Lancastria in the 1840s' *Transactions of the Institute of British Geographers* Vol 45 (1968) pp. 143-57.

[50] *NSA* VIII. p. 91

[51] *NSA* VIII. p. 223

[52] *NSA* VIII. p. 224

[53] *NSA* VIII. p. 226

[54] D. Cannadine, *Victorious Century. The United Kingdom 1800-1906* (2017) p. 330

[55] Jamestown's long terraced rows were not built until the 1860s.

[56] Figures taken from the *scottish-places.info* website. *Quoting from* F.H. Groome (ed) *Ordnance Gazeteer of Scotland: A study of Scottish Topography, Statistical, Biographical and Historical.* (1882-85)

[57] *Census.* population tables II , Vol I England and Wales Divisions VII-XI. Scotland. Islands. 1851
p.20; pp. 933-7

[58] C.G.Doherty,* 'The Growth and Decline of the Bleaching, Printing and Dyeing Industry in the Vale of Leven', *Scottish Industrial History.* Vol 8:2 (1985) pp. 4-14.
* (should read: 'Docherty')

2 Industries, Orr Ewings and Dennys

Vale of Leven

The villages of the Vale of Leven were built to accommodate workers in the bleach, print and dye works which were being established along the river. They were factory colonies: Renton, Alexandria and Jamestown had been built for no other purpose, while Bonhill village grew rapidly as a result of industrialisation. As the eighteenth century ended, the industry was adapting to printing on calico made from cheap cotton supplies abundantly available from the United States. This was replacing linen made from flax, which was regarded as a less reliable raw material. In the first half of the nineteenth century there was expansion as new processing techniques were introduced and markets opened up. By 1850, 'Turkey Red' dyeing and mechanical cylinder printing had been added to bleaching, block printing and yarn dyeing operations carried out in the vicinity. As factories expanded to meet demand employment opportunities blossomed. In the 1860s there were eleven 'works' along the River Leven involved in cloth bleaching, printing and dyeing. Yet, less than half a century later, amalgamations and closures were necessary to save the works from extinction and a reduction in workforce led to an exodus from the printwork reliant villages.

The Vale of Leven's factories specialised in 'Turkey Red' dyeing which

was of a different character to mass produced grey cotton manufacture. It used high technology in large and sophisticated working units, but also employed a higher percentage of skilled male workers from design to pattern cutters, dyers and printers.[1]

In the Vale, around 20% of male printworkers were in this well paid category, but the vast majority of workers both male and female, were not so fortunate. Low wages and poor working conditions were commonplace. Processes may have been 'sophisticated' but they involved considerable dangers.

In Dalquhurn, 130,000 gallons of bulls' blood per annum had once been used in the printing and dyeing process and its use continued, even as chemical dyes were introduced. Madder root along with rancid olive oil and sheep's dung, all of which had been extensively used in the 1840s for preparing cloth before dyeing, were still in evidence in 1869.[2] Whether using natural or artificial products, the dyeing process produced harmful liquids and unpleasant, often noxious, vapours. Those who worked in this industry faced hazardous conditions daily - often with serious consequences. Female print workers were known as 'jeely eaters' because their hands were permanently stained red.[3] Apart from the toxic liquids involved in the dyeing process, the high temperatures that were required to dry dyed cloth led to frequent fires (see Chapter 5).

As the industry evolved, naturally occurring dyes such as 'alizarin' made from the madder root, were being replaced by chemical dyes although cloth dyed by 'natural' methods still commanded the highest prices.[4]

In 1881, John Christie (part owner of the Alexandria Works) wrote to 'business contact dyers' that some men were suffering swollen and pustulated hands and arms from an unknown cause in the production process.[5]

However, the printworks owners remained largely unconcerned about working conditions. They were happy to employ children even as successive Factory Acts were limiting their use. In 1847 when the '10 hours' Act was passed, child labour may or may not have been 'relatively insignificant' across industrial Scotland but it was still present and continued to be used in the printworks well into the second half of the century.[6]

Dye workers later campaigned in support of the subsequent 1860 Act 'limiting hitherto atrocious hours worked by blistered children' and eventually founded a Scottish union at Dundee in 1888.[7]

It has been suggested that the power exercised by the printwork owners produced a docile workforce.[8] Certainly, the owners immersed themselves in the daily lives of their workforce and their families.

There were four principal firms in the Vale during the latter half of the nineteenth century, and all were involved in printing, dyeing and bleaching: James Black & Co, John Orr Ewing & Co, William Stirling & Sons and Archibald Ewing & Co. Between them they provided work for over 6,000 people . The owners and managers of these firms lived close to their factories and were intimately involved in the locality, influencing political cultural and social life. Sir Archibald Orr Ewing was the local Conservative Member of Parliament from 1868 to 1892, and Alex Wylie, a partner in William Stirling & Sons was member between 1895 and 1906 as a Liberal Unionist. They were elders in the kirk, patrons of the many societies which proliferated in the area, providers of educational facilities and donors of public halls, reading rooms and a public park. The dominant recreational and cultural activities in the locality consisted of Educational Societies, Mechanics' Institutes, Masonic Lodges, music societies and bands, sporting clubs, a Burns Club, a Co-operative Society and a Unionist and a Liberal Association.[9]

John Christie, who had earlier written of his concerns about the effect of the production process on the hands and arms of his workforce, 'gifted' the thirteen acre Christie Park to the people of Alexandria in 1902, but closer inspection reveals that the workers' annual bonus was diverted to pay for it.[10] To his credit, seven years earlier Christie had paid an outstanding debt of £300 to the owners of the Bonhill and Balloch bridges, helping to abolish tolls as the bridges were declared 'free to all as a highway'. The tolls had been a contentious issue with workers having to pay if they crossed the Leven between Bonhill and Alexandria, and their abolition benefitted both workers and management. The bridge owners are reported to have received a total of £30,000 in compensation.[11]

The people of the Vale may have 'enjoyed' the patronage of printwork owners but there were few signs of submissive behaviour. It is not surprising that calico printers in the West of Scotland 'particularly in Glasgow, Campsie and the Vale of Leven' had a militant reputation when faced with works' owners who fought the implementation of each measure designed to limit working hours and to improve working conditions.[12]

The Vale has a long history of industrial activism. In the late eighteenth century the introduction of 'piece work' resulted in protests, violence and imprisonment. In the early nineteenth century there was strong support for Chartism, while strikes and industrial disputes increased towards the end of the century. There was a major strike in 1911 and after the First World War, there was support for radical politics and Communist Party candidates in local elections.[13]

In September 1875 at the Queen's Hotel, George Square, Glasgow, Archibald Orr Ewing, printwork owner and local MP, gave evidence to the Royal Commission enquiry into the operation of the Factory and Workshop Act. This testimony provides an unflattering insight into Orr Ewing's attitude to labour relations. He told the enquiry that he was

MP for Dumbartonshire and senior partner of the firm of Archibald Orr Ewing and Co, turkey-red and yarn dye workers, Vale of Leven... that his ... business employed 1,728 people and that almost every process of our dye works is conducted by machinery, which has enabled us to dispose with certainly 50% and perhaps nearly 75% of the labour force since I began the business.[14]

The Factory and Workshop Act in question aimed to end Saturday afternoon working. Orr Ewing explained that turkey red dyeing was a continuous process and that he would be as well closing the works for the whole day. (Half day working on a Saturday was already established by the Factory Act in other branches of industry). When asked to consider giving a 'whole holiday every fortnight' instead, Orr Ewing replied:

our goods are very subject to spontaneous combustion and on Sundays we are obliged to keep people watching them. An entire holiday would involve the loss of a day's wages to the work people and would be conducive to the habits of idleness which are already sufficiently common. [15]

As the *Glasgow Herald* reported it,

his point was well taken though his further argument that a half day on a Saturday would simply make the workforce idle, generated less sympathy.[16]

Orr Ewing railed against government interference in trade where it was 'not necessary' and suggested that block printing was declining because of the 'difficulty of obtaining juvenile labour'. He thought that 'it would be wise legislation to limit the number of hours which children and young people were employed so that they might not be worked excessively', but according to the *Lennox Herald*, he 'deprecated any further limitations in the trade to which he belonged'. Furthermore, he thought it 'would be wise both for the sake of education and labour that no child under ten years of age should be employed... and instead of having half timers in such a business as (his) where work was *not hard and quite healthy,* that children should be allowed to work ten hours one day and that the next day should be entirely devoted to education'.

He also observed that 'his workforce did not live very near the work; accommodation for lodgers in the district was bad; and the sanitary arrangements were bad'.[17]

Orr Ewing and the other printwork owners not only dictated pay and conditions, they strived to control wider aspects of community life and attempted to keep workers and their families on a tight rein. In the parliamentary election of 1868, when Orr Ewing was first elected as MP for Dunbartonshire, he was initially opposed by Liberal, George Campbell, who was supported by local Loch Lomond laird Sir James Colquhoun. A disputatious campaign led to claim and counter claim about efforts to coerce those workers who had the vote. The *Lennox Herald* printed a letter alleging that Orr Ewing's factory shop sold meat which was 'dearer than that brought by van from Dumbarton each day' and that food money was taken from workers' pay 'without quantity or price specified'.[18] This latter practice known as 'trucking', was outlawed in many trades in 1831 and extended to almost all manual working by 1887.[19] Campbell was later to withdraw his candidature and Orr Ewing was elected unopposed.

Fortunately, the extremely successful Vale of Leven Co-operative Society founded in 1861, had branches in all four printwork settlements and in Balloch and was of great benefit to ordinary working people who came to depend on the 'Co-op'.[20]

It is easy to disparage the actions and attitudes of works' owners, including Orr Ewing, but they also sought to improve living conditions. In addition to building houses for their workers, they promoted 'recreational and cultural activities'. They gave money to the local presbytery and helped fund the building of a Catholic chapel for the Irish workforce and their families.[21]

There were two notable crisis points for the bleaching, printing and dyeing industry as it moved into the second half of the nineteenth century. In 1857, in the midst of a nationwide depression, the Western Bank, which had offered considerable financial support to cotton industrialists, closed.[22] This was followed by the American Civil War of 1861-1865 which severely disrupted cotton supplies and amply demonstrated the problems of over reliance on a foreign, raw material. The resulting loss of confidence, perhaps for the first time, exposed the weak foundations of the Scottish textile industry - but it did not signal its end.[23]

Leone Levi writing in 1863, stated that in 1860 the USA exported 2,579,000 bales of cotton to Britain which was nearly 80% of total cotton imports. By 1862 this was down to 72,000 bales as importers frantically looked to Brazil, the Caribbean, the Mediterranean and especially the East Indies, to address the shortfall, but they had difficulties in filling the phenomenal gap left by the American producers.[24] This shortage forced an increase in the price of cotton and applied pressure to an industry that was already exporting low price goods to important markets such as India.[25] Supply had been in excess of demand for several years and profitability could only be sustained by lowering prices. In the Vale of Leven a tangible result of this slump was the shedding of labour. Alexandria's Ferryfield Works was closed in 1864 and reopened only after extensive renovation in 1871.[26]

Beyond these crises, the industry moved into a steadier phase, although the cautious tones of many reports suggest that six years after the Civil War had ended confidence had yet to be restored.[27] Block printing in particular was still in a 'depressed state', which was understandable as mechanical printing methods were becoming more prevalent. This was emphasised by Bremner, who provides a detailed description of the operations at Dalquhurn and Cordale works in the late 1860s when the Dalquhurn Works dyed both cloth and yarn 'turkey-red'.[28] All of the yarn and more than half of the cloth was exported in 'plain red state' and the remainder of the cloth was then transferred to Cordale to be printed. Bremner states that turkey-red dyeing in the Vale of Leven began in 1828. This probably accounts for the sharp increase in population between 1831 and 1841. The cloth printed in these works came chiefly from Glasgow and Manchester. The Dalquhurn Works processed 18,450,000 yards (600,000 pieces) of cloth and 600,000 to 800,000 pounds of yarn per annum. Dalquhurn employed about 1000 people, 'around two thirds of whom are women, a considerable proportion of whom are Irish'.[29] A further 500 men, women and children were employed at Cordale.[30]

The Vale firms exported all over the world, especially to India, but also to the Far East, some Pacific islands, West Africa and South America.[31]

The works continued to expand up until the 1890s. In that decade the Vale's cloth finishing industry, suffering from the same fundamental, structural defects as the textile industry in general, encountered severe difficulties. Low wages upon which the industry relied, were not enough to sustain profitability. Investment in machinery had been slow and piecemeal and technical advances had been pioneered elsewhere. New chemical dyes may have been more efficient than 'turkey-red' dye which was still manufactured using naturally occurring substances but 'artificial' dyes were not wholly adopted, partly because true 'turkey-red' goods, products of 'a highly specialised and sophisticated industry', were of better quality.[32] Initially, specialisation in turkey-red products protected the Vale's trade from the vagaries affecting the cotton manufacturing industry but as the Vale became increasingly 'overdependent on a small number of specialised goods' it led to its 'inevitable decline'.[33]

Trade had been increasingly affected by foreign competition especially from the USA, where readily available cotton supplies could be processed cheaply. Furthermore, India was producing and printing its own cotton goods and had imposed tariffs on foreign imports. The result was a significant reduction of what was once a lucrative market for the Vale's products.

Towards the end of the century the Vale of Leven firms split into two groups, severing at a stroke the close ties between the printwork owners and the communities they had built, lived in and dominated.

The majority of firms including Dalquhurn and Cordale in Renton, Dillichip in Bonhill and the Alexandria, Milton and Levenside works in Alexandria/Jamestown amalgamated in 1897 to become the United Turkey Red Company.[34] Thereafter Dalmonach and Ferryfield works were acquired by the Manchester based Calico Printers' Association.[35] The intention of the former was to avoid a takeover by the latter. Both businesses were ultimately unsuccessful in their attempts to offset decline and the shares of the new CPA group dipped after a few months. The amalgamations had broken the direct relationship that the factory owners had with their workforce and the number of printworkers was gradually reduced as the industry suffered a lingering decline. Still, it remained the principal industry in the Vale during the first half of the twentieth century. The United TurkeyRed Company and the British Silk Dyeing Company (founded in 1929), 'modern diminished representations' of the bleaching, printing and dyeing industry, employed 1,904 in 1951. That compared to a workforce of 6,000 in 1875 and 4,574 in 1911.[36]

Dumbarton

In the second half of the nineteenth century industrial growth in Dumbarton was vigorous in marked contrast to earlier decades when the Vale's works were expanding rapidly and the glassworks, the burgh's biggest employer, stuttered towards closure.

The impact that shipbuilding had on Dumbarton was dramatic, as Irving, writing in 1860, states:

the foundation of the whole prosperity of the town is unquestionably the shipbuilding trade and particularly that branch of the trade concerned in the construction of iron-steel vessels.

He pinpoints 1844, five years after the *New Statistical Account of Dumbarton Parish* was written, as the time when:

… a change began to take place. Vessels were then built not only of larger tonnage, but as the use of iron in the construction of vessels came to be more generally known an entirely new branch of the trade took root in Dumbarton.[37]

It is no coincidence that Irving should select 1844 as the beginning of Dumbarton's industrial renaissance, as it was then that Denny and Rankin's yard on the west bank of the Leven at Woodyard was to become the first home of Denny Brothers who dominated industrial life in Dumbarton. In this era they were possibly the most progressive and innovative shipbuilders on the Clyde, which in itself was renowned for the production of high quality and technically advanced vessels.

Figure 2:1 below shows the chronology and location of the Dumbarton yards.[38] All of the shipyards that existed in Dumbarton with the exception of MacMillan and Sons, had Denny family involvement at some stage.

In 1849, the Dennys went into partnership with Tulloch's firm which made ships' engines. Tulloch and Denny became Denny and Company in 1862. Dennystown Forge was located on the west bank of the Leven north of the railway line. South of the railway line, a new housing development Dennystown, owned in part by Peter and James Denny, was ready for occupation in 1855.

MacMillan and Sons originally had a yard at Brewery Lane but it was when they moved in 1845/6 to the 'Dockyard' immediately east of the Parish Church that they prospered. They constructed more than 800 vessels here, both sailing and steam ships, some of which were larger than 7,500 tons in weight.[39]

The phenomenal rise of shipbuilding in Dumbarton was paralleled the length and breadth of the Clyde from Glasgow to Greenock as iron hulled steamships gradually replaced wooden sailing ships. As late as the 1850s shipbuilding contributed very little to the British economy. A change began in the 1860s, and by the 'last decades of the nineteenth century Clyde shipyards produced roughly one third of British output' which in turn had 'a world market share of of over 80% by the 1890s'.[40] The average, annual tonnage launched on the Clyde between 1871 and 1874 was 250,000 tons. The Clyde still led Britain's shipbuilding industry, with an average annual launching of 565,000 tons in the 1909-1913 period.[41]

Meanwhile Dennys maintained their position in the vanguard of Scottish shipbuilding by being the first firm to construct an ocean going vessel built of mild steel. This was the powerful 'Rotomahana' built for New Zealand's Union Steamship Line in 1879. In that year half of the Clyde's steel ship tonnage came from Dennys yard as the company promoted the use of the new alloy.[42] A year later Dennys 'established an awards scheme' where workers were encouraged to suggest ideas for improvement. Sums of 'up to £10' were offered as a reward. In four years there were 101 successful claims.[43] In 1883 Dennys opened an experimental tank which was used to test model prototypes against wave and water conditions. It was the first commercial tank in the world.[44] Dennys also initiated 'variable speed trials' of their vessels, a practice that quickly became standard across the industry.[45]

The experimental tank was not only used by Dennys. Other shipbuilders used it too: indicative of co-operation between yards, which stood in stark contrast to the Vale's factories where production secrets were closely guarded. The owners of the printworks were rivals who fought 'bitter court battles over copyright and design theft'. Cooperation here was confined to 'collective action when it came to trade disputes with workers'.[46]

The shipbuilding industry was not immune to economic depression and, like the bleaching, printing and dyeing companies in the Vale of Leven, it too had suffered with the failure of the Western Bank in 1857.[47] One year earlier, the end of the Crimean War signalled a slump at Dennys when 'three-quarter time and reduced staffs became the order of the day'.[48]

In 1860, according to the 'Denny Lists' : 'the majority of vessels (built were) passenger liners and high class cargo steamers'. The Lists also indicate that Dennys constructed a number of blockade runners and 'disguised warships' for the Confederate States of America in the early 1860s, so that the:

great shipbuilding boom at the time of the American Civil War helped Denny more than most and thereafter the firm appears to have been fairly solidly established.[49]

The War not only provided a market for the light, fast 'blockade runners', designed to outrun the US vessels imposing an embargo on the Confederate ports, but it removed a competitor. Output from US shipyards was severely affected by the conflict and Dennys, along with other yards on the Clyde and Tyne and Wear, benefitted from the lack of competition.[50]

During recovery in the 1860s, William Denny and Brothers moved their operations from Woodyard to the Leven Shipyard on the east side of the river, adjacent to MacMillan's. It was by far the biggest shipyard in the burgh, swallowing up the smaller Victoria Yard which had existed on this site (see Chapter 4). In the next decade, construction of shallow draught steamers designed for use on tropical rivers became an important Denny specialism so that by the eighties the company 'had become seriously involved in the building of the type of ship they were associated with more than any other'.[51]

Dennys interest in shipbuilding was extended to include investment in shipping companies and 'between 1844 and 1914 the Denny partners were connected at one time or another with at least nineteen shipping companies'.[52] They had a long and successful collaboration with the Glasgow based shipping firm Patrick Henderson and Company but their most significant venture was to be with the Irrawaddy Flotilla Company. Dennys took over 20% of shares in the original company founded in 1865 but built no ships for it until the company reformed in 1876 with Peter Denny as chairman. In the following sixty years William Denny and Brothers built over 250 vessels for the company and although some of the vessels were small and included barges, it was a highly lucrative association.[53] In another innovation, many of the ships were built in sections and shipped to Rangoon to be reassembled.[54]

The profits that Dennys made from the construction of small river craft for the Irrawaddy Flotilla Company and others specialising in river trade, was much higher in percentage terms than for larger ocean going vessels. The craft were simpler and 'in some cases could even be mass produced' so that Dennys could continue the practice of sending ships' component parts abroad to be assembled at the ports from which they operated. 'Building river craft ...ultimately proved the most remunerative sector of their operations'.[55]

Dennys shipbuilders certainly fitted the definition of a successful 'specialist' company. However, indicators of the economic decline in shipbuilding could be identified, albeit faintly, as early as the 1890s.

Dennys were amongst the most progressive firms in accepting and developing the latest technology ...The firm's record of contracts over the forty years before 1914 is of almost unqualified profits earned, but there is a qualification which indicates the appearance of problems before 1914 ... From ship 170 launched in 1874 to ship 1007 launched in 1913, only 73 were recorded as leading to unprofitable contracts. In many cases the amount of the loss was small and the aggregate over the forty years before 1914 was only £226,609 but the distribution of the loss is more important. The incidence increased in the later 1890s and became even more frequent in the twentieth century.[56]

During the second half of the nineteenth century serious problems were on the distant horizon and Dennys was a successful, inventive, progressive and thriving company. In Dumbarton, shipbuilding companies came and went throughout the period, most of them involving members of the Denny family, although MacMillan's yard operated on the same site from 1845/6 until 1932.

Dennys success did not preclude discord. Like the printwork owners in the Vale, the Denny family sponsored educational and recreational pursuits, they opened reading rooms, gifted public parks and channelled a sense of community through safe and distracting pastimes. Nonetheless when it came to industrial relations they were as ruthless as they were benevolent.

Unemployment became:

a frequent, but quite unpredictable occurrence, as the behaviour of the Scottish economy was increasingly bound up with world trade and commerce. As an instance of this, the number of men employed at Denny's Dumbarton in 1858 was 1,122, yet the following year it had fallen to 408. This fluctuating pattern proved persistent, for in 1875 Denny's workforce was 1,321, but shrank to 558 in 1876.[57]

These were dramatic fluctuations but to take a longer view of employment patterns, Dennys had 555 employees by 1860. If this figure is assigned a notional value of 100, then this value rose to over 240 by 1863 and only dipped below 200 in one year up to 1870. Between 1876 and 1879 inclusive, the value was below 200 but thereafter it was not less than this throughout the 1880s. This, in spite of a countrywide depression which saw a decline in the gross tonnage of ships launched on the Clyde in the second half of that decade.[58]

In Scotland the principal response to economic difficulties was always to reduce labour costs. The volatility of the figures above attests to the practice of casual hirings and firings which primarily affected unskilled labourers.[59]

It has been suggested that in the two decades before the beginning of World War One the formerly 'Liberal' Denny family became increasingly 'Conservative'. They decided to join other employers in collective action against the spread of union disputes throughout the Clyde area'.[60] Four decades before this, the Dennys were involved in anti-union action. In 1856, 'William Denny and Brothers [i.e. Dennys] and other Dumbarton shipbuilders, with the exception of Peter Denny and Daniel Rankin', decided to 'lock out' union members. This cost Dennys over £7000 pounds in penalties for non-delivery. Blackleg labour was brought in from the North East of Scotland. Some of the blacklegs were assaulted by striking workers who were subsequently jailed. This resulted in a riot as the jail in Quay Street was attacked and the arrested men released. The escaped prisoners fled the country to avoid trial.

The unions were eventually recognised but events of 1856 left a bitter legacy.[61] Nine years later, another serious and protracted strike saw the bulk of shipyard joiners and blacksmiths, whose wages had been reduced, leave the burgh for work elsewhere.[62]

Nonetheless, a successful Dennys was the key to Dumbarton's prosperity, and the agglomeration of ancillary industries such as engine works, ropeworks, foundries and forges which were largely, or wholly, reliant on the shipyards, provided still more work to bolster the burgh's economic wellbeing. The most enduring of these was the Dennystown Forge, established in 1854, which finally closed in 1979.

Dumbarton Burgh was the county seat and administrative centre of Dunbartonshire. The municipal buildings and sheriff court were located there. By 1891, it had a larger middle class population than the Vale of Leven, with more 'professional and managerial' workers and a better developed retail trade. In contrast to the Vale, its economic health was to endure into the twentieth century. Dumbarton's population continued to rise, while in the Vale, growth stalled between 1891 and 1901 as the printworks hit troubled times.

Figure 2:1 below, from J Burrow and co (eds) Denny 1844-1932 (1933) shows a complex network of establishments, companies and chronologies which underline the pervasive influence of the Denny family in Dumbarton's industrial past.

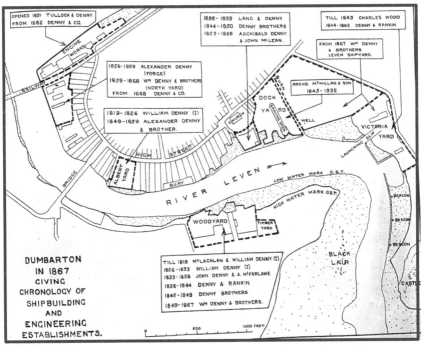

Figure 2:1 Dumbarton in 1897, Giving Chronology of Shipbuilding & Engineering Establishments.

NOTES

[1] S. Nenadic and S. Tuckett, *The Turkey Red Printed Cotton Industry in Scotland. c 1840-1940* (2013) p. 4

[2] D. Bremner, *The Industries of Scotland, their Rise Progress and Present Condition.* (1869. Reprinted in 1967) p. 300

[3] Nenadic and Tuckett, *The Turkey Red Printed Cotton Industry* p. 14

[4] Ibid. p. 38

[5] Ibid. p. 10

[6] J. Butt, 'Labour and Industrial Relations in the Scottish Cotton Industry during The Industrial Revolution' in J. Butt and K.G.Ponting, (eds) *Scottish Textile Industry* (1987) pp. 139-60

[7] J.T. Ward, 'Textile Trade Unionism in 19th century Scotland', in Butt and Ponting, Ibid. pp. 126-38

[8] R. Gallacher, 'The Vale of Leven 1914-1975: Changes in Working Class Organisation and Action' in T. Dickson, (ed) *Capital and Class in Scotland* (1982) p. 187

[9] Ibid. pp. 187-8

[10] Lennox Herald *(hereafter LH)* 6 August 2019

[11] J. Agnew, *The Story of the Vale of Leven* (1975) p. 62

[12] Ward, 'Textile Trade Unionism' p. 136

[13] Gallacher, *'The Vale of Leven 1914-1975'*

[14] *LH* 11 September 1875

[15] Ibid.

[16] Nenadic and Tuckett, *The Turkey Red Printed Cotton Industry* p. 29

[17] *LH* 11 September 1875

[18] *LH* 5 September 1868

[19] See Oxford Reference at *oxfordreference.com* 'Truck Acts' and Cannadine *Victorious Century* p. 296

[20] J. Agnew, *The Story of the Vale of Leven* pp. 51-2 *www.valeofleven.org.uk*>alexandria3html. The Dumbarton Co-operative Society was founded at the same time.

[21] J. Melling, 'Scottish Industrialists and the Changing Character of Class Relations in the Clyde Region c.1880-1918' in T. Dickson (ed) *Capital and Class in Scotland*, p. 84 citing U.T.R papers, UGD 13 1 / 8, Letters 10.6.1869-1111.12.1878.

[22] I.G.C. Hutchison, *Industry, Reform and Empire Scotland, 1790-1880* (2020) pp. 52-3

[23] Cooke, *The Rise and Fall of the Scottish Cotton Industry* p. 82

[24] L. Levi, 'On the Cotton Trade and Manufacture as Affected by the Civil War in America'. *Journal of the Royal Statistical Society* (1863) Vol 26 No 1 (pp. 26-48). See pp 38-41

[25] The Vale factories' specialist manufacture of high quality 'turkey-red' goods did mean that they were better placed to survive the 'famine' than those which produced cheaper goods.

[26] *LH* 24 June 1871

[27] *See LH* 1871

[28] Bremner, *The Industries of Scotland*, pp. 295-304

[29] Ibid. p. 301

[30] Ibid. p. 304

[31] N. Tarrent, 'The Turkey Red Dyeing Industry in the Vale of Leven' *in* J. Butt and Ponting (eds) *Scottish Textile Industry* pp. 37-47

[32] Ibid. p. 45

[33] Cooke, *The Rise and Fall of the Scottish Cotton Industry* p.205

[34] *LH* 30 October 1897

[35] A.F. Jones, and G.N. Hopner, *On Leven's Banks* (1980) pp. 39-48

[36] M.S. Dilke and A.A.Templeton (eds), *The Third Statistical Account of Scotland*, Volume 6 The County of Dunbarton (1959) p. 60 and p. 90 (Hereafter referred to in footnotes as TSA Vol 6).

[37] J.Irving, *The Book of Dunbartonshire (1860)*

[38] J. Burrow, and co. (eds), *Denny 1844 - 1932* (1933)

[39] J. Shields, *Clyde Built: A history of shipbuilding on the Clyde* (1949) p. 108. MacMillan's is referred to as McMillan's in some sources.

[40] J. Schwerin, 'The evolution of the Clyde region's shipbuilding innovation system in the second half of the nineteenth century'. *Journal of Economic Geography* (2004) 4 pp 83-101. p. 87

[41] A. Slaven, *The Development of the West of Scotland 1750 - 1960* (1975) See Chapters 5 and 7.

[42] R.H.Campbell, *Scotland since 1707. The rise of an Industrial society* (1971) p. 230

[43] Schwerin, 'The evolution of the Clyde region's shipbuilding' quote from p84, citing C. MacLeod, Negotiating the rewards of invention: the shop floor inventor in Victorian Britain. *Working paper University of Bristol, mimeo.*(1998)

[44] The Denny Tank is all that survives of the company and is now a Scottish Maritime Museum.

[45] J. Shields, *Clyde Built: A history of shipbuilding on the Clyde* p.106

[46] Schwerin, 'The evolution of the Clyde region's shipbuilding' p. 94 and quote from Nenadic and S. Tuckett, *The Turkey Red Printed Cotton Industry* p. 13

[47] Irving, *The Book of Dunbartonshire* pp. 293-4

[48] *The Denny Lists* Volume 1. (1973) p. 1

[49] Ibid.

[50] Schwerin, 'The evolution of the Clyde region's shipbuilding' p. 87

[51] *The Denny Lists* p. 2

[52] P. Robertson, 'Shipping and Shipbuilding. The Case of William Denny and Brothers', *Business History* Vol 16 Issue 1. (1974) pp. 36-47

[53] Ibid. p. 39

[54] Shields, *Clyde Built* p. 108

[55] Robertson, 'Shipping and Shipbuilding' pp. 43-7

[56] R.H. Campbell, *The Rise and Fall of Scottish Industry* (1980) p. 64

[57] Hutchison, *Industry, Reform and Empire* p. 80

[58] Schwerin, 'The evolution of the Clyde region's shipbuilding' pp.89-96. See figure 1. p.89.

[59] R. Rodger, 'Employment, Wages and Poverty in the Scottish Cities 1841-1914' pp. 25-63 in
 G. Gordon, (ed) *Perspectives of the Scottish City* (1985)

[60] Melling, *Scottish Industrialists* pp. 94-100

[61] MacPhail, *Dumbarton through the Centuries* pp. 67-9

[62] *Dumbarton Herald.* August 1865 (Hereafter *DH* in footnotes)

3 The Expansion of Settlements in the Vale of Leven

Introduction

It was around 1850 coinciding with the arrival of the railway, that Alexandria became the principal settlement in the Vale of Leven. Like Renton, it was a factory colony that had grown up around 'the Grocery' on the Dumbarton to Luss road which ran along the west side of the valley. It grew towards the factories on the river and down towards the 'Bawbee Bridge' built in 1836, linking Alexandria to Bonhill village on the east bank of the Leven.[1] By 1864 (and the publication of the 1st Edition of the Ordnance Survey large scale maps of the area), Alexandria was larger than Renton in both physical size and population. It had expanded to become the main shopping and service centre for the whole of the Vale. Bonhill, like its neighbours had grown along a main road, in this case the turnpike road linking Dumbarton to Stirling. Further north, the settlement of Jamestown had been augmented by Archibald Orr Ewing who had built houses there for his workers at the nearby Levenbank printworks (later to become part of the Milton Works). It was a basic factory settlement consisting of several long terraced rows and described in 1884 as a 'model village which within our memory consisted of one or two insignificant houses only'.[2]

By the 1890s, the villages, particularly Renton and Alexandria, had experienced a good deal of expansion and in the latter case, old buildings in the centre of the village had been demolished and replaced by larger and more substantial red sandstone terraces.[3] There had even been the beginnings of a movement of people away from the town centre towards the periphery.[4] All four villages had continued their growth along predominantly north - south axes between the river and the steeply rising land beyond it. New planned housing units had been added to the southern ends of both Renton and Alexandria and, while some 'middle class' housing was now evident in all of the villages, it was most prevalent in Alexandria. The location of this housing was noticeably similar in each village. It was situated behind the village, that is further away from the river, the works, the main road and 'working class' housing. In Renton and Alexandria, the middle class housing tended to lie mainly to the west and south of the village centres. In Bonhill and Jamestown on the east bank, they were to the east and north.

A Comparison of the First and Second Editions of Ordnance Survey Maps of the Vale of Leven published in 1864 and 1899 (see Figures 3:1, 3:2, 3:3 and 3:4)[5]

These maps were published at scales of 6 inches to 1 mile and 25 inches to 1 mile. The 1864 map was surveyed around 1860 and the 1899 map was surveyed in 1896-97. Therefore the survey date, rather than the publishing date, is used generally when describing the townscapes.

The Printworks

Over the period 1860-1896, the most striking change in the industrial landscape was the increased size of the printworks, most dramatically in Alexandria and Jamestown, although almost all of the existing works showed signs of expansion. Jamestown's Levenbank Works, the most northerly factory, had nearly doubled in size and, with the Low Levenbank Yarn Works had been become part of the Milton Works that had been built behind Milton and Napierston Terraces.

In Alexandria, the expansion was most notable where the Croftengea Works had joined the Levenfield Works to its south, forming part of the extensive Alexandria Works which covered over fifteen acres of land. The relatively small Charleston Engraving Works, which had nonetheless almost doubled in size since 1860, had also been subsumed by the Alexandria Works.

In contrast, the Ferryfield Works to the south of the town close to Bonhill bridge, had changed little in that time except for a siding linking it with the railway system.[6] Directly opposite Ferryfield on the east bank of the river at Bonhill was the Dalmonach Works which had hardly grown since 1860. Together these works were to become part of the Calico Printers Association of Manchester during the decline of the 1890s. Dalmonach had however, been linked to the railway system by a 630 yard spur which ran through the Levenbank Works and also served the Milton Works.

Further south in Bonhill, the small Kirkland Works which had been bought by a Mr J Pender of Manchester in 1868 had disappeared, as had the Atherston Dyewood mill.[7] In contrast, the Dillichip Works had grown almost fourfold since 1860. The Dillichip bridge built in 1875, provided it with a link to the railway system between Renton and Alexandria.

The Renton works, Cordale and Dalquhurn, had also expanded considerably since 1860. Dalquhurn (off maps to the south) of was now, with the Alexandria works, the biggest in the Vale. Cordale was linked to Dalquhurn by a railway siding which ran along the river towpath and from there onto the main line.

Prior to the railway, goods were moved to and from the Vale by 'gabbart on the Leven, or by carts on the roads'.[8]

The Urban Environment

By the late nineteenth century, Alexandria was a small town that had grown rapidly since the 1860s, when it had already overtaken Renton as the largest village in the Vale. However, it was in the last two decades of the century when the most significant urban expansion took place.[9]

As in Renton, the first rows of workers' houses in Alexandria ran from the main Dumbarton to Luss Turnpike road eastwards, down towards the river and works. In 1841, Alexandria centred on North Street and Alexander Street. Thereafter it spread rapidly southwards towards the 'Bawbee Bridge', which had been built in 1836.

Bank Street had been laid out by 1833 to link the main road with Bonhill Ferry, when Bridge Street was only 'a proposed new road'. Subsequently it was built to link the bridge with what was then Main Street. The area within the triangle of ground formed by the three streets was well developed by 1860, when Bridge Street marked the southern limit of Alexandria - with the exception of a few large houses such as 'Parkneuk' built along the riverside facing Bonhill. By 1896, there had been further additions. To the north was Wilson Street, a broader street than its two southern neighbours consisting, for the most part, of two storey, red sandstone terraces. To the south, building on Main Street had been continued on its west side with the addition of several large detached houses, including St Mungo's Episcopal Manse and its church which was the southernmost building in the town. On the eastern side of Main Street, two storey, red sandstone, terraced rows had been built. The southern side of Bridge Street, west of the railway line had been developed since 1860. A hotel sat on the corner of Bridge Street and Main Street and significant house building had taken place south of this and west of the railway.[10] Most prominently, Middleton Street had been added parallel to Main Street. It contained small detached and semi detached cottages at its northern end and substantial two storey, terraced rows at its southern end. All of the buildings were constructed with red sandstone.

After 1879, Middleton Street and the streets linking it to Main Street formed a considerable housing development aimed at the skilled, working class and middle class in Alexandria.[11]

The 1891 census shows that the occupations of household heads in Middleton Street included skilled printworkers and engravers, as well as tradesmen and owners of small businesses such as joiners, grocers, bakers, a butcher, a 'dairy keeper' and a shoemaker. There were teachers, a clerk, a 'bookseller/printer', a railway signalman, an 'Inspector of Poor' and a 'steamboat captain', living in the street. Many of the householders were long established residents of Alexandria whose employed teenage or young adult children lived with them. It was a populous street. For example, two families, each of eight people lived at 91 Middleton Street, three households consisting of thirteen people lived at number 115, and at number 215 there were five households comprising thirty four people. Although still heavily dependent on the printworks, the town was diversifying. Shopkeepers, clerical, administrative and other service workers lived there, as did a growing number of professionals, including doctors, lawyers and bankers who were there to service the needs of the growing town. West of Middleton Street were the beginnings of Smollett Street, with detached properties including 'Rowanlea House' where Jane Cullen lived on 'private means', employing two 'live-in' domestic servants and Alexandria House where Englishman Arthur Ledgerwood, a 'Forgemaster' to trade, lived with his family and three servants.[12]

Alexandria was ideally placed to become the principal village in the Vale of Leven, not only due to the success of its printworks, but because it occupied a bridging point on the Leven opposite the long established 'parish' village of Bonhill. There was gently sloping land on which to expand. It was not constrained by the steeper slopes which restricted Renton's, and to a lesser extent, Bonhill's growth and it was a 'central place' convenient for Bonhill, Jamestown, Renton and Balloch.

As Figure 3:1 shows, as early as 1860 Alexandria had superior amenities to Renton, Bonhill and Jamestown with three schools, four churches, a post office, a gas works and a railway station. By 1896 as Figure 3:2 shows, a hotel, two public halls (one of which was the grand Alexandria Public Hall built in 1862), two banks, a football ground, a reservoir and a cemetery had been added along with another school and two more churches.

In 1841, Renton sat between the Dalquhurn Works to the south and the Cordale Works to the north. Houses were constructed along Main Street on the Dumbarton to Luss Road and there were three streets, Stirling Street, Thimble Street and Burn Street, running off Main Street towards the River Leven. Back Street parallel to Main Street on its western side, had existed since the 1820s and by 1860 had, like Main Street, an almost continuous row of houses on either side of the street. The Cordale Estate that contained both Cordale House and the Cordale Works, precluded houses being built further north on the east side of Main Street. Access to the Cordale Works was via the river tow path while Cordale House, occupied by the Works' proprietors, was reached by a sweeping, tree lined drive which ran from a lodge house on Main Street north of Stirling Street.

By 1860 (Figure 3:3), the village did not extend much beyond its 1841 boundaries. There had been a variety of two storey houses consisting of short, terraced rows and cottages built at the north end of Main Street on its western side facing the Cordale Estate, a trend that was to continue up until, and after 1897. The biggest change in the 1841- 60 period was the building of the railway to the west of the village, along the break of slope, beyond which the land rose more steeply towards the summit of Carman Hill.

By 1896 (Figure 3:4), building coverage had increased in the northern part of Renton in Main Street, Burn Street (the western part of which was now renamed 'King Street'), Thimble Street and Stirling Street. Additions tended to be small scale, although some rebuilding and redevelopment had taken place. To the south of the village additions had been more striking. In 1860, the village ended abruptly at the 'Mission Church' on Main Street. By 1896, when the United Presbyterian Church occupied that site, building on Main Street had been extended southwards by about 150 yards.[13] This extension was renamed Lennox Street, and along this stretch, streets were constructed on either side. This new 'planned unit' was impressively laid out with wide streets, red sandstone houses, a new church, four public buildings and halls, including a Masonic Lodge and Drill Hall.

By 1864, above the north western edge of Renton, Carman Loch had been extended to form a large reservoir. It provided vital supplies of drinking water for the village, at a time when insanitary conditions were having a serious effect on public health.[14]

As the oldest hamlet, or clachan, in the valley Bonhill always retained links to its rural surroundings, in spite of the influx of printworkers. By 1860, much of the housing was situated along the Main Street on the Dumbarton to Stirling road. It had spread southwards from the ferry crossing / bridging point on the river to the Dillichip Works. By 1896, Dillichip Terrace, a long, continuous row of two storey houses had been built to serve the works opposite. The built up section of Bonhill's Main Street ran south for three quarters of a mile from the bridge, linking it to Alexandria. The prime location of workers' houses was initially along the east side of Main Street and in Burn Street, with a few older cottages in the 'back lane' and on the west side of Main Street, near the river where the Manse was located. By 1897, George Street had been built between Main Street and the 'back lane' to its east ,where the land begins to rise steeply.

In 1860, Bonhill's amenities were inferior to those of Renton and Alexandria. Three churches and two schools were shown on the map, one of which was the Dalmonach Works school which closed in 1870.[15] By the end of the century the other school had been replaced by a larger, public school, by which time a post office, bank and public hall had been added to the village.

Jamestown had been extended prior to the survey of 1860, and was largely formed of 'long ranges of two or three storey settlements erected by Archibald Orr Ewing employer of almost all who reside there'.[16]

It was sited directly east of Orr Ewing's Levenbank Works on the Dumbarton to Stirling Road, north of Bonhill. The first section of its long characteristic terraced rows, Levenbank, that ran south towards Bonhill, had been built by that date. There were few amenities apart from the school and a railway station on the Forth and Clyde Junction line that ran from Balloch to Stirling. Orr Ewing had opposed the building of a pub in 1870 but was quite happy to sell liquor in his own store.[17] By 1896, with the extension of the Levenbank Works and the growth of the Milton Works, there had been the addition of the impressive Jamestown Parish Church and church hall in the north of the village. Like many of the buildings in the Vale they were constructed of locally quarried red sandstone. The original Levenbank terraced row had been extended by the addition of another, longer terrace, and by Milton Terrace. All of these were on the east side of the main road. A fourth terrace, Napierston Terrace, had been built along the Auchencarroch Road at its junction with the Dumbarton - Stirling Road.

The Orr Ewing had been largely responsible for a substantial growth of terraced housing in both Jamestown and Alexandria, but not all of the workers' houses were built to the same specifications. There were 'clear gradations of quality to complement the workplace hierarchy' and it was certainly the case that 'continued employment' was 'a condition of tenancy'.[18]

In all four villages, most of the housing developments described above were built in the latter part of the 1860 to 1897 period.

The Railway

The Caledonian and Dumbartonshire Railway opened in 1850, and ran from the western terminus of the Forth and Clyde canal at Bowling, a steamer port linked to Glasgow. The new line ran westwards to Balloch via Dumbarton, with stations at Renton, Alexandria, Balloch and Balloch Pier.

For the Vale, the boost to trade, industry, workforce mobility, and tourism was enormous. In these early days the journey from Balloch to Glasgow took 1½ hours, ½ an hour by train to Bowling and 1 hour by steamer to Glasgow. The cost varied from 11d to 1/6d.[19]

The railway was augmented in 1856 by the Balloch to Stirling line belonging to the Forth and Clyde Railway Company which had a station at Jamestown, and, more importantly in 1858, when the Glasgow, Dumbarton and Helensburgh Railway was opened. This had the effect of extending the Balloch - Bowling line to Glasgow, providing a further boost to both freight and passenger transport.[20] In 1860, only one of the works, Croftengea, was linked to the railway by a siding but this was to change rapidly as the larger works connected to the line from 1861 onwards[21] (see section The Printworks, above).

NOTES

[1] Jones and Hopner, *On Leven's Banks* p. 21

[2] D. McLeod, *Dumbarton, Vale of Leven and Loch Lomond* (1884) p. 129

[3] Jones and Hopner, *On Leven's Banks* p. 22

[4] *LH* 16 May 1891

[5] For information on Ordnance Survey maps and mapping see R. Hewitt, *Map of a Nation: A Biography of the Ordnance Survey* (2011)

[6] Ferryfield had been closed between 1864 and 1871

[7] *LH* 9 May 1868

[8] Jones and Hopner, *On Leven's Banks* p. 55. A 'gabbart' or 'lighter' was a barge used to transport goods up and down the river.

[9] An update of the *first edition Ordnance Survey Map* (1864) dated 1879 appears in J. Irving, Book of Dumbartonshire Vol 1

[10] This became the Griffin Hotel, which survived into the twenty-first century.

[11] Irving, *Book of Dunbartonshire.*

[12] Smollett Street is referred to as Smollett Road in the 1891 Census.

[13] Jones and Hopner, *On Leven's Banks* p. 71. The nearby Gaelic Church built in 1856, was still in existence in spite of the continuing decrease in those of Highland birth and the negligible number of Gaelic speakers. The congregation moved to a new church in Latta Street Dumbarton in the early twentieth century.

[14] Vale of Leven History Project. *www.valeofleven.org.uk/ renton3.html*

[15] *LH* 25 June 1870

[16] McLeod, *Dumbarton, Vale of Leven and Loch Lomond* p. 129

[17] *LH* 30 April 1870

[18] Melling, *Scottish Industrialists* p. 84. and footnote 81 which cites U.T. R. papers UGD 1 / 8 Letter 20.2.1879.

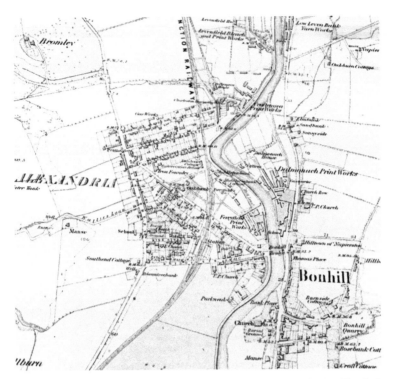

Alexandria and part of Bonhill. Fig 3:1 above - 1860. Fig 3:2 below - 1896.

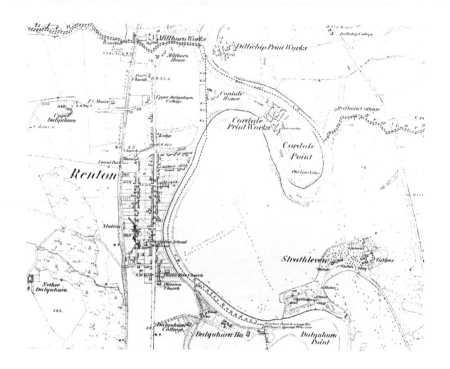

Renton Fig 3:3 above - 1860. Fig 3:4 below - 1896.

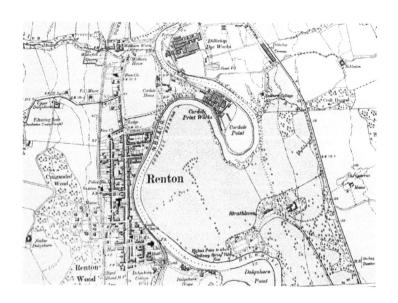

54

Photo 1 Dillichip Works, Bonhill

Photo 2 Bridge Street Alexandria from the Leven c. 1911

Photo 3 Burn Street, Bonhill

Photo 4 Renton, in the 1890s. Southern end of Main Street, looking north

Photo 5 Mitchell Street Alexandria, showing printworkers cottages

Photo 6 Jamestown Dam

4 Urban Growth in Dumbarton

Introduction

Prior to 1850, there was little need for urban expansion in Dumbarton. Most of its people lived in the old medieval core of the burgh around High Street, College Street and Church Street (see Chapter 1, Figure 1:2). As the population began to grow rapidly, open spaces within this confined area were given over to housing as accommodation became cramped and overcrowded. Housing was urgently required for industrial workers who were flocking to the burgh.

Local industrialists were agents of urban growth. The Dennys were responsible for building the first substantial 'planned unit' of housing in Dumbarton, which marked a continued expansion on the west bank of the river and into Cardross Parish. This development, Dennystown, constructed in the 1850s was:

designed to house some 210 families, or around 1,000 persons, in rows of two storey blocks ranged around three large courtyards ... By the standards of the period the Dennystown houses were fair sized, parlours or living rooms measured 15' x 11' 6", bedrooms 10' 10" x 9' 3". The dwellings were of 1, 2, 3 or 4 apartments and the estate streets and squares were lit by gas. The back premises were supplied with wash houses, coal cellars and privies and a water supply was designed to be provided to each of the three courtyards but the pipes and water troughs were not installed until 1861. The provision of a direct water supply to each house had to wait for a further twenty years and the impetus given by a growing official concern with public health and a typhoid epidemic in the Dennystown in 1880. By this time the estate had passed out of the hands of the Denny family and for some years prior to 1881 the deterioration of Dennystown and the high level of mortality associated with the area had been a cause of concern to the local authority. [1]

When Irving, writing in 1857, stated that more work had been done in Dumbarton in two or three years than in the previous generation, he was doubtless referring to Dennystown, but at the same time there had been piecemeal redevelopment taking place in the High Street.[2] The machinery of municipal enterprise was increasingly evident as the Victorian era progressed. Projects included: a cemetery (1854); riverside embanking reclamation work (1858); a gravity fed system bringing water from the Kilpatrick Hills (1860); the building of a large academy and burgh hall (1865-66) and a reservoir (1874).

By the 1870s, Dumbarton was expanding eastwards to where the ground had been very poorly drained and liable to flooding prior to the deepening of the Clyde. Many of the houses here would be built by the Dumbarton Building Society.[3] The need to accommodate skilled tradesmen employed at the adjacent Leven Shipyard, encouraged Peter Denny to take an interest in the society, and in 1873, he 'handed over property and ground to the value of £1,470 on a loan for 5 years at 4% per annum'.[4] Thereafter, the society took possession of brick cottages and building sites belonging to him in Leven and Clyde Streets.[5] Osborne is in no doubt as to the mutually beneficial effects which subsequent developments had for both the owner occupiers and for Dennys: a process which inhibited the mobility of the inhabitants and encouraged stability.[6] Labour mobility had cost Dennys skilled manpower during earlier industrial disputes in both 1856 and 1865 when many workers left the burgh.[7] House owning anchored skilled workers to their homes, and the manual working elite, to the fore in the new building society, were among the main beneficiaries of its activities. The society was unsuccessful in its attempts to buy land on the periphery of Dumbarton and 'again Mr Denny was approached for ground at Knoxland, and he agreed to give 10,016 square yards at a price of £1,972'.[8] By 1884, 22.3% of the society's house owners were carpenters, 15.6% joiners, 15.6% platers and 12.2% were riveters.[9] Even the smallest one room and kitchen houses were occupied by skilled men. No labourers are to be found on the building society's list.

This was the development of 'Newtown' and Knoxland, the second noteworthy expansion of the burgh in 30 years. It was markedly superior to Dennystown in layout, facilities and design. It consisted of a variety of house types: there were grey sandstone tenements; terraced cottages and two storey terraced rows, unlike Dennystown which consisted almost entirely of brick built tenements.

This had the effect of producing a strongly 'skilled manual' profile to Dumbarton East where 'unskilled' industrial workers, 'labourers' and the Irish were all 'under-represented' by 1871.

Grander housing was constructed on the edge of the town, notably at Kirktonhill overlooking Dennystown and the river, and on the Bonhill and Round Riding Roads to the north east of the old town. These houses tended to be inhabited by professional classes of the type found in many small Scottish burghs, as well as those in higher managerial positions in the shipyards.

In spite of ambitious building projects and the prosperity engendered by shipbuilding, for many the reality of living in Dumbarton meant cramped rooms close to, or in the High Street or College Street ('The Vennel'). This was the overcrowded heart of the burgh, where it was not unusual to find 'closes' housing more than one hundred inhabitants.[10]

A Comparison of the First and Second Editions of Ordnance Survey Maps of Dumbarton Burgh published in 1864 and 1899. (See Figures 4:1, 4:2, 4:3, 4:4, 4:5 and 4:6)

As for the Vale of Leven, these maps were published at scales of 6 inches to 1 mile and 25 inches to 1 mile. The 1864 map was surveyed around 1859-60 and the 1899 map was surveyed in 1896-97.

Over the period from 1860 to 1890 the burgh's population had more than doubled.[11] There had been both internal redevelopment and more importantly, substantial additions at the periphery.

The Urban and Industrial Environment

For the purposes of description, the High Street is divided into four sectors corresponding to *Census Enumeration Districts*. These are not geographically exact but are described as:

South West - on the 'Leven' side from the Parish Church, including Church Place, to Dumbarton Cross (i.e. where Quay Street and College Street meet the High Street);[12]

South East - as above on the 'landward' side.

North West - the buildings on the 'Leven' side of the street running from Dumbarton Cross to the old bridge and beyond into Artizan;

North East - as above but on the eastern or 'landward' side of the street;

In 1860, the highest building densities were along the High Street, particularly around Dumbarton Cross, parts of Quay Street and College Street immediately adjacent to it.

College Street had been built upon for about 200 yards of its length on both sides of the street but with very little 'backland' infilling.

Church Street has almost continuous development on its west side from High Street to College Park Street which has an incomplete row of buildings on its south side .

Strathleven Place has some larger houses in evidence. These are substantial middle class, detached and semi detached properties which include two manses.

Effectively, the east - west running railway line and the north - south running 'Mill Burn', represent the northern and eastern extent respectively, of the continuously built up area of Dumbarton east of the River Leven.

Beyond these boundaries are the beginnings of the burgh's expansion at Castle Street which extends on to Glasgow Road for 150 yards from Church Street and on Bonhill Road north of the railway. In both cases there are scatterings of much larger houses, with those around Bonhill Road having extensive grounds and gardens.

By 1896, there were many more buildings and much infilling in the core of the burgh. Extensive outward expansion is also evident. Buildings on College Street now extended for over 300 yards from the

High Street to its junction with College Park Street by which time this had a continuous row of buildings on its south side.

Conspicuous infilling had taken place in the area bounded by the curve of the High Street, Church Street and the railway line.

There were significant changes to land use on the 'landward' side of the High Street. There was marked infilling in the segment bounded by High Street, the western side of College Street and the recently built Risk Street. Prior to that these areas had been gardens.

It was a similar situation in the area between College Street and Church Street bounded by the High Street in the south and College Park Street in the north. Gardens and cultivated land had largely been replaced by buildings which included a cattle market, a theatre and a timber yard situated behind the pre-existing tannery. There was now continuous building coverage along College Park Street and round into College Street.

'Back houses' were to be found throughout the old medieval core of Dumbarton and many were of poorer quality than the tenements which fronted the street. They accommodated a mass of people living in cramped, sub-standard, badly constructed, and makeshift dwellings.[13]

New streets had been laid out since the 1860s. These included:

- Risk Street running west from College Street to Artizan which was almost continuously built on along one side of the street

- McLean Place running from Church Street eastwards. In the 1860s, it had been a lane which separated the County Buildings and prison from open ground to the north. By the 1890s, it had a row of grey sandstone tenements, and at its eastern end, St Patrick's Primary School which opened in 1887[14]

The school hall still exists and is now the parish hall of St Patrick's Church.

In Church Street there had been infilling on the corner with Castle Street. The substantial grey sandstone tenements built there still stand. Just to the north of this, Dumbarton Academy had relocated from the west side of Church Street, across the road, into substantial buildings which would become the Burgh Hall.[15]

The eastward expansion of the burgh, the impact of the railways, and increasing industrialisation are the clearest signs of Dumbarton's transformation over the second half of the nineteenth century.

Buildings in Castle Street had been demolished to accommodate an extension of the gasworks.

The extensive area south of Castle Street/Glasgow Road, largely undeveloped in 1860, was by 1896, dominated by William Denny and Brothers Leven Shipyard (opened 1867) which extended down to the castle. 'The shipyard (iron)', the 'Dock Building Yard (wood)' and the 'Victoria Shipbuilding Yard' all shown on the 1864 map, have been swallowed up by the massive Leven Yard which extended to over 40 acres.

This end of the burgh is scored with railway lines and sidings running into the Leven Yard and the yards immediately south and east of the Parish Church. The most enduring yard was occupied by Archibald MacMillan and Sons (from 1845-1932). It is described as an iron shipbuilding yard on the 1864 map. By the 1890s it had been considerably extended. The 'Graving Dock' was still in existence but a large tidal basin had been cut between this yard and the Leven Yard, and yet another substantial basin had been cut in the latter, further south near the mouth of the river.

The Newtown/Knoxland development was built to the east of the Leven Yard on land that had been undeveloped in 1860. Its parallel streets run at right angles south from Glasgow Road. From west to east: housing on Leven Street and Clyde Street, comprised in the main, of tenement rows and terraced houses; immediately east of this lies Wallace Street, a broader street with lower density, semi-detached, 'cottage style' housing and three storey terraces; east again, is Victoria Street forming in part, the western side of Knoxland Square which has substantial cottage rows on its south side; Bruce Street helps to form the eastern edge of the square, and beyond that Buchanan Street, follows the course of Gruggie's Burn.

There is continuous building on the south side of Glasgow Road between the entrances to Leven Street, Clyde Street, Wallace Street, and Victoria Street.

This expansion was not merely a housing estate, but a successful attempt to forge a new community. Aimed specifically at emerging 'middle class' and 'skilled working class' residents, it had wide streets, and there were open spaces planted with grass and trees. This was especially true at the eastern end of the developments around the tree lined Knoxland Square, where there was a church, school and bandstand. The 'Newtown', bounded by Glasgow Road to the north, Leven Street to the west, Castlegreen Street to the south and Buchanan Street/Gruggie's Burn to the east covered some 25 acres. The site was not developed as a 'planned unit'. Land was built upon as it became available, and not all of it was developed by the Dumbarton Building Society. This helps to account for the variety of house types and building styles occurring in such a relatively small area. In contrast to comparatively affluent Knoxland, Bankend, a tenement built immediately east of Gruggie's Burn quickly became a poor and overcrowded dwelling place.

The area of Dumbarton burgh 'over the bridge', immediately west of the river in Cardross Parish, was the site of Dennystown a housing development, begun in 1853. By 1860 it had become almost surrounded by industry. To the north, the railway line separated it from Dennystown Forge and Levenbank Foundry, while at its southernmost end was a boiler and engine works complex built on either side of the western end of the bridge. A tannery, a glue works and an iron foundry were situated to the east, between the tenements and the river. Tanneries and glue works were often located near each other as both used animal hides and glue works also used animal bones which had to be boiled in the process. Victorian glue works and tanneries were notoriously malodorous and the smells from these factories, along with the smoke and smells and airborne pollutants from the foundries must have been unpleasant for the residents of Dennystown who lived very close by.

Westbridgend, the road that leads from Cardross Road to Dumbarton Bridge and which marked the western boundary of Dennystown, was also well developed by 1860. There were several blocks of tenements on its eastern side, this in stark contrast to most of its western side, where immediately south of the Black Bull Inn was the United Presbyterian (UP) Church and manse. Between the manse and the bridge there were two very grand houses, Bellfield and Levenford. Each was built only 30 or so yards from Westbridgend, but crucially, on high ground, which gave them open views to the east and the Kilpatrick Hills high above the burgh. The houses overlooked Dennystown which was built downslope to the river. Both had substantial grounds and gardens guarded by lodge houses close to the road. Levenford was built for shipbuilder James Denny, and in the 1861 census he is recorded as living there with his family and four servants.

By 1896, Dennystown Forge had more than doubled in size, and there had been further tenement building north of the UP Church (which had been impressively rebuilt in 1888).[16] A public school, erected in 1876, was just behind these buildings. However, the biggest change on the west bank was a large increase in the number of homes for the professional and managerial classes at Kirktonhill, an extensive area of high status, low density, housing which had been built a discreet distance from the manual workers' homes. It is located south west of the bridge on a hill that runs down to the shores of the Clyde and lies adjacent to the western edge of Levengrove Public Park which was previously the estate and home of the Dixon family who had once owned the Glassworks. It was gifted to the burgh by shipbuilders Peter Denny and John MacMillan and opened in 1885.[17] More professional and managerial class housing had been built on Oxhill Road. The road had been laid out by 1860 and though not as grand or extensive as Kirktonhill, by 1899 it contained large detached and semi-detached properties.

The 1864 map named some the prominent buildings which were present, but these are not named on the 1897 map.[18] Foremost among these was the Parish Church rebuilt in 1811. An enduring symbol of Dumbarton's religious heritage, it occupies the site of an early medieval church dedicated to St Patrick.

A Free Church set back from the 'south eastern' section of the High Street had been extended since the 1860s.

The school which had once adjoined St Patrick's RC Church had been replaced by one at McLean Place. In 1903, the church itself would be replaced by the present building on Strathleven Place.

The United Presbyterian Church ('the UP church' on the maps) was situated on the corner of High Street and Church Place. By the 1890s there was a 'Union Church (Episcopalian)' on the corner of Glasgow Road and Leven Street at the western edge of the new Knoxland development. The prominent yellow sandstone St Augustine's Episcopal Church which still stands on the High Street, was built in 1873. An earlier Episcopalian Church dedicated to St Patrick, had been opened in 1847 and its foundation had involved both Scots and Irish Episcopalians.[19] There were smaller 'parish' churches built at Dalreoch in 1873 and Knoxland in 1884.[20]

The County Buildings in Church Street now housed the Sheriff Court and had been extended since 1860. In between the County Buildings and the new Academy on Church Street stood the Denny Working Men's Institute (1892).

By the second half of the nineteenth century the southern end of the High Street was home to three banks. In 1860, the Commercial Bank was on the 'Leven' side of the street and the Bank of Scotland on the 'landward' side. They were still there in 1897, when the fine red sandstone British Linen Bank was opened close by at 17-21 High Street.

In 1860, the aptly named 'Steamboat Tavern' sat on the quay near Quay Street. The Elephant Hotel which was demolished in the 1930s, was located on High Street near Quay Street. The Steamboat Tavern does not appear on the later map but by then there were three other public houses in the western sector of the High Street. One of these was the Elephant and Castle, which after Glencairn House (built in 1623) was the second oldest building remaining on the street until it was finally demolished in 2017. There were a further three pubs to the north of the Cross.

An extensive area of middle class housing had been laid down along Bonhill Road, Alexander Street and Round Riding Road, comprising mainly of large semi detached and detached houses.

The Railway

The railway age had arrived in Dumbarton by 1850 with the opening of the 'Caledonian and Dumbartonshire Railway' which ran from Bowling to Balloch via Dumbarton. In return for allowing the railway company to run their line across 'Broad Meadow', the burgh received £1000 to be used for embanking the Leven and to begin reclamation of 'the Drowned Lands'.[21] The river had burst its banks in the sixteenth century and the flooded land was never drained. The accurate 1832 map produced by the Government's boundary commission shows the extent of the flooded area prior to reclamation (see Figure 1:2). By 1860, this land had been improved, but was shown as 'rough grazing' on the 1st Edition map, most likely because it had not fully dried out and remained boggy.

The 'Caledonian and Dumbartonshire' line which followed the route now taken by the Sustrans Cycle track into the burgh from the east, was linked to Glasgow eight years later (see previous section on the Vale of Leven). This network was eventually taken over by the North British Railway Company. Its 'intense' rival the Caledonian Railway Company added a further line into Dumbarton from Glasgow in 1896. This line followed the current route from the east into the burgh. The company built Dumbarton East station to cater for the growing suburbs in this part of the burgh. The lines conjoined between this station and the railway bridge over Bonhill Road/Strathleven Place. A jointly run line continued to its terminus at Balloch, while the North British Line extended from Dalreoch to Helensburgh and beyond.[22]

There had been no railway sidings in 1860, but by 1897 the east end of the burgh was scored with them. There were two goods stations lying just north of Castle Street/Glasgow Road: one run by the 'Dumbarton and Balloch Joint Line' and the other by the 'Caledonian Railway'. Multiple sidings ran from the Caledonian Line between

Dumbarton Central and Dumbarton East to the goods stations and MacMillan's yard immediately behind the Parish Church.

By 1897 appreciable changes had taken place north of the embanked railway line which largely separated the urban from the rural part of the burgh. The 'Drowned Lands' had been fully reclaimed and were the site of improved pasture land, a slaughter house and an ornamental pond. What is now known as 'the Common' was termed 'Meadow Park', and there was a footpath linking Church Street to the Cottage Hospital, the line now taken by Townend Road. Dumbarton Golf Course was laid out directly north west of the ornamental pond in 1888.

NOTES

[1] B.D. Osborne, 'Dumbarton shipbuilding and workers' housing 1850-1900', *Scottish Urban History* Vol 3 (1) (1980) p. 4

[2] J. Irving, *The History of Dumbartonshire: From the earliest period to the present time* (1857) p. 296

[3] J.Lyon, *Jubilee Souvenir of Dumbarton Building Society. 1873 - 1923 Fifty Years History* (1923) p. 2. The Society was initially known as the Dumbarton Land and Buildings Investment Company. It became the Dumbarton Building Society in 1878.

[4] Ibid. p. 3

[5] Ibid. p. 5

[6] Osborne, *'Dumbarton shipbuilding and workers' housing'* p. 9 cites census and valuation returns for the Newtown area which show that in a sample of occupants, 82% of owner occupiers were still at the same address seven years after the 1881 census, compared to 32% of those who were renting.

[7] See Chapter 2, and also J. Foster. et al, 'Sectarianism, Segregation and Politics in Clydeside in the later Nineteenth Century' p. 89 in M. Mitchell, (ed) *New Perspectives on the Irish in Scotland* (2008)

[8] Lyon, *Jubilee Souvenir of Dumbarton Building Society* p. 6

[9] Osborne, 'Dumbarton shipbuilding and workers' housing' p. 9

[10] Under-recording of inhabitants was very common, and it is certain that the numbers living at many addresses were concealed from the census enumerator.

[11] Minor boundary changes contributed to this growth.

[12] The area the immediate vicinity of the Parish Church leading to the High Street is known as Church Place.

[13] Census enumerators were expected to provide brief details of the district which they surveyed. In Dumbarton, especially in the High Street and College Street, there was frequent reference to addresses 'including closes and back houses'.

[14] MacPhail, *Dumbarton Through the Centuries* p. 84

[15] The facade of this hall was retained for many years after the Burgh Hall closed and it now fronts the newly located Council Buildings opened in 2018.

[16] MacPhail, *Dumbarton Through the Centuries* p. 77

[17] J. Hood, *Old Dumbarton* (1999)

[18] On the 2nd Edition OS map some were indicated by abbreviations like PH for Public House or Ch for Church.

[19] I. Meredith, 'Irish Migrants in the Scottish Episcopal Church in the 19th Century', in Mitchell (ed) *New Perspectives* p. 61

St Mungo's Episcopalian Church was opened in Alexandria in 1877 and it too was founded by both Scots and Irish Episcopalians.

[20] MacPhail, *Dumbarton Through the Centuries* pp. 77-81, p. 85, *gives a comprehensive history of church building in nineteenth and early twentieth century Dumbarton.*

[21] Ibid. p. 69

[22] D. Spaven, *The Railway Atlas of Scotland. Two Hundred Years of History* (2015) Maps Ch3

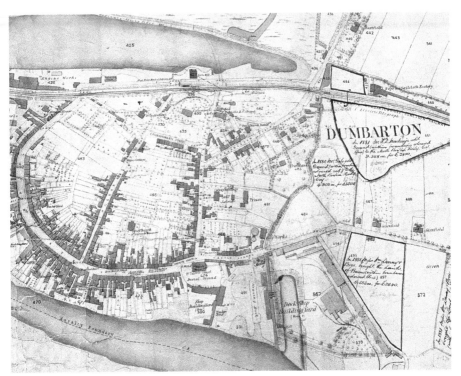

Dumbarton. Figure 4:1 above - 1860. Figure 4:2 below - 1896.

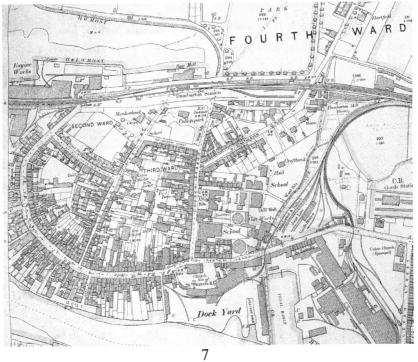

Figure 4:3 (above left) and Figure 4:4 (above right) show West Bridgend in 1860 and 1896 respectively. Dumbarton Bridge is just off the maps at the middle right where it adjoins West Bridgend

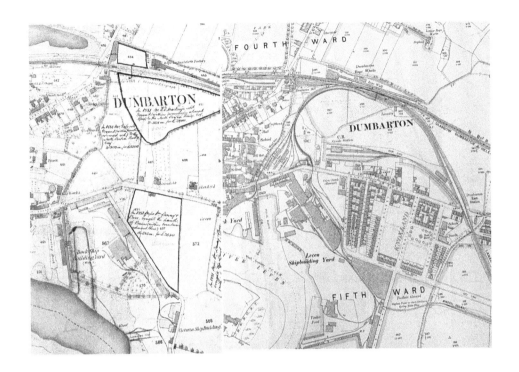

Figures 4:5 (above left) and 4:6 (above right) show the east end of Dumbarton in 1860 and 1896 respectively. The growth of the Leven Shipyard, the housing developments at Newtown/Knoxland and the railway sidings are all apparent in the 1896 map.

Photo 8 Knoxland Square

Photo 7 Corner of High Street and
College Street c.1894

Photo 9 Leven Shipyard in 1909

Photo 10 Dennystown in the early twentieth century

Photo 11 Dennystown Forge c.1902

5 Surviving in a Hostile Environment: Population Growth, Employment, Living and Working Conditions

Population Growth

In the period from 1861 to 1891 the Vale of Leven and Dumbarton were communities with young and quickly growing populations. Thousands of incomers were attracted to the area and over this thirty year period the population in the Vale rose from around 11,000 to over 19,000, while in Dumbarton, starting from a lower base of 8,200, the population had reached nearly 17,000 (see figure 5:1). This growth was fuelled by both natural increase and robust in-migration. The influx of young adult in-migrants led in turn to a high birth rate. In the Vale throughout this period, over one third of the population were children of fourteen years and under, whereas those aged forty-five and over accounted for less than one in five of the residents.[1]

Dumbarton displayed a similar population distribution, but if anything, there was a slightly smaller proportion of over forty-fives.[2] Heavy in-migration was a more recent phenomenon in Dumbarton, with a substantially larger ratio of migrants to locals among the younger adult population and correspondingly fewer people in the older age ranges. These figures are comparable to those for other Scottish towns[3].

In all economic migrations, young, often unattached, and healthy adults make up the bulk of those on the move. At all four census years considered here, in the 15-44 age range, females outnumbered males in the Vale of Leven whereas the opposite was the case in Dumbarton. This was a reflection of contrasts in the jobs market where the printworks employed many young women, whereas in Dumbarton heavy industry attracted young men.

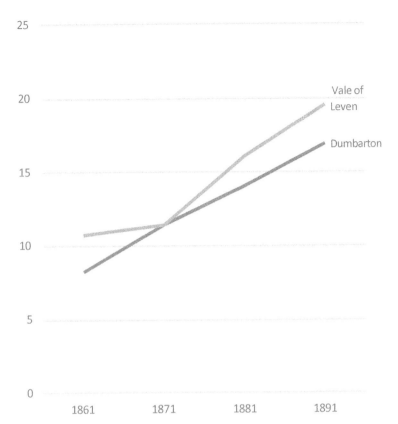

25

20   Vale of
                                                      Leven

                                                      Dumbarton

15

10

5

0
        1861   1871   1881   1891

Figure 5:1 - Population Growth: Dumbarton Burgh and
the villages of the Vale of Leven 1861-1891 (in thousands)

Health and Housing

Rapid population increase put an enormous strain on infrastructure. As Chapter 3 describes, the Vale's townscapes expanded to cope with this surge, but progress was not always steady. Conditions in Renton were definitely poorer than in the rest of the Vale. It had fewer houses with a direct supply of water and on average, fewer rooms per house than the other three settlements. Nonetheless, as the Medical Health Officer states in his 1891 report:

Of even more importance ... is the number of persons per room. Wherever the habit prevails of keeping lodgers, rooms are specially apt to be overcrowded...and when a sufficient staff of inspectors is appointed a considerable part of their work ...will be the visiting of houses with let in lodgers

He comments on progress that had been made in the Vale since 1881:

In Jamestown the persons per room have decreased from 2.77 to 1.94, in Bonhill from 2.37 to 2.20, and in Alexandria from 2.12 to 1.84...In Cardross parish, Renton in 1881, had 2.65 per room, and in 1891 2.33 persons. It still, therefore, lags behind the rest of the Vale of Leven, and when we come to examine its death-rate from all causes, and especially from zymotic (infectious) diseases, the facts will be found to correspond' [4]

Death rate statistics available for the latter portion of this period show that Renton was more akin to Dumbarton than to the neighbouring parish of Bonhill, which contained the other settlements.[5] Bonhill village did have its own problems, notably in Burn Street, which was named for the burn that ran down the middle of the street separating one row of houses from the other. Untreated sewage 'finds its way into the (Leven) by means of the burn of Bonhill which is simply an open sewer, and very offensive in hot weather'.[6]

The preponderance of 'fever' (typhus) cases reported here was no coincidence. There had been two outbreaks reported in the 1860s, and even as late as 1891 a typhus epidemic in Renton was narrowly averted.[7] It was a disease that had almost disappeared around twenty years earlier, and its unexpected reappearance was an unpleasant surprise for the health authorities. In the March of that year there had been an initial case in Napierston Terrace, Jamestown, but this had been contained. A more serious outbreak occurred in Renton a few months later.

The Medical Officer himself had visited

a house consisting of two small apartments in a crowded locality, there were no less than twelve inmates, constituting two families. One of the inmates was a woman with a baby two or three days old. In this house there were four cases.

The source of the outbreak could not be identified, but the illness had begun in August, a month before it had been diagnosed. These cases were in the Henderson and Fraser families at 134 Back Street, Renton. Four more

were discovered, one at McCrae's, 18 Burn Street, another at Murray's, 18 Burn Street, one at Bell's, 6 Lennox Street and one at Haddow's, 68 Back Street. These were at once sent to hospital ... other five cases occurred in the above mentioned houses, there being thus 17 cases in all, constituting the outbreak

The authorities acted swiftly and thoroughly, as all of the infected were hospitalised. The baby had been unaffected and was looked after by a nurse. Bedding and clothing was either burned or disinfected. The houses were fumigated and lime washed and the windows left open to air the premises. There had been plans to quarantine the patients in an out of town reception house, but local feelings mitigated against this course of action. Notices were posted throughout the Vale warning of typhus and instructing people in prevention of the disease. It was a very thorough response which stopped the spread of typhus and a clear example of the growing power and effectiveness of community health measures, which would have been unthinkable earlier in the century. Typhus was to flare up again at the end of the year, this time at a 'tramps lodging house' in the 'slums of Alexandria'. It killed both the landlord and his wife, along with one other person, before being contained. It had infected eleven people in all, fewer than in Renton, but with three fatalities.[8]

Nevertheless, the rurality of Bonhill parish, its well planned villages where the printworks' owners 'provided houses for their workers, which, in the initial stages, were of reasonable quality' and the ease with which expansion could be directed, all served to keep it comparatively healthy.[9] So in spite of an expanding population, problems of overcrowding in the Vale were not as bad as in Dumbarton and lodging was not as prevalent. Printwork owners understood that to retain a workforce in a relatively remote location housing had to be provided, but working class housing was basic and contained few amenities. According to one individual, his family of seven moved to Govan Drive, Alexandria in 1915, where they inhabited a room and kitchen with a toilet on the stairhead shared with three other families. In Jamestown, Milton Terrace for instance, also exhibited atrocious conditions well in to the twentieth century, when according to Communist Party election literature, it contained '96 houses, 433 inhabitants and only 17 privies'.[10]

Conditions were far from ideal, but the comparatively small sizes of the villages, their relatively low housing densities and proximity to the countryside tended to ameliorate wretched conditions and 'although there were squalid areas, it is important to stress that, overall, this area was not as bad as some' in inner cities, nor indeed Dumbarton.[11]

Michael Anderson, states that:

Differences in geographical location have at times also had consequences, especially for mortality: towns at river mouths often had higher death rates than those higher up rivers, for example, and those with access to good water supplies from local springs or nearby mountain slopes were much better off than those which used wells or slow running lowland rivers.[12]

From that description, the Vale was in a much healthier location than Dumbarton which was built near the mouth of the Leven: albeit a fast flowing river, it was tidal at this stage. Large amounts of noxious effluent discharged by the printworks were carried downstream to within a few yards of Dumbarton High Street's houses and wells. As late as 1891, all raw sewage from more than 19,000 people living along the banks of the Leven to the north, the sewage from Dumbarton itself with a population of nearly 17,000, and discharge from all of the other industrial and agricultural operations in the valley, ended up in the Leven.[13]

In Dumbarton, the rapid growth in population is indicative of net in-migration and of industrial prosperity which signalled an abundance of jobs in shipbuilding and its associated foundries and machine shops. Benefits percolated throughout the economy. Houses were needed and housebuilding schemes provided employment for masons, joiners, plumbers, slaters, plasterers and painters. Shopping and transport facilities were required as well as a whole range of public and professional services, stimulated not merely by urban growth but by the improvement in educational, public health and local government standards.

Industrial prosperity did not bring an improvement in living conditions for the bulk of the population. Indeed, quite the reverse, as housebuilding failed to keep up with the rapid growth in population. Initially, local industrialists were the main agents of house building, but they could do little to assuage the dire housing shortage that resulted in overcrowding and dreadful sanitary conditions. Building firms in towns like Dumbarton tended to be small scale operations, capable of correspondingly limited developments and unable to tackle the larger projects that the situation required.[14] Consequently, the dark side of nineteenth century industrialisation was all too apparent in Dumbarton. The burgh's demographic characteristics reflected not only the industrial success of shipbuilding and heavy engineering but also the ravages of poor housing, cramped living space, inefficient water supplies and perfunctory sewage disposal. Death rates were between 20 and 26 per 1,000 on average.[15] This was similar to the rates experienced in other small Scottish towns but was not as high as those in the cities, where the sheer extent of sub-standard and overcrowded housing proved to be an important factor.[16] Housing developments of a modest size by city standards, had beneficial effects in a smaller town like Dumbarton, but the pressure of a rapidly growing population continued to place enormous strains on the housing stock.

Infants and young children were the most at risk. High birth rates compensated for high infant mortality rates. In a burgh whose population had nearly doubled from 1861 to 1891, there was little change to that pattern over the period, as sanitary improvements struggled to make any significant impact on public health. Improved hygiene and stricter planning controls were offset by rapid population growth where in-migration fuelled by industrial success led to pressure on the physical fabric of the burgh. This manifested itself in the number of 'made-down'[17] houses and apartments. Cellars and outhouses were also used for habitation and the makeshift infilling of open spaces, gardens and vegetable plots with 'back houses'[18] meant that in the High Street and its immediate environs, space was rapidly choked with all manner of structures.

Local newspaper reports highlighted the correlation between death rates, infectious diseases and Dumbarton's congested urban environment. In 1863, typhoid and smallpox epidemics had ravaged the town and, in a report highlighting this, there was also mention of the poor sanitary conditions, overcrowding and the difficulties which the 'labouring classes' had in getting any kind of shelter.[19] Again, in March 1864, reports linked the 'alarming numbers' of diseases to inadequate sanitation and unregulated building on long, narrow 'gardens' to the rear of the tenements. There was also the suggestion that not enough was being done 'to enforce the Police Act and Nuisances Removal Act' by local authorities.[20] Substandard construction methods and the haste with which tenements were erected were referred to in June of that year.[21] The desperate need for accommodation was due to a population increase of 2,000 since 1861. The result of this pressure was a frightening increase in death rates. The *Dumbarton Herald* reported that the quarterly return for Dumbarton up to September 1864 showed death rates at 48.4 per 1,000 compared to the 'small towns' average up to June 1864 of 27.7 per 1,000.[22] The intense population pressure on such a physically restrictive location was no better seven years later, as well meaning legislation was ignored or circumvented. In one case a submission to build 'dwelling houses and a workshop on backland' was upheld by a sheriff despite doubt over its legality under the General Police Act. The *Lennox Herald,* reporting the case, commented that if the Act were to be obeyed 'there would be no building in the town'.[23]

Around the same time, James Birkmyre of 'Glasgow road' was accused of a contravention of the Act 'having put up several buildings at his property without consent' and 'with allowing these, though virtually cellars, to be occupied as dwelling houses'. The 'ceilings were only 6 feet 3 inches or thereby in height' but the cellars 'had been converted into dwelling houses at a time when there was a great scarcity of such accommodation'.[24] Similar situations occurred in many of Scotland's industrialising burghs 'where even the interventionist burgh authorities were reluctant or powerless to control' the standard of housing and unhygenic conditions which led to disease and early death.[25]

In essence, developments like Dennystown and later, Newtown and Knoxland, only prevented the situation from deteriorating, so that by the late nineteenth century public health problems still confronted those who lived in the old overcrowded heart of the burgh .

Vale of Leven: Male Employment (see Appendix 1, Table 5:1)

- In 1861, 61% of all employed males living in the Vale of Leven worked in the bleaching, printing and dyeing industry.

- This dropped by over 10% in the next ten years, recovering again by 1881 to almost 1861 levels, before slipping back to just over 50% by 1891.

- No other sector of male employment came close to matching the numbers working in this industry. Taken together, 'shipbuilding', 'iron and steel trades' and 'machinery' only employed 6% - 8.5% of the male workforce, not dissimilar to the numbers in the building trades. Around 4% - 7% of employed males were in the nebulous 'general labouring' category which often indicated no fixed employment.

In the 1861-71 decade population growth slowed. Most of the growth in Bonhill Parish was in Jamestown. The population of Bonhill village had barely changed.[26] There were 196 more people living in Renton than previously.[27] These figures indicate that in this ten year period natural population increase had not, for the most part, replaced the many people who had deserted the Vale of Leven for a life elsewhere. It may not only have been the uncertain economic climate which prompted their departure, as outbreaks of disease, such as typhus in 1864 and cholera in 1866, were markers of an unhealthy environment.[28] The printworks dispensed with, at the very least, 300 - 400 male workers. At the same time they hired a minimum of 150 - 250 females who were cheaper to employ.[29] These were hardly dramatic changes over a decade, but they signalled a greater reliance on female labour, as well as a less successful period for the printworks.[30]

This was the decade when the American Civil War (1861-1865) was fought. United States' warships enforced a blockade of the secessionist Confederate ports along the Atlantic seaboard, primarily aimed at preventing the export of cotton and other raw materials. Surprisingly, the Confederate Government itself imposed an embargo on cotton exports, reasoning that the loss of supplies might bring Britain and France into the War on their side.[31] Unfortunately for them this tactic did not have the desired effect.[32]

It is ironic that while the effects of the conflict were being felt in the Vale, Peter Denny, a few miles down the road in Dumbarton sought to profit from it by building light, fast ships for the Confederate states. These were the 'blockade runners' built to evade the Union ships enforcing the embargo of southern ports.[33]

Curiously, reports in local newspapers did not provide much evidence of hardship in the Vale. More attention was focused on mill villages such as nearby Duntocher, where cotton cloth was produced and where three of its four mills closed down in the 1860s. There were, in addition, articles on the difficulties faced by the cotton mills in Lancashire but little mention of the Vale of Leven, where cloth was was not manufactured but where it was was bleached, dyed and printed.[34]

The outbreak of hostilities had led to much local trepidation. By September 1861, just over five months into the conflict, the *Dumbarton Herald* reported . . . 'The dreaded cotton famine . . . which the Civil War had led us to anticipate is now being felt'.[35] There were further warnings on the subject early in 1862.[36] However, by July of that year the *Herald* indicated that problems were more severe in Lancashire than in the Vale of Leven.[37] By September, printwork owner John Orr Ewing speaking at a meeting in the Alexandria Works, stated that there was enough unbleached cloth, 'grey goods still on hand' but warned that the shortage of cotton and the rising prices that this precipitated, did not augur well for the future.[38] Although there was always a tendency for the printworks to be less busy in the winter, in the autumn of 1862 it was admitted that short time work would be much more likely in the coming months.

By the spring of 1863 there was some cause for optimism. The people had been 'pretty well employed' and in the past winter, the scarcity of employment 'common in most districts where similar branches of trade are prosecuted was at no time very severely felt'.[39] This was in contrast to the difficulties experienced in the calico producing mills.[40] The 'cotton famine' threw many out of work. Immigration was one response and, as the *Dumbarton Herald* reported in July 1863, the Glasgow Relief Fund Committee helped 250 of the city's unemployed, cotton operatives and their children to emigrate to Canada.[41]

For the remainder of the war the general tone of remarks on the 'state of trade' suggested that it was holding up reasonably well in spite of the difficulties.[42] What is unusual by present day standards, is the lack of reference to a reduction in the labour force or to the slowing of growth. The workforce reduction over the course of the 1861-71 decade was small but even if that had occurred largely in the 1861-1865 period when the war was being waged, it may not have appeared to be dramatic. The absence of comment in the local press on unemployment or underemployment underscores the volatility of the situation: an increase in jobs when the order book was healthy and the shedding of labour, erratic and part time working when it was not. The Ferryfield Works which had lain idle for the best part of seven years, from 1864 to 1871 was only mentioned in the local press when it reopened.[43] This suggests that it was not uncommon for works to close for short periods when orders were not forthcoming. Clearly, substantial variations in the labour force and population turnover were so typical of the times that they did not merit the interest of local journalists. In 1871, the same journalists were surprised by the slow population growth in Bonhill over the previous decade.[44] There can be little doubt that the depression caused by the war had an adverse effect on local trade, but cotton cloth was sourced elsewhere, including from India, where trade links already existed, and where there was a demand for the Vale's high quality products.[45]

By 1881, much of the confidence lost in the 1860s had been restored, and around six in ten of all employed males living in the Vale of Leven worked in the printworks, a very similar proportion to 1861. This is all the more impressive as the population had risen by over 4,500 in the decade since 1871, with males making up just less than half of that number.[46] Consequently, other sectors of employment assumed less importance. The relative attractiveness of the heavy industries waned as did other occupations such as those in the clothing trade.

By 1891, when extreme difficulties resulting in merger, closure and decline were still six or seven years away, there was a hint that the printworks were not as buoyant as in 1881. Nonetheless, the works still accounted for just over half of all employed males in the Vale. The industrial base was very narrow and there were no alternative forms of factory employment, although shipbuilding once again increased its share of employed males. Other sectors of employment were not independent of the printworks. Transport, trading, public and professional services were there to meet people's needs and the people were there because of the printworks. The catastrophic decline of the printworks in the 1890s ensured that the communities would suffer, as out-migration caused the population to drop by nearly a thousand in the 1881-91 decade. This exodus affected all four villages, with Bonhill suffering the biggest loss of 318 people.[47] With no major alternatives, the Vale remained chronically dependent on bleaching, printing and dyeing into the twentieth century.

Vale of Leven: Female Employment (see Appendix 1, Table 5:2)

The female employment structure was more straightforward than that for males and the sample indicates that:

- In each census year around half of all females over 14 were in paid occupations, the exception being 1861 when the figure was slightly lower.

- The Vale's bleach, print and dye works were by far the biggest single employers of female labour, with between 75% and 80% of all employed females working there over the period.

- No other major occupational category accounted for more than 10% of women employed outside the home.

- The percentage of the total female population over fourteen years of age employed at the printworks rose steadily from 1861 to 1881, with a slight dip towards 1891. This is in contrast to the male pattern where a very definite percentage decline took place between 1861 and 1871.

The overall proportion of women in work was considerably higher than the Scottish average where, for much of the nineteenth century, a quarter of women were in paid employment. Figures for Dundee in 1881, which are cited as an exception, show that 57% of women were in this category. This was not much higher than the figure for the Vale, and like the Vale it involved textile work. In Dundee, women accounted for three-quarters of all jute workers.[48]

In the Vale, industrialists decided to hire more women as they were cheaper to employ than men and although the factory owners could hardly be accused of overpaying the male workforce, skilled male printers commanded relatively good salaries. As 'machine printing' began to supersede 'block printing'[49] and mechanisation eased the physical burden all along the production line, it still required women to undertake hard and demanding labour in challenging working conditions.

The vast majority of female printworkers were regarded as unskilled or semi-skilled. Their occupations are often described in the *census enumerators' books* in broad terms such as 'printworker' and 'worker in dye works'.

By comparison, other sectors of employment were very small indeed. Some women were servants in the houses of the middle classes, especially in Alexandria which had become the biggest of the villages and was now the retail and service centre of the Vale. Small numbers of women were employed as milliners or dressmakers, many working at home, in back shops or in 'sewing rooms', for low, piece work rates. Conditions were often poor and the working day was long. The *Lennox Herald* told of 'toiling in close, unwholesome rooms for 13-16$\frac{1}{2}$ hours per day during the busy season'.[50] Job security was non existent, therefore if employees got pregnant, fell ill or had to give up work temporarily, there were others only too willing to take their place. The *Herald* bemoaned the working conditions and lack of alternative employment for women.

Conditions were no more pleasant in the printworks, with high temperatures, steam and noxious chemicals in the air. Permanently stained hands were only one manifestation of the unhealthy working environment. Hours were shorter and pay, on average, higher, than in 'sewing rooms', but the laborious work was only for the young and fit. In 1861, which is not atypical, four out of every five women employed in the print and dye works were under 25 years old. As women married and had children, they were less likely to be employed in a full time occupation outside of the home. For women in later nineteenth century Scotland there was

a trend to limit formal participation in paid work outside the home after marriage. By a process of official prohibition…and the emergence of new

88

notions of 'respectability' which placed stress on the central role of the male breadwinner, married women became increasingly tied to the home.[51]

Women were forced to give up formal employment when they got married, but were forced back into work if they were widowed and had to support themselves and their children.

Dumbarton: Male Employment (see Appendix 1 Table 5:3)

By 1861, the shipbuilding industry in Dumbarton was assuming greater importance. The year before, Irving had described the transformation brought by the shipyards.[52]

- In 1861, 25% of employed males worked in the shipyards, but this was to rise to 40% by 1891.

- The foundry trades along with iron and steel workers in general, made up the next biggest sector of employment (between 12% and 15% of employed males).

- Taken together, the foundry trades, iron and steel workers and those working in 'machinery' were largely reliant on the shipyards. These three categories 'shipbuilding', 'foundry and iron and steel trades' and 'machinery' accounted for 45% of the employed males in 1861, 55% by 1871, 61% in 1881 and perhaps slightly higher in 1891. (In 1901 when employment statistics were published for employed males in the burgh of Dumbarton, 62% of employed males worked in 'mines, metals and engineering').

This was all against a background of sustained population growth. In the thirty year period 1861-91, the population of the burgh had more than doubled, rising from just over 8,200 to 16,900, so that the numbers of those employed in the yards grew even more spectacularly than the percentage figures suggest. Dumbarton's foundries were not completely reliant on local shipyards. There is no need to look too far for evidence of this as Dennystown Forge remained operational for sixteen years after the last ship had left Dennys' stocks.

Throughout the second half of the nineteenth century shipbuilding was the mainstay of Dumbarton's economy. Most of the Dumbarton yards had a connection with the wider Denny family but Denny Brothers, based at the Leven Shipyard since 1867, was pre-eminent. It was one of the foremost shipbuilding companies on the Clyde with a record of innovation and technical excellence (see Chapter 2). There were small scale manufacturing concerns in the burgh. There was a ropeworks, partly, but not wholly, dependent on the shipyards. Other industrial premises included sawmills, a glue factory, a tannery, a grain mill and a gasworks. There were artisans and craftsmen working in, for example, blacksmithing, tailoring, carpentry and baking. Many were supplying local shops and businesses in what was, after all, the most enduring urban centre in Dunbartonshire.

Local building firms were involved in important housing projects in the burgh, firstly at Westbridgend (Dennystown) and later at the 'Newtown' and Knoxland area to the east of the old burgh core. There was employment to be had in public works such as the building of the academy and burgh hall, and in redeveloping the buildings which fronted the High Street. However, as described earlier in this chapter, behind the emerging modern façade, were long strips of land that were witness to the altogether less attractive process: that of plot repletion, where the open ground was being rapidly covered by hastily constructed 'dwellings' that were often small, dark, ill ventilated, poorly constructed and lacking in basic amenities; no more than urban bothies, often tacked on to existing buildings which were themselves overcrowded and insanitary.

Ironically, building workers engaged in this 'jerry-built' activity, found that their jobs were about as secure as some of the hastily erected buildings they constructed. Job descriptions recorded by census enumerators, such as 'house and ship painter' or 'house and ship carpenter' emphasise the fluidity of the labour market. Sudden hirings and firings affecting both skilled and unskilled workers were commonplace. On the other hand, across the period there was a definite decline in the proportion of men designated in the census returns as 'general labourers'[53] which perhaps reveals that the casual or sporadic nature of employment was diminishing in Dumbarton as the shipyards were taking on more unskilled men.

As the burgh rapidly industrialised after 1850, and employment other than in heavy industry assumed less importance, it remained 'the county town' of Dunbartonshire, the centre of the county's administration and its main market town. It was home to a small but important group of public and professional employees, such as those working in the law, education and local government, as well as shopkeepers, traders, craftsmen and artisans.[54]

Dumbarton: Female Employment (see Appendix 1 Figure 5:4)

The female employment sector in Dumbarton was less developed than the male sector. The reasons are not difficult to find: there were comparatively few jobs for women in a burgh dominated by heavy industry.

- In the 1861 sample, around one third of all women and girls over 14 were designated as employed outside the home. This figure dropped to about a quarter in 1871, which was around the Scottish national average for the period.

- By 1881 and 1891, the figure had returned to just less than a third. This, a direct consequence of the relatively large number of Dumbarton domiciled women now employed in the Vale's printworks.

- By 1881 printworking had become Dumbarton's most important source of female employment, with around 500 women journeying to work in the Vale each day.

The problem in Dumbarton was a lack of employment opportunities rather than lack of need. Women who were seeking work had little to choose from. In 1861 and 1871, domestic service was the largest employer of female labour; a few women were employed in clothing, dressmaking and retailing and small numbers were employed in professional and public services, which usually meant teaching or clerical work.[55] In common with women in other parts of Scotland, many gave up paid employment when they married and had children.[56] Work such as housekeeping, cleaning, sewing and knitting was common and often necessary to supplement meagre household incomes.[57] Given that much of this was casual in nature it was not always acknowledged or recorded.

Bleaching, printing and dyeing, insignificant in 1861, eventually overtook domestic service at the 1881 census as the biggest employer of female labour in Dumbarton and it remained so in 1891. Around this time of every ten Dumbarton women who were 'employed', three or four were working in the Vale of Leven's printworks and not in the burgh. This meant a daily commute to the Vale of Leven, especially to Renton the village closest to Dumbarton's western edge. This journey would have taken 35 to 45 minutes to complete on foot from Dennystown where many of the printworkers lived. A journey to Bonhill from the High Street would have taken over an hour .

In spite of the difficulties that the industry encountered in the 1891-1901 period, about 6% of Dumbarton's females aged 10 and over were recorded as being employed in 'textiles and fabrics' at the latter date. This included not only printworkers but those employed in 'sewing rooms' and doing 'piece work' at home.[58]

Printworking was probably preferred to domestic service in spite of the travelling involved. The work was not always steady, but the hours were shorter and the wages better. There were definite contrasts in the profiles of those employed in either sector. Most women were likely to be in employment in their teens and early twenties. This was overwhelmingly so in the print and dye works, where the vast majority of operatives were between 14 and 24 years of age. Domestic service embraced a wider age group, almost half were aged over 25.

Printworking was a short term, mainly pre-marriage occupation. Domestic service often involved servants who 'lived in' the houses where they worked. These were mainly the larger residences on the periphery of Dumbarton. In addition, there were older women employed as domestic servants many of whom were widows who needed to support themselves and their families. Some 'lived in', others were employed on a part-time basis.

Child Labour

The Vale of Leven

The use of child labour was a notable feature of the textile industry in the eighteenth and early nineteenth century, when children were paid low wages to perform menial tasks. In the printworks the most common job done by children was that of 'tearer' which involved spreading dye paste onto a printing block before use. Until 1871, as many as 2% to 4% of the total printwork labour force (male and female) were children under ten. The number of people working in the printworks in 1875 is estimated at 6,000, which would suggest that approximately 200 under tens were employed there as late as 1871.[59] This is at odds with most estimates for the Scottish cotton industry where, 'by 1847, child labour, subject of factory legislation in 1833, was relatively insignificant'.[60] (The figures above are lifted from the sample of 500 Vale of Leven families taken from the 1871 *census enumerators' books*). In 1881, there was still a sprinkling of children under ten employed in the Vale's printworks, but no child of this age was in recorded employment at the 1891 census.

The story was different for the 10-14 year olds.

- In the first half of the 1861-91 period, a quarter of the females employed in the industry were girls of fourteen and younger.

- Boys between ten and fourteen comprised less than one in five of the male workforce over the same period.

- As late as 1891, one in ten of the workforce was a child between ten and fourteen years of age.

The 1872 Education Act, which made universal primary education compulsory, may have had the effect of limiting the number of children employed, but some works' owners circumvented that by providing schools, sometimes within the factory grounds themselves, so that children could be educated whilst retaining their jobs. The most famous example of that in this area was the Dalmonach School, built in the 1830s and adjacent to works of the same name.[61]

It was not that there was no primary schooling prior to the Act. On the contrary, there was a wide range and variety of provision throughout Scotland, but overall this was patchy. Predictably, 'the urban poor (and) some industrial communities' as well as the Western Isles, had the worst levels of literacy.[62]

Very few children were employed other than in the print and dye works. Some of them were 'general messengers' or 'servants' but even as early as 1861, no child under ten was recorded in employment other than in the factories.

Dumbarton

In Dumbarton, there were few very young children recorded in employment throughout the second half of the nineteenth century.

- In the sample only one male child in the 5-9 years age cohort in 1861 was designated as employed.

  At no other time was a child of that age, male or female, recorded as being in work. Doubtless, there were those who did casual work and menial tasks for very little reward.

- Up to one in four boys in the 10-14 age group were employed but were not heavily concentrated in any one sector. Fewer girls in this age cohort were employed, mainly because there were no opportunities for them to work in heavy industry.

- Shipbuilding occupied between a quarter and a third of 10-14 year old boys in work.

- 'Rivet boy' and 'message boy' were common designations, but most were listed in vague groupings such as 'miscellaneous' or 'general dealing'.

The dye works not only employed children from the Vale. A small number from Dumbarton were also employed there. No Dumbarton children were among the printworkers in the 1871 sample, but they are recorded in small numbers in the 1881 and 1891 samples. This parallels the occupational pattern of Dumbarton's female residents working in the Vale of Leven. Of the 39 Dumbarton boys in the 10-14 age bracket recorded as being in employment in the 1881 sample of 500 households, seven of them were working in the Vale's factories.

The printwork proprietors may have been less scrupulous than their counterparts in heavy industry, but in general, Victorian attitudes were accepting of the need for child labour. The decision to employ children or not partly depended on the nature of available work, as was the case in the employment of women. Heavy industry was physically demanding in a way in which printworking was not, and this ensured that fewer Dumbarton children were recorded as employed. The yards and foundries appeared less inclined to recruit children than the textile industry where it had long been a notable feature.[63]

Working Conditions

Life could be hazardous for the men, women and children who worked in the factories, foundries and shipyards. The effects of dyes on the hands and arms of printworkers have already been highlighted, but the impact of the dye works environment on the respiratory system is less well documented, although the first Medical Officer of Health's Report on the County of Dunbartonshire indicates that in 1891, deaths from respiratory diseases (and whooping cough) were far higher in Renton than all other districts in West Dunbarton.[64] Poverty and overcrowding played a major role in this. But factory conditions undoubtedly contributed.

High temperatures required in the dyeing process resulted in evaporation and condensation of noxious liquids ingested by the workforce. Bremner, writing in 1869, states:

...yarn is dyed by a hand process and the (female) operatives engaged in that department have a most unhealthy and disagreeable occupation. They have to stand over cisterns of scalding, steaming liquor and keep the yarn in constant motion by shifting and turning the rods on which it hung.[65]

Temperatures of 150F (66C) were required during the process but it was 'never over 90F (32C) when people were present'. Dyeing had to be halted in severe winter weather when these temperatures could not be reached.[66] 'True Turkey Red dyeing must stand pressure boiling with sodium carbonate, followed by bleaching with sodium hydrochlorite kept alkaline by soda ash, as well as a weak caustic soda boil and soap boiling'...with the increasing use of synthetic dyes and simpler processes there was less need 'for sometimes rather unpleasant ingredients'[67] such as bulls' blood, supplied in leaky barrels, which was a constant source of irritation during the summer.[68]

The contrast between the hot house conditions inside the works and the temperature outside had the added effect of causing colds and respiratory problems. Working in the heat and noxious atmosphere of the print and dye works was certainly not conducive to good health.

'Contemporary' witness statements include the following:

you could almost tell (when the works were coming out) what department people worked in from their colour. Some were pure white while others had red or blue arms.

Dermatitis was rife in the print shop. I knew a man who had dermatitis from the top of his head to the soles of his feet'.

Running water and showers were not available and protective clothing was only issued in extreme emergencies.

Many of the dyes contained a dangerous mixture of substances such as lead, chromium, arsenic, mercury and copper.[69]

Maintaining high temperatures also caused fires … 'sometimes with loss of life'.[70] Among the fires reported was an incident in January 1875, when four storage buildings were destroyed at Dalquhurn. It was a Saturday afternoon and no employees were in the vicinity, but as a result, workers were temporarily laid off, and £4000-£5000 worth of cloth was destroyed.[71] The *Glasgow Herald* reported in October 1876 that four fires had occurred within six months at William Stirling's (Dalquhurn) works,[72] and in 1873, a building was burned to the ground at the Alexandria Works.[73] These were noteworthy, but not isolated, cases. Prior to this, the *Dumbarton Herald* had reported that there had been: two 'fatal fires' at Levenbank and Dalmonach in 1860; no fewer than four fires at Croftengea between January 1860 and June 1861 and, in 1865, a fire at the Alexandria works which destroyed a drying store and its contents.[74]

Health and safety were not major concerns and accidents involving machinery were commonplace. Serious industrial accidents were reported regularly in the local press throughout the period. Doubtless, many incidents deemed less egregious went unreported.

Taking the first three months of 1875, the year in which Archibald Orr Ewing later pled his case at the Royal Commission enquiry into the operation of the Workshop and Factory Act, two serious accidents involving children took place in the printworks. In February 1875, Hugh Hamilton, a boy of thirteen who lived in Jamestown had both arms 'severely crushed' in a machine at the Levenbank Works where he was employed, and Jessie Eadie 'aged about thirteen' had to have her right arm amputated when the wheel of a truck passed over it in the Alexandria Works.[75] In operations which involved dealing with very hot liquids, scaldings were frequent occurrences. Deaths due to scalding were reported in 1868 and in 1874.[76]

The printworks employed more child labour than the shipyards, but the latter were not immune to serious accidents involving children, and at the start of that same year, a boy, Dougald Campbell, son of John Campbell, a riveter who lived in Renton, fell into the hold of a ship at Dennys. The *Dumbarton Herald* reported that 'a fatality' is now 'feared'.[77]

Over the early months of that year there were reports of a case in which John Lowe, a caulker living in Dennystown, was suing shipbuilders John MacMillan and Sons over the death of his son. The boy who was eleven years old, was 'illegally employed' in the yard as a 'rivet catcher' and was burned to death whilst engaged in catching hot rivets in a ship's 'cross yard'. The 'cross yard', the *Dumbarton Herald* explained, was a 'tube or pillar and measured ten and a half inches at the narrow end' and 'the child had been induced to enter the tube, red hot rivets (were) passed down to him causing his clothes to catch fire. He died as a result of his injuries the next day'.[78]

Shipyard workers such as riveters and caulkers operated at dangerous heights on scaffolding which afforded little protection. Rivet squads were engaged in particularly hazardous work. They were employed in 'teams' and often engaged in 'piece work', where the team was paid on the basis of the number of rivets they managed to fit per day. The quicker they could work, the more they earned. In the team, the 'rivet heater' ensured that the rivet was red hot; it was then thrown to the 'rivet catcher', usually a young boy carrying a bucket and wielding tongs; he passed the red hot rivet to a 'holder on' who used a device to hold the rivet in place while it was hammered in by the riveter. It was a risky business and when the red hot rivets missed their intended targets it resulted in frequent accidents including burnings and blindings. Ulster born William Devlin, a young man working in a Dumbarton shipyard rivet squad, was blinded in one eye. Many years later he told a story of when his foreman had asked him to 'run his eye' along a beam: Devlin claimed that he had popped out his glass eye and promptly obliged.

A Low Wage Economy

In spite of the contrasts, the Vale and Dumbarton had much in common with other industrial towns and cities in Scotland. People in the industrial heartland were subject to circumstances which impeded progress and blighted lives. Scotland's economy was predicated on low wages. When industries encountered difficulties the first response of their owners was to lay off workers. Thus 'the cause and the course of poverty was determined by … irregular employment'. Unskilled factory workers were shed with comparative ease whereas skilled workers were largely retained. In dependent occupations such as 'portering, navvying, messengering, (and) carting' there was an 'elasticity of demand' where operatives were

engaged on an hourly or half daily basis. This presented considerable scope for accommodating changes in output with none of the risk being borne by the entrepreneur. The adjustment was through labour costs only.[79]

In Scotland it is estimated that at this time 'around one-fifth to one-quarter of the adult labour force in larger towns worked on a casual or seasonal basis'.[80]

The implications are clear: with over 50% of the male workforce in the lowest social strata in the Vale and between 35%- 40% in a similar position in Dumbarton, along with almost all female workers who were in irregular and low wage employment, life was precarious for large numbers of people. Regular wages, required to house and feed a family, could not be guaranteed. Hardship made it difficult for people to afford a place to stay and the house tenure system in Scotland aggravated the problem as longer leases 'were the norm' compared to England's shorter leasing system which was much more attuned to the volatile economic circumstances endured by the poorer working class population. Long term leases for people in low status jobs were untenable.[81] The system was circumvented by informal arrangements such as sub-letting and casual lodging which gave rise to intense overcrowding, dirt and disease (see Chapter 11). Defaulting on a lease had legal consequences. Families left their homes without warning and the 'midnight flit' was a familiar response to prospective legal action.[82]

Problems with leasing were not the only reasons why people deserted their homes. Significant numbers of people called to appear at Dumbarton Sheriff Court on minor charges such as drunken or anti-social behaviour, left the area to escape punishment which was then imposed *in absentia*. One instance involved a group of people involved in a 'party row' case. A 'party row' where 'party songs' were sung - 'party' being a West of Scotland euphemism for 'sectarian'. The *Lennox Herald* reported that 'ten to twelve' people who were due to appear in court had absconded.[83]

NOTES

[1] *Thesis,* Chapter 8 p. 119 Figure 8:1

[2] Ibid. p. 141 Figure 9:1.

[3] M. Anderson, *Scotland's Populations from the 1850s to today* (2018) p. 189 Table 10:1

[4] *scotlandsplaces.gov.uk*. Medical Officer of Health reports 1891 - Dunbartonshire. p. 19

[5] Death rate statistics for the 1880-1889 period show that Dumbarton's mean rate over the period was 20.581 per 1000. Bonhill Parish recorded a mean of 18.080 over this period, and Renton over the 1883-1889 period recorded 19.735. Renton had the highest annual death rate recorded for any of the local settlements, including Dumbarton, in 1886 with a figure of 24.040 per 1000. Source: *scotlandsplaces.gov.uk*. Medical Officer of Health reports 1891 - Dunbartonshire. p. 69

[6] Ibid. p. 29

[7] *DH* 15 November 1862; *LH* 17 September 1864

[8] Medical Officer of Health reports 1891 pp. 48-51

[9] R.J.Findlay, 'Urbanisation and Industrialisation: West Dunbartonshire since 1750', Ch 4 p. 71 in I. Brown, (ed) *Changing Identities Ancient Roots*

[10] Gallacher, 'The Vale of Leven 1914-1975' p. 190 citing Communist Party local election literature, (1928); P. Abercrombie and R.H. Mathew. *The Clyde Valley Regional Plan* (1946) p. 276

[11] Findlay, 'Urbanisation and Industrialisation' p. 71

[12] Anderson, *Scotland's Populations p. 95*

[13] Medical Officer of Health reports 1891 p. 29

[14] Hutchison, *Industry, Reform and Empire.* p 104

[15] The current death rate for Scotland (with a much older population than in the nineteenth century) is 10.3 per 1000.

[16] The rates in Scotland's four largest cities were 28.1 in 1861 and 23.3 in 1881. The Scottish averages for the same dates were 21.5 and 19.7 respectively. Hutchison *Industry, Reform and Empire*. p. 96, citing M.W. Flynn et al, *Scottish Population History* (1977) p. 382

[17] Where houses and rooms were further subdivided to accommodate more occupants in the same available space.

[18] Dwellings in Dumbarton High Street, as described by a census enumerator in 1871.

[19] *DH* 12 December 1863

[20] *DH* 19 March 1864

[21] *DH* 4 June 1864

[22] *DH* 17 September 1864

[23] *DH* 6 April 1871

[24] *LH* 1 April and 8 April 1871

[25] E.A. Cameron, *Impaled Upon a Thistle. Scotland since 1880.* (2010) p. 12

[26] *LH* 20 April 1871

[27] Figures taken from the *scottish-places.info* website. Quoting from Groome, *Ordnance Gazeteer of Scotland* (1882-85)

[28] Agnew, *The Story of the Vale of Leven*. p. 36

[29] These figures are based on the sample estimates from those listed as bleach, print and dye workers and resident in the Vale at the 1861 and 1871 censuses. They do not include printworkers living in Dumbarton or Balloch, and as such will be underestimates.

[30] W.W. Knox pinpoints this period as marking a 'turning point in the sexual composition of the labour force in spinning' in *Hanging by a Thread. The Scottish Cotton Industry c1850-1914* (1995) p. 20. See also *Thesis*, Chapter 8 Fig 8:4, where rough estimates are obtained by comparing the small age-specific rise in the male and female adult population with the percentage changes in printwork employment over the 1861-71 decade.

[31] See also Chapter 2

[32] J.M. McPherson, *Battle Cry of Freedom. The Civil War Era.* (1988) Ch12 pp. 383-86

[33] For a list of ships built both on order and on speculation see the *Denny Lists* Vol 1

[34] At this time local newspapers did not confine themselves to local news but reported on British and world events too, often lifting reports from other journals.

[35] *DH* 29 September 1861

[36] *DH* 2 March 1862 and 15 March 1862

[37] *DH* 12 July and 26 July 1862

[38] *DH* 27 September 1862

[39] *DH* 11 May 1863

[40] *DH* 20 December 1863

[41] *DH* 25 July 1863

[42] *DH* 20 June 1863; 11 June 1864; LH 16 July 1864; 30 July 1864

[43] *LH* May 1871

[44] *LH* 20 April 1871. This figure included 'landward' areas as well as Alexandria, the developing village of Jamestown and the village of Bonhill which lost population over this period.

[45] Nenadic and Tuckett, *The Turkey Red Printed Cotton Industry* p. 100

[46] Groome, *Ordnance Gazeteer of Scotland* and *Thesis*, Chapter 8. Figure 8:1 p. 119

[47] *Census: Population report Scotland.* Vol I 1891 p. 117 *and Population Scotland* Vol I 1901 pp. 45-6

[48] Hutchison, *Industry, Reform and Empire* pp. 84-5

[49] R. Holloway, *Leaving Alexandria (2013)* p. 27 Richard Holloway mentions that his father worked as a ' block printer' in the early twentieth century.

[50] *LH* 18 June 1864

[51] T. Griffiths, 'Work, Leisure and Time' in T. Griffiths and G. Morton. *A History of Everyday life in Scotland 1800-1900* (2010) pp. 188-9

[52] See Chapter 2.

[53] These were not 'unskilled factory workers', but often those without regular employment.

[54] *Thesis*, Fig 9:2. p. 144

[55] *Thesis*, p. 147

[56] Anderson, *Scotland's Populations* Table 7:5 p. 106

[57] Hutchison, *Industry, Reform and Empire* p. 83

[58] Anderson, *Scotland's Populations* Table 7:5 p. 106

[59] *TSA* Vol 6 p. 60

[60] J. Butt, in Butt and Ponting *Scottish Textile Industry*, Ch 10 p. 142

[61] Jones and Hopner, *On Leven's Banks*. p. 64

[62] T. M. Devine, *The Scottish Nation. A Modern History* (2012) p. 398

[63] Cooke, *The Rise and Fall of the Scottish Cotton Industry* p. 23 refers to William Stirling's works in Renton, where the 'industry relied heavily on child labour'.

[64] scotlandsplaces.gov.uk. Medical Officer of Health reports 1891 - Dunbartonshire. This was the first report of its kind. (Statistics for Dumbarton Burgh were beyond the remit of the report and are largely excluded from it).

[65] Bremner, *The Industries of Scotland*, p. 300

[66] Cooke, *The Rise and Fall of the Scottish Cotton Industry*. p. 110

[67] Tarrant, 'The Turkey Red Dyeing Industry in the Vale of Leven' pp37- 47 in Butt and Ponting (eds) *The Scottish textile industry*

[68] Nenadic and Tuckett, *The Turkey Red Printed Cotton Industry* p. 25

[69] West Dunbartonshire Arts and Heritage. Sunday Strolls and Sagas - Turkey Red Memories. Posted on Twitter/Facebook 17 April 2022.

[70] Nenadic and Tuckett *The Turkey Red Printed Cotton Industry* p. 29

[71] *DH* 14 January 1875

[72] *Glasgow Herald* 2 October 1876, cited in Nenadic and Tuckett, *The Turkey Red Printed Cotton Industry* p. 29

[73] Nenadic and Tuckett, *The Turkey Red Printed Cotton Industry* p. 10

[74] *DH* - 15 November 1860; 1 March 1860, 5 April 1860, 10 May 1860, 27 June 1861; 2 December 1865

[75] *DH* 4 March 1875 and LH 2 March 1875

[76] Agnew, *The Story of the Vale of Leven*. p. 61. Other fatalities were recorded at Dalquhurn in 1863 (*DH* 12 July 1863) and Alexandria Works in 1866 (*DH* 16 August 1866)

[77] *DH* 21 January 1875

[78] *DH* 20 May 1875. See also reports from 4 March and 13 May 1875.

[79] Rodger, 'Employment, Wages and Poverty' p. 46

[80] Hutchison, *Industry, Reform and Empire* p. 106

[81] Ibid.

[82] Ibid.

[83] *LH* 13 May 1871

6 A Restless People

Introduction

In the second half of the nineteenth century, Scotland's population structure was not dissimilar to that of the world's poorest countries today. Over a third of the population was under fifteen years of age, with far fewer adults reaching old age. From 1851 to 1911 this had not appreciably changed. Scotland remained a high birth rate / high death rate / high infant mortality society throughout that sixty year period. Between 1861 and 1891, both the Vale and Dumbarton conformed to this national pattern.[1]

One striking feature of the country's demography was the very high level of population mobility. Movement within, into and out of Dumbarton and the Vale was commonplace and sustained at levels that we would not recognise in Scotland today. There was a tremendous churn of people. Scots who had been born outside of the area, those who were 'locally' born - many of whom were children of migrants - and the Irish, were all readily inclined to move.

There were distinctive contrasts between Dumbarton and the Vale. Both were subject to high rates of population mobility, but in the Vale, young women outnumbered young men and in Dumbarton the opposite was the case.[2] The difference was largely due to net in-migration. Young women were attracted to the Vale of Leven by the abundant work available for them in the printworks, whereas in Dumbarton, jobs in shipbuilding and heavy industry attracted young men.

Over the period, Dumbarton suffered from a higher death rate than the Vale of Leven, where only Renton came close to equalling the burgh's figures. There can be no doubt that poor housing, overcrowding and the lack of sanitation were to blame for this disparity. As published census reports show, Dumbartonians lived, on average, in more confined spaces and with more people 'per house'. It was common for tenement rooms to be 'made down', that is, subdivided by constructing partitions within rooms to provide more accommodation, thus making more use of already limited space. The street and tenement layout and sheer density of housing in the burgh exacerbated the problem. The long narrow plots of land which ran back from the street had been laid out centuries before. Initially they had contained the burgesses' houses and the 'backlands' were used to keep livestock and grow crops. As in Glasgow, industrial success caused a housing crisis. Plots were swamped with buildings of variable quality: sheds, cellars, workshops and outhouses were used to accommodate people. The 'closes' and 'pends' that linked the tenements and 'backlands' were dark, cluttered and insanitary.

The River Leven is broad, fast flowing and around 90 metres (100 yards) wide at Dumbarton. As an industrial river it was capable of breaking down and dispersing a lot of the effluent discharged into it, but it is also tidal south of Renton, and this regularly slows its flow. At high tide, water can pool and be pushed back upriver. The dye works upstream discharged thousands of gallons of polluted water into the river each day. One witness said:

I was fascinated by the dyes going into the water. It wasn't just a wee spot of dye, the whole river was discoloured with different designs all over the place, yellows running into purples, running into reds, running into oranges.[3]

This, added to human and animal waste from the rapidly growing settlements along the Leven's banks, resulted in a heavily polluted and pungent watercourse running immediately behind the overpopulated High Street.

Wage rates in shipbuilding were, in general, higher than in print working but if the cost of accommodation was also higher in Dumbarton, then much of that benefit was lost. Maps and plans of the settlements (especially the large scale Ordnance Survey maps, see Chapters 3 and 4), show that there was more open space and lower housing densities in the Vale of Leven, although Renton was always worse off than the other villages.

Conditions were far from perfect in the Vale. Overcrowding and insanitary conditions were undoubtedly a problem there too, but a more substantial and better planned housing stock, subject to less population pressure, unquestionably contributed to a healthier standard of living.

In spite of this, Dumbarton's heavy industry was a more attractive prospect than printworking. Throughout the period a small but significant number of the Vale's employed males, around 5%-7%, worked in shipbuilding or iron and steel trades. Allowing for the fact that there was a small iron foundry in Alexandria, it is clear that men were prepared to travel to Dumbarton for employment, or who were indeed forced to locate or lodge in the Vale because accommodation in Dumbarton was difficult to find. Most of these workers lived in Renton or Bonhill. This was in part, a consequence of the dire housing situation in Dumbarton, which forced workers to lodge in the outlying villages.[4] In contrast, there were very few male print and dye workers living in Dumbarton.

Migration and Population Change in the Scottish Context

In the nineteenth century, Dunbartonshire displayed an extremely high turnover of population, even by the standards of West Central Scotland:

heightened … since it was a transit zone between the Highlands and Islands on one side and the expanding industries of Clydeside on the other [5]

Dunbartonshire straddled the Highland Boundary Fault. Major route ways ran through it, taking people from Stirlingshire, Argyllshire and the north west, into the industrial heartlands of Central Scotland. In its lowland section, it contained printworks, shipyards, iron foundries, mines and engine works. It was connected to a network of steamer ports. Dumbarton especially, had a history of trade with the Highlands and a connection with Ireland. By the 1850s, the western portion of Dunbartonshire was also well connected by rail to Glasgow. Population movements within the 'shire were significant too, with an overall drift from the rural northern and upland parishes to the industrialising south and especially to the banks of the Clyde.

This movement was being replicated all over the Central Belt of Scotland. By 1850, Scotland was the most urbanised country in Europe after England and Wales: all the more remarkable given that previously, Scotland had lagged behind much of Western Europe in this regard.[6] In both Dumbarton and the Vale of Leven there was rapid population growth throughout most of the second half of the nineteenth century, built on the successes of their respective industries. Between 1861 and 1871, the County of Dunbartonshire lost 2.7% of its population to net out-migration. Cotton mills closed across the county and in-migration to the Vale of Leven certainly stalled, although Dumbarton's growth was unaffected. In contrast, Lanark and Renfrew gained 5.6% and 8.5% of their respective populations, through net in-migration, while Stirling, Ayr and Argyll recorded substantial losses of 8.5%, 15.1% and 14.3% respectively.[7] Rural parishes were losing population to industrialising parishes and to emigration.

In the next decade there was a dramatic change. Only Dunbartonshire and Renfrew, of all the counties in Scotland, showed large net inflows of people and in 'the major overseas emigration decade of the 1880s, *only* Bute and Dunbartonshire had any net in-migration at county level'.[8] Bute's small increase in population was not due to industrialisation but to the growth in 'commuting, holidaying and retirement' settlement. A similar process occurred in Helensburgh, a planned, middle class town, which saw its population rise from 2,800 in 1851 to 7,700 by 1881.[9] Dunbartonshire's population continued to grow in the 1890s and into the first decade of the new century, when it again bucked the trend in what was another period of heavy emigration from Scotland.[10]

The growth in Dunbartonshire's population was not evenly spread across its industrial hubs. Between 1831 and 1841 Bonhill Parish's population rose by more than 3,000, as a direct result of the growth of the bleach, print and dye works. In Dumbarton, over the same decade, the population increase was under 800.[11] It was not until 1871 that Dumbarton's population exceeded that of Bonhill Parish. Population in the Vale of Leven, that is Bonhill Parish which contained Bonhill village, Alexandria and Jamestown - and Renton, which was part of Cardross Parish - rose from around 11,000 in 1861 to over 19,000 in 1891, with growth being markedly slower over the 1861-71 decade. Between 1891 and 1901, the Vale's population declined by 960 due to the difficulties faced by the printworks.

The most spectacular population growth in Dunbartonshire was not in Dumbarton nor the Vale, but at Clydebank, nine miles up river from the mouth of the Leven. It had been a greenfield site in 1870 but had a population of 10,000 a decade later, due to the success of J and G Thomson's shipyard which was moved from Govan to accommodate the building of Princes Dock. The world famous sewing machine manufacturer, I M Singer and Company, built an extensive factory here in the 1880s.[12] In consequence, by 1920, Clydebank's population had risen from zero to 37,500 over less than fifty years.

Migration was a vital component of population growth in Dunbartonshire throughout the second half of the nineteenth century.[13] As in other lowland counties, there was a high turnover of population. In the 1861 to 1891 period, population growth in Dunbarton, Renfrew and Lanark was 'driven by in-migration' and aided by natural increase.[14] For a relatively small county in both area and population, Dunbartonshire attracted large numbers of migrants, but at the same time, large numbers left the county to go elsewhere. Population movement between Dunbartonshire and the counties in the industrial Central Belt was at a high level throughout this period.

For example in 1851, Lanarkshire was home to 2,575 people under the age of twenty who had been born in Dunbartonshire, while at the same date 2,148 Lanarkshire born 'under twenties' were living in Dunbartonshire.[15]

Movement of course, was not only conducted across county boundaries: people moved within their counties of birth too. 'Moving home was a highly pervasive feature of life' both within Dunbartonshire and throughout Scotland.[16] In 1851, 'almost half' of the population and 'nearly two thirds of those aged 20 and over were living in a parish or a town or city in Scotland different from that of their birth'.[17]

These astounding figures describe a phenomenal rate of movement throughout Scotland, but they cannot capture its dynamic nature. The statistics compare a person's place of birth with their location in 1851. They do not capture moves made in the interim, including leaving and then returning to one's place of birth. While they include those born in Ireland and other countries, they do not account for the many Scots who left the country for other parts of the UK or abroad. During the second half of the nineteenth century and into the twentieth century, Scotland lost more people per head of population to emigration than almost any Western European country, with the exception of Ireland.[18]

Migration and the Vale of Leven

The villages in the Vale of Leven were founded during the first phase of industrialisation as textile processing centres. The fresh water that printworks required in abundance was readily available. The Leven, fed by Loch Lomond, provided an inexhaustible supply which facilitated industrial expansion. A major problem was the lack of an indigenous labour supply, and in common with other textile colonies, labour had to be imported, initially on a seasonal basis.[19] It has been suggested that much early migration to factory villages was essentially short distance, within half a day's walk from home.[20] However, seasonal Highland labour was employed too, and such migrations often became permanent as improvements in technology allowed the industrial process to be continued all year round.

From the 1850s onwards, movement was certainly not confined to 'half a days walk'. The majority of in-migrants were 'neighbouring Scots'.[21] There were sizeable numbers from Ireland (around 10% of the sample population in any census year from 1861 to 1891). As the scale of production increased, it was to become centred in large factories like Dalquhurn/Cordale, Milton and the Alexandria Works. Across Britain, cottage industry was declining. Many of the smaller and more remote operations closed down, as the streams on which mills relied could not sustain industrial expansion. Communications and transport improved dramatically. Word of mouth was no longer the only way the working classes communicated with one another. Improving levels of literacy helped people gain a wider knowledge and keener appreciation of available employment opportunities and literate migrants sent letters home. Companies placed job adverts in newspapers. In 1873, William Stirling's company at Dalquhurn and Cordale, made 'concerted efforts' to attract girls from Southern Ireland who were 'strong' and 'willing to work'.[22] Barriers to movement were also lowered as, thanks to the growth of railways in particular, travelling times decreased.

By 1861, in-migration was an important and established process, both in satisfying the increasing demands of the textile processing industries and in replacing those who were going elsewhere. Even in the most favourable economic and industrial climate, population mobility and inter-county migration were so commonplace that people thought little of moving to another town or village for minimal advantage. The standard of housing was poor overall and when hardship struck, the inability to pay for the most basic accommodation encouraged the workforce to be very mobile. Employers such as the Orr Ewings and Dennys built 'tied houses' for their workforces, but if you ceased working for an employer, you no longer had a place to live. Unfortunately for the industrialists, factory workers did not become sedentary to order, and if a better opportunity was perceived elsewhere, neither the job they had, nor the house they lived in, were sufficient to make them stay. People travelled light, having little in the way of personal possessions to tie them down. There are numerous local examples of workers leaving *en masse* for employment elsewhere, such as the departure of joiners from Dumbarton after a strike in 1865 (see Chapter 2).

Initially, housing provided by employers enticed people to this relatively remote greenfield site. Provision of housing was an essential ingredient for the success of industrial operations in the Vale of Leven. William Stirling moved his business from Glasgow to the Vale in the eighteenth century, principally to offset the cost of 'high' wages, but he needed to build Renton to house his workers.[23] Employers like the Orr Ewings had to provide houses in the clachans of Alexandria, Bonhill and Jamestown. It became less common for employers to act directly as builders and landlords as the nineteenth century progressed. In Dumbarton, skilled workers were tied to houses that they bought from the local building societies, set up or encouraged by the Dennys and other businessmen.[24]

It is estimated that about half of the Vale's population in 1851 was not born locally.[25] Even this bald statistic hides the fact that the majority of locally born people were children and youths, many being the sons and daughters of in-migrants. Of the Vale's native born population, more than half were children under 15 years old. This is indicative of recent in-migration which had seen the population of the Vale climb steeply in the previous two decades.

Figure 6:1 at the end of this chapter shows the estimated migrant and local born population from 1861-91. This demonstrates that net in-migration slackened in the 1861-71 decade. There was a resurgence in the following decade, but from 1881 to 1891, the pace of in-migration slowed slightly. Towards the end of this period, the graph shows that the Vale was increasingly growing its own population and becoming less dependent on in-migration. The overall pattern is a barometer of industrial fortunes in the Vale. Growth faltered through the first half of the 1860s. The Western Bank failure (1857) was but one sign of the depression being endured in the UK, and as a result of the American Civil War (1861-1865), cotton supplies collapsed. The industry recovered in the 1870s but there were signs of problems in the 1880s and into the 1890s. By the late 1890s the industry suffered a severe slump resulting in net out-migration. Migrants and potential migrants to the Vale of Leven were often rootless and prepared to move wherever economic advantage could be gained. Many, if not most, responded to opportunities available in specific locations.

- The printed Census Reports for the Vale of Leven show more female than male in-migration.

- In each census year (1861, 1871, 1881, 1891) there are approximately six women for every five men in the 15-54 age group which comprises the majority of the working population. This is a direct response to the number of jobs for females that were available in the printworks.

- In 1861's sample population, for every 100 females in the 15-54 age group who were born locally, there were over 140 who had been born elsewhere. This dropped to just below that figure in 1871, increased to over 160 in 1881 and was around 155 in 1891.

- The figures chart a definite increase in female in-migration after 1871.

- There were fewer men than women in this age group across the period, but initially, an even higher proportion of these were in-migrants.

- The sample for 1861 shows that for every 100 locally born males in the 15-54 age group, there were 175 born elsewhere.

- In contrast to the female ratios, there was a steady proportional decline after this with ratios of 100:153 in 1871, 100:146 in 1881 and 100:127 in 1891, as more work in the textile industries was being undertaken by women.

Censuses are taken at ten year intervals, and as such, cannot shed light on the complexity of short term population movement. The population was highly mobile and moving house was a regular occurrence. In-migrants did not always stay put, but moved on to new destinations, some went back to places where they had lived and worked before, others returned home. Those who were born in the parishes of Dumbarton, Bonhill or Cardross (Renton) are described as 'natives' or 'locals' here, but those who remained in this small corner of Dunbartonshire into adulthood were hardly sedentary. People moved house in response to changing circumstances: when they lost their jobs; had become more and more reliant on sporadic, casual or part time employment; when they could no longer afford the rent they were paying; when a lease expired; or when a better offer came along. A tenant defaulting on rent could have his possessions, such as they were, confiscated, and that was a very good reason for leaving the area hurriedly and without notice if circumstances took a turn for the worse.[26]

For those who stayed, there were lots of short distance moves, within a street, a village or a district. Many had crossed parish boundaries more than once, as the recorded birthplaces of their children indicate. Furthermore, large numbers of people who were born locally were children of migrants, and, with little attachment to their place of birth, would think nothing of moving on.

One way of gauging the migratory trends of those born locally is to 'follow' the number of natives recorded from one census to the next.[27] Across this period, large numbers of locals 'disappeared', either through death or migration. Even allowing for those who had died, there was still a substantial net loss each decade of around 30% to 40% of locally born adults aged 15-44 recorded at one census, who had moved out of the area by the next one.[28] What cannot be quantified are the numbers who left and then came back, nor the overall pattern of individual movement in the inter-censal years. The out-migration of locals decade by decade is discussed further in Chapter 9.

Figures for in-migrants, whether from other counties in Scotland, Ireland or elsewhere are *net* figures, that is the number from a county or a country present at one census, compared to the number from that county or country at the next.[29] They too cannot reveal anything about migratory patterns between census years. The census can only be used to compare the overall *number* of in-migrants from a specific location at one census point with those recorded at that location at a subsequent census.

What these raw figures disguise is that in-migrants were even more likely to move on than locals. Those who were last to arrive were often the first to leave.[30] A new arrival may have found it more difficult to secure stable employment and accommodation than a settled incomer or a local. Employers were more likely to dismiss strangers than well established locals or migrants whom they both knew and trusted.

Evidence, particularly from local newspapers and other contemporary sources, suggests that employment cycles, and the shift between relative posterity and relative austerity, were often very short term or seasonal. The problem for working people in the Vale was that they depended on a very narrow industrial base. Other than the bleach, print and dye works, there was no comparable alternative employment.

The consequential closure of the Ferryfield works in 1864 drew little comment, though more often, slumps in trade meant that workers were laid off temporarily, or moved to part time working. In winter, for example, it was sometimes difficult for the works to achieve the very high temperatures required in the dyeing process.[31] Some of the printworkers would find that employed days were being overtaken by idle ones, or that there were longer periods of inactivity and shorter working days. Income earned by their children, who were also employed in the printworks, declined. Many household heads supplemented their incomes by taking in boarders or lodgers who worked alongside them. Young, unattached lodgers were more footloose than householders, and more likely to look for work elsewhere. In such circumstances, choices came into sharper focus: accept casual work, part-time work or under-employment and wait for things to improve, or move away. The evidence is that many did the latter.

Migration and Dumbarton

Dumbarton may have been a 'Royal Burgh' but for most of its history it hadn't been a very successful one. While the Vale industrialised, grew and prospered in the first half of the nineteenth century, Dumbarton faltered. It was home to traders, shopkeepers, artisans, craftsmen and administrators as befitted a county and market town, but had hosted no large scale employers since the closure of the glassworks in the 1830s. It was only in the 1850s that Dumbarton truly joined the industrial age as shipbuilding, with its attendant engineering and foundry works, began to assume a greater significance. Migrants arrived looking for work in heavy industry. In contrast, the long established textile works to the north were entering a period of difficulty. Dumbarton's industrial growth was to continue almost unchecked throughout the second half of the century. It had a steadier population growth than the Vale, although the Vale's population continued to grow rapidly. Dumbarton's population rose steeply in 30 years, from around 8,200 in 1861 to nearly 17,000 by 1891. By 1911 it was 20,600, around four times higher than it had been in 1851.[32] The speed and immediacy of growth and the demand for labour, ensured that there were always more 'migrants' than locally born people living in the burgh over this period and, as with the Vale of Leven, many of the 'locals' were the children of migrants (see Figure 6:2 at the end of this chapter).

Most migrants of working age were men employed in heavy industry - principally shipbuilding. Dumbarton was an increasingly important destination for migrants as the second half of the century began. It attracted large numbers of young, single men who were prepared to move independently and speculatively, whereas families were more liable to move if the situation regarding availability of work and lodgings was known to be favourable.

- In 1861, of all the male migrants in the 15-54 age group, over one third of them were in the youngest of the four 'ten year' cohorts, the 15-24 year olds. This indicates a very recent surge in migration.

- The ratios of locally born males to migrants in the 15-54 age group was about 100 to 440 in 1861. A remarkable figure: more than four migrants were present for every locally born male in this age group.

- Thereafter, this decreased fairly quickly, to 100:360 by 1871, 100:240 by 1881 and 100:200 by 1891. This was against a background of steady population growth in which a natural increase in the number of locally born residents was making a greater contribution.

- However, in 1891, the 15-54 age bracket still contained two male migrants for every locally born man.

- These figures were far higher than anything experienced in the Vale over the same period, but it of course had a longer history of conspicuous in-migration than Dumbarton.

Female migration to Dumbarton was less about job opportunities and was more dependent on movements of families, whereas in the Vale of Leven many young single women had moved into the area to find work. In Dumbarton, according to the sample, three in every ten women were in recorded employment outside of the home, but in the Vale, half of all women were employed, and by far, the majority were earning their living in the printworks.

In Dumbarton, like the Vale, the situation was very fluid. Migrants would come and go. They were more likely to be footloose than locals, and yet around one in four locally born males in the 15-54 age group had left Dumbarton in each of the three decades considered here: a substantial number, but it was markedly fewer than were leaving the Vale over the same period.

Shipbuilding was a flourishing concern, but the workforce was not sedentary. A simple scenario where a successful industry attracts and retains a workforce did not apply here, nor did it apply to any of the shipbuilding towns along the Clyde. Dumbarton was only one hub in a network. Communications along the Clyde were good, and travel became cheaper, and much quicker, with the development of the rail system. By the second half of the nineteenth century it was possible to go from one end of the western industrial belt to the other in a few hours at most, the only problem being the cost of the journey.

When Thomson's relocated their Govan shipyard to a rural site on the north bank of the Clyde, there was no accommodation for the workforce, and so before the rapid growth of Clydebank, men commuted to the yard. Most travelled by train, thus as early as the 1870s, working class railway commuting was established in the West of Scotland.[33]

Ease of movement may have been improving, but housing in Dumbarton was not. It was of poor quality: there was not enough of it to satisfy demand, and, inevitably, this led to overcrowding and costly rents. For many industrial workers and their families the standard of accommodation would have been a factor in deciding whether to stay or to go. In Dennystown, which did not have the poorest housing stock in the burgh, a joiners' dispute in 1865 resulted in most of the workers leaving the area to seek jobs elsewhere. Of 160 household heads who were present in Dennystown in 1861, only four remained in 1871.[34]

Doubtless, the dire housing situation in Dumbarton had its part to play in population mobility. People attracted by the job prospects found that they were in competition with many others for adequate accommodation. Even as late as 1891, one quarter of Dumbarton's population, around 4,500 people, lived in the High Street which is only around ⅓ of a mile (550 metres) long. Very high population densities were also recorded in adjacent streets such as College Street ('the Vennel') and Quay Street which ran north and south respectively, from the High Street at Dumbarton Cross. Developments at Dennystown, 'over the bridge' to the west, and those in the Newtown/Knoxland to the east of the town, were to an extent alleviating the problem, but the latter had been designed to house skilled workers and did little to ease the plight of labourers and the unskilled. Dennystown had been intended for skilled workers, but overcrowding had led to a rapid decline in its status.

The very nature of shipbuilding encouraged workers to 'follow the job'. As a ship was being built, a variety of tradesmen were required for various stages of the production process. Riveters and caulkers were needed in the initial stages of constructing the hull and superstructure of a ship; engineers and mechanics were needed to assemble and instal engines, propellors and other moving parts; whereas ships' carpenters and painters were more in demand when a ship was being 'fitted out'. Workers moved between Clyde yards to take advantage of available opportunities. Increasingly, the circulation of workers became wider, involving not only the Clyde yards, but those in places such as Belfast, Barrow, and Tyne and Wear.[35]

One individual who was part of this flow was shipwright's son Roderick Chisholm, born in Dumbarton in 1868. By 1881 his family had moved to Old Kilpatrick and ten years later they lived in Clydebank, by which time Roderick was a ships' draughtsman. Shortly after this he was working at Harland and Wolff in Belfast. He rose to become one of their chief draughtsmen, working on the designs of the Titanic and its sister ship, the Olympia. He was one of nine men selected for the 'Guarantee Team' that would sail on the Titanic's maiden voyage, none of whom survived its sinking. [36]

Clearly, people did not confine their movements to Scotland. In the decade beginning 1881, there was an overall population loss recorded in the 'Western Lowlands' of Scotland due to emigration, both to other parts of the UK and abroad.[37] Emigration to the 'New World' was an important facet of population movement throughout the nineteenth and into the twentieth century, with the USA being the most important destination for both Scots and Irish.[38] Local newspapers ran adverts encouraging emigration: describing opportunities, listing shipping timetables and fares, including assisted and non-assisted passages, to Australia, New Zealand, Canada, South Africa and the USA. Many people living in Dumbarton and the Vale left for these destinations, just as they were to do in the decades immediately after the Second World War.

Adverts for assisted passage to Otago, on South Island, New Zealand, placed by the prominent Glasgow shipping firm of Patrick Henderson and Company, featured regularly in the *Dumbarton Herald* and *Lennox Herald*. In January 1871, for example, 'agricultural labourers, shepherds, tradesmen, fishermen and their families and female domestic servants' were being sought.[39]

Here, the Denny connection was significant. The Dennys had invested in Henderson's and built several ships for them, including a 'blockade runner', one of several Dennys built during the American Civil War (1861-1865). They also joined them in a number of other ventures including the purchase of Confederate States of America Bonds. Patrick Henderson even named one of his ships the 'Peter Denny'.[40]

Henderson's had begun to carry passengers and freight to Otago where the Free Church of Scotland had established a colony. Monthly sailings (in season) from Glasgow were begun in 1864, and by 1878 the company was also running sailings from London.

Along with Peter Denny, Henderson's supported the Otago Steam Ship Company which operated on the run from Otago to Tasmania.[41]

In April 1871, the *Lennox Herald* reported the safe arrival in Otago of the ship 'Agnes Muir' ninety three days after it had left the Clyde in December 1870.[42]

Population Growth and Migratory Trends

Figures 6:1 and 6:2 below, show the growth of the migrant and locally born population in the Vale of Leven and Dumbarton over a thirty year period.

It is striking that although Dumbarton and the Vale are near neighbours, there were distinct differences, not only in the birthplaces of their inhabitants, but in the proportions of 'locals' and 'migrants' in their respective populations. There were proportionally fewer locally born people living in Dumbarton because of a strong and sustained surge of in-migration. Figure 6:2 shows that the growth of 'local' and 'migrant' populations ran almost parallel. The burgh slowly became more dependent on its own indigenously bred population as the percentage of locally born rose from 42% of a population of around 8,200 in 1861 to 48% of 16,900 in 1891. But the number of migrants living there was still higher than that of those locally born.[43]

As figure 6:1 shows, there was a higher percentage of locals living in the Vale than there was in Dumbarton. About half of the population of the Vale in 1861 was born locally when the total population was around 11,000 and that had risen to 55% of nearly 19,000 in 1891. As the locally born population grew slowly in the 1861-71 decade, the number of migrants almost levelled out. There was a steeper growth in the number of migrants over the next decade, after a surge of in-migration which involved substantial numbers of Irish women. The ebb and flow of population in the Vale's villages is hardly surprising, given that the bleach, print and dye works had suffered serious setbacks in the late 1850s and early 1860s and were entering a less productive period in the 1890s. In the first half of the nineteenth century, the Vale had experienced a period of heavy in-migration. In contrast, Dumbarton's industries did not flourish until the 1850s when it too began to attract lots of incomers. The demand for labour in heavy industry coincided with the immediate post Famine rush of the

Irish to Scotland. Alongside this, Irish navvies were already working nearby on the railways. Such circumstances contributed to the significant growth in Irish immigration to the burgh.

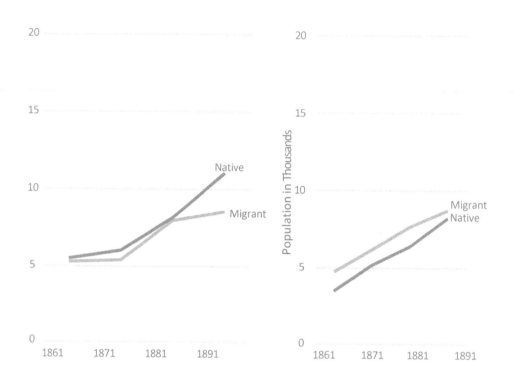

Figure 6:1 Vale of Leven:
'Native' and 'Migrant' Population (000s)
1861-1891

Figure 6:2 Dumbarton:
'Native' and 'Migrant' Population (000s)
1861-1891

[1] Anderson, *Scotland's Populations* pp. 189-191. Table 10:1 shows the percentage of the Scottish population under fifteen years of age in 1851 was 35.6 and 36.6 in 1881. The 1881 sample estimates for the Vale and Dumbarton are 33.5 and 37.5 respectively.

[2] In each census from 1861 to 1891 women in the Vale of Leven between the age of 14 and 44 outnumbered men in the same age group, whereas in Dumbarton it was the reverse.

[3] *@WDCHeritage* 17 April 2022

[4] *DH* 19 March 1864

[5] Slaven, *The Development of the West of Scotland* p. 141

[6] Anderson, *Scotland's Populations* p. 97

[7] Ibid. p.130. These figures represent net-migration which is measured by comparing the number of migrants recorded for a location at the beginning and end of a period (after allowances are made for expected mortality rates) e.g. a decade, as measured by the decennial census.

[8] Ibid. p.131. Dunbartonshire in the 1881-91 decade saw a net in-flow of 7%, whereas Bute's net in-flow was only 0.3%.

[9] Ibid. p. 97

[10] Ibid. p. 132

[11] *Thesis*, pp. 7-8

[12] *TSA* Vol 6 pp. 232-33

[13] Migration is defined here as any movement of population across county or national boundaries. However, all those born in Dumbarton, Bonhill and Cardross Parishes are regarded as 'natives', 'locals',or 'locally born', whereas those born in other Dunbartonshire Parishes are regarded as 'neighbouring' or 'nearby' Scots'.

[14] Anderson, *Scotland's Populations* p. 132

[15] Ibid. p. 164

[16] Ibid. pp. 139-40

[17] Ibid. Quoting figures derived from the National Sample of the 1851 Census of Great Britain which, for Scotland, consisted of 54,000 people from 158 systematically sampled enumeration districts, and samples from 25 randomly selected institutions.

[18] Ibid. p. 142

[19] See Chapter 1

[20] D.G. Lockhart, 'Patterns of Migration and Movement of Labour to the Planned Villages of North East Scotland' *Scottish Geographical Magazine* Vol 98 (1) (1982) pp 35-49

[21] See Introduction: Nomenclature.

[22] Nenadic and Tuckett, *The Turkey Red Printed Cotton Industry* p. 5, citing University of Glasgow Archives. UGD/13/1/8/229.

[23] Cooke, *The Rise and Fall of the Scottish Cotton Industry* p. 23

[24] Osborne, 'Dumbarton shipbuilding and workers' housing' pp. 2-11

[25] Those born in Bonhill, Cardross and Dumbarton parishes are regarded here as 'locals'.

[26] Hutchison, *Industry, Reform and Empire*. p. 107

[27] *Thesis*, Chapters 11 and 12

[28] *Thesis*, Ch 11. Age specific estimated death rates are used to calculate an approximate number of deaths that would occur in this group over a ten year period.

[29] In this study those born in Dunbartonshire outside of Dumbarton, Bonhill and Cardross parishes are considered as 'neighbouring Scots', not 'locals', but this does not allow for movements between the local parishes to be tracked, although it was very common for people born in one local parish to be living in another.

[30] C.G.Pooley, 'Residential Mobility in the Victorian City' *Transactions of the Institute of British Geographers* NS 4 (1979) pp.258-77

[31] Cooke, *The Rise and Fall of the Scottish Cotton Industry* p. 110

[32] It should be noted that Dumbarton's burgh boundaries were widened over this period.

[33] Adams, *The Making of Urban Scotland*. p. 92

[34] Osborne, 'Dumbarton shipbuilding and workers' housing' pp. 2-11. See also Chapter 11 here, where the change in Dennystown's profile from 1861 to 1871, is described in more detail.

[35] D.M. MacRaild, *Irish Migrants in Modern Britain 1750-1922* (1999) p. 108

[36] *BBC Radio 4 Today* programme 4 March 2023. (1hr 53minutes in) and *encyclopedia-titanic.org*

[37] M. Flinn, et al, *Scottish Population History from the Seventeenth Century to the Nineteen Thirties* (1977) pp. 464-65

[38] T. M. Devine, *To the Ends of the Earth. Scotland's Global Diaspora 1750-2010* (2011) p. 125

[39] *DH* 5 January 1871

[40] 'Shipping lines involved in New Zealand Immigration' *https:// sites.rootsweb.com/~nzbound/lines.htm* . This was not Dennys only connection with New Zealand. See Chapter 2

[41] Robertson, 'Shipping and Shipbuilding' p. 38

[42] *LH* 22 April 1871

[43] The figures from sample show that around 44% of the 8,253 population in 1861 to over 48% of the 16,927 population in 1891 were born locally.

7 The Incomers

In the previous chapter, the ebb and flow of people to and from Dumbarton and the Vale of Leven was examined. Here, the focus is on where those individuals were from and what they faced when they arrived.

Lowland Scots Migration.

Until recently, the movement of Lowland Scots from rural areas into the industrialising villages, towns and cities of Central Scotland has been largely neglected, with greater focus being on the more dramatic Irish and Highland migrations.[1] However, the lowland counties contributed more people to the growing urban settlements in Scotland's Central Belt than any other group. 'Neighbouring Scots' made up approximately 30% to 32% of the Vale's population throughout the 1861-91 period, as opposed to 23% to 27% for Dumbarton. These figures indicate a sustained in-migration that was maintained throughout the second half of the nineteenth century, as the settlements along the Leven Valley continued to grow vigorously.

Scots from nearby counties who moved to this area are regarded as 'incomers', but problems of assimilation were slight. By their weight of numbers they altered the complexion of the burgh and the Vale. Lowland Scots may have shared a common nationality, language and religion with the locals, but it would be wrong to consider them as a homogenous group. They were employed in a wide spectrum of occupations and covered a broad range of social classes, unlike the Irish who were 'over-represented' in manual work and in the lower social strata. The 'neighbouring Scots' came from many different environments: for example, from rural highland and coastal areas of Argyll; industrial towns in Lanarkshire; the City of Glasgow; agricultural parishes in Ayrshire; and mill villages in Renfrewshire and

Stirlingshire. In common with all lowland counties, there was also a drift within Dunbartonshire from rural and upland areas to the industrialising towns and villages, as well as a movement from Dunbartonshire to other nearby counties. There is evidence that some moved in an effort to find work in occupations or in industries similar to those that they were leaving behind, but for those who came from farming backgrounds, work on the land was neither available nor, in most cases, desirable. Ties to the land had been broken forever. Many migrants were footloose: the birthplaces of their children a catalogue of towns in the West of Scotland.[2]

As they were born relatively close by, the movement of Lowland Scots to urban areas could be considered less traumatic. Not all new arrivals had to search for accommodation, as they often lodged with friends or relatives who were instrumental in finding them employment - although it involved dislocation and alienation for some. The work available in prospering towns and cities was a clear attraction. It offered the promise of better wages and shorter hours than farm work, but the reality of conditions in mills, factories and foundries was in stark contrast to the outdoor work which they had left behind. Industrial work was pressured, noisy, dirty and dangerous. Working in crowded factories could be a daunting experience, where a perfunctory nod to the health and safety of workers was the best that could be expected, and where accidents were commonplace.[3] Couple this with the burden of moving from a rural to an urban environment: finding accommodation; living in cramped circumstances, perhaps among strangers; a basic lack of privacy; and, encountering squalid conditions which were sources of disease. Many had no choice other than to leave their homes. Tenant farmers were evicted as population increase and changes to farm practices meant that they were no longer required to work on the land and 'to be without work was also to be without a place to stay'.[4]

In spite of the conditions to be endured in mills and factories, towns and cities were alluring, promising not only employment opportunities but a varied leisure and social life which was unavailable in the countryside. In what little free time they had, male workers in Dumbarton and the Vale of Leven could get involved in a wide array of activities which included sports such as rowing, bowling, quoits and particularly, football, which by the later decades of the century had

firmly established itself... as the leading passion of the working class male Scot. Its growth coincided with decades in which a sustained improvement in living standards along with a reduction in working hours widened access to leisure on a regular basis for a large section of the population. [5]

Football, both as a participation and a spectator sport, was encouraged by Saturday half day working, introduced in the 1870s.[6] In the early years of nationally organised football, Vale of Leven, Renton and Dumbarton football clubs were among the most successful teams in the country, with Scottish Cup winners Renton beating the FA Cup winners West Bromwich Albion, in what was billed as the 'World Championship' in 1888.

There were of course, ample opportunities for drinking, music and dancing, but local industrialists, clergymen and politicians in their paternalistic ways encouraged sober and 'worthy' pursuits among the middle and 'respectable' working classes. There were subscription libraries (before the advent of free public libraries at the end of the century), art clubs, choral and music societies, church activities and outings. Both Liberal and Conservative Associations had 'rooms' in the area. The Masonic Order was well established as was 'The Dumbarton District Lodge of Loyal Orangemen'. All of the above feature in local trade directories and almanacs published in the 1880s and 1890s.[7]

Leisure time, initially the preserve of the middle classes and the male 'labour aristocracy', had been extended to include most working class males by the later decades of the century. Working class 'housewives' did not enjoy the benefits of reduced factory working hours that led to more free time. For them:

the day lacked formal boundaries, but rather was punctuated by the insistent, yet intermittent requirement to fulfil household chores, interspersed with periods when duties were less pressing. If these interludes were the nearest that most women came to 'leisure time', they were often filled by activities vital to maintaining the fabric of the household such as mending clothes or shopping for the next days meal.[8]

Neither could the poorest people indulge themselves in much leisure time, as they worked where and when they could.

The movement from the rural and upland parishes of Central Scotland to its flourishing industrial heartlands gained pace, and even when conditions in the countryside became more conducive to staying put, the momentum of migration, once set in motion, was difficult to resist. This relocation was aided by improvements in communications. The people in rural districts were keenly aware of the potential opportunities, as they were in contact with those already there. The rail network was the principal means of transport.

Highland Migration

Those 'neighbouring Scots' from Argyll were part of the Highland migration southwards to the industrial belt. Some Highlanders were distinguished from the Lowland Scots by their Gaelic language. By the second half of the nineteenth century there were few bilingual or 'Gaelic only' speakers in Dumbarton or the Vale.[9] Those from Argyll comprised around 2-3% of Dumbarton's population and in the Vale their proportion of the population dropped from over 6% in 1861 to under 2% in 1891.[10] It was a stream of migration which had begun in the eighteenth century with the start of 'clearances', and had been strong in the early nineteenth century when the industrialising lowlands attracted Highland migrants. Printwork owner Archibald Orr Ewing stated in 1875, that forty years earlier

an immense number of Highlanders were employed, but now nearly half were Irish… the habits of the people were more simple: perhaps they consumed less drink and lived on a more nutritious diet.[11]

The failure of the potato crop in Ireland was paralleled by a similar event in the Highland Crofting counties in 1846, but the latter was on a smaller scale. The famine it triggered was longer lasting than the Irish famine, but much less deadly. A consequence of the Highland famine was that movement to the industrial south did increase, but it did not become a large scale permanent shift, in spite of the fact that 'perhaps a third of the entire population migrated permanently from the western mainland and the Hebrides between the early 1840s and the later 1850s'.[12] Many Highlanders emigrated, and a 'sharp increase' was recorded in passenger numbers leaving the principal Scottish ports for North America, Australia and New Zealand.[13]

Irish Immigration

There has been a continual ebb and flow of population between Ireland and Scotland since prehistoric times. Celtic peoples from Antrim settled in Argyll around 400 AD. In 563 AD, Columba came from Ireland, founding his community in Iona, he set about converting the indigenous population to Christianity. In the seventeenth century the British Crown promoted the plantation of Scots settlers to Ulster and the removal of the Catholic natives from the best land. The Famine years and their aftermath brought thousands of Irish immigrants to the industrial heartland of Central Scotland seeking work and security. In the late nineteenth and early twentieth century there was a circulation of shipyard workers between Belfast and Clydeside. This enduring relationship has bound Scotland and Ireland together, with ties to Ulster being particularly close.

In the pre-Famine era, Irish immigrants were no strangers to Scotland where they sought out work, but their stay was often temporary in that they provided a pool of harvest labour.[14] In places like the Vale of Leven, they would work not only in agriculture but in the open air bleachfields, returning home in the murky months when bleaching by sunlight was impossible. Those who stayed in Scotland tended to cluster in the rural south west, in Dumfries and Galloway and Ayrshire: the counties closest to their native land. The situation evolved as the nineteenth century progressed. James Handley estimated that in the mid 1840s up to 25,000 harvest labourers arrived in Glasgow during the summer season, and many were beginning to prolong their stay in Scotland.[15] Seasonal annual migration did not cease during the 'Famine' nor afterwards, as thousands of temporary migrants continued to travel to Scotland, initially to work in agriculture, but also to take up jobs in industry and construction. It has been estimated that 35,000 to 40,000 temporary migrant labourers arrived in the UK each year in the period between 1880 and 1900 and not all were agricultural workers.[16]

Temporary migrants could become permanent settlers:

For many of these it was in fact the prelude to a less easily reversible departure. It provided both a taste for life elsewhere and a means of indulging that taste. Indeed seasonal and permanent migration were often complementary rather than alternative experiences'[17]

Permanent migration did not begin with An Gorta Mor. The Irish had been arriving and staying in ever increasing numbers throughout the first half of the nineteenth century. The 1841 Census shows that there were around 126,000 Irish in Scotland to be found largely in the industrialising Central Belt of the country. Many were linen workers, both Protestant and Catholic, drawn to areas of cloth production such as Blantyre, Paisley and Glasgow, and to areas like the Vale, which was becoming one of the most important cloth bleaching, printing and dyeing centres in the country. The Irish were employed in large numbers as 'navvies' firstly in the construction of canals and then in the railway building era of the mid nineteenth century.

The 'Great Famine', the 'Great Hunger' or An Gorta Mor, emanating from successive failures of the potato crop, lasted from 1845 to 1852.[18] As the catastrophe unfolded, the Irish poured into Britain, impelled by conditions at home and drawn to an industrialising country by the chance of employment, by a growing web of family and community connections, and, indeed by the prospect of eventually making their way to America.[19] Emigration soon became 'a long term response to a short term calamity'.[20]

Tom Devine describes:

The Great Irish Famine of the 1840s, [as] not only the greatest human disaster in nineteenth-century Europe but, proportionally, more lethal than the majority of famines in modern times. The calamity killed one-eighth of the entire population or just over a million people…Emigration from Ireland had been taking place on a substantial scale from the early eighteenth-century and the Great Famine massively accelerated the scale of that exodus. An estimated 2.1 million men, women and children left for overseas destinations in the decade between 1845 and 1855 with 1.5 million sailing for the USA, another 340,000 for British North America (later the Dominion of Canada) and between 200,000 and 300,000 settling in Great Britain…fewer than

131

100,000 came to Scotland during those crisis years. In relative terms, however, this was an enormous and unique burden for a small country which contained only around 2.8 million inhabitants in 1845.[21]

The extent of the British Government's inadequate response to the Famine is subject to ongoing debate, but it is interesting to note that it is estimated to have spent under £10 million on what was initially a loan for famine relief, compared to around £70 million spent on pursuing the Crimean War in the 1850s and about £20 million, over time, in compensating plantation owners in the West Indies after the abolition of slavery in 1833.[22]

There were three main emigrant routes to Britain from Ireland:

- the Northern, from Ulster and Northern Connaught to Scotland.

- the Midland, from Connaught and most of Leinster via Dublin to northern England and the midlands of England.

- the Southern, from south Leinster and Munster to London, often via Bristol.[23]

The northern route into Scotland carried many Protestant as well as Catholic migrants who brought very different religious and political beliefs with them.[24]

At the height of the Famine in 1847, the vessels arriving in Glasgow carrying goods, mainly livestock, and human cargo, came principally from Larne, Belfast, Dublin, Derry and Limerick. Larne and Limerick contributed 352 and 134 ships respectively. These were all sailing ships which were smaller and slower than steam ships. Out of a total of 291 ships from Belfast, 221 were steamers. Likewise, the majority of Derry's ships were steamers - 177 out of 206. Dublin's 91 steamers, from a total of 114 ships, were on average larger and heavier than those from Belfast or Derry, and in all probability carried fewer immigrants.[25] Exports of farm products did not stop during the Famine. Indeed the export of livestock increased. 'In total over three million live animals were exported between 1846-50, more than the number of people who emigrated during the famine years'.[26] Poor refugees fleeing from famine would share space with cattle on the crossings to Britain.

The arrival of thousands of poor, starving and disease ridden immigrants posed major problems for Glasgow, the main port of disembarkation in Scotland. It is estimated that in 1847, 50,000 refugees were set down on its streets.[27] Typhus, often referred to as 'fever', and other diseases caused by poverty, overcrowding and poor sanitation were hardly unheard of prior to this date, but, as in Liverpool, the Irish in Glasgow were deemed responsible for the typhus epidemic.[28]

The *Glasgow Herald* of 22 March 1847 told its readers that...

the great majority of cases of typhus which have occurred may be traced to the masses of diseased and famished Irish which have been thrown amongst us...

Thus at the outset, the blame was unequivocally laid on the Irish famine refugees.[29] Fears of typhus carriers arriving in Scotland prompted the authorities in Glasgow to request that Irish ships be inspected at Greenock, before travelling on to the city. When this measure failed, the Glasgow Parochial Board asked the Home Office to apply the inspections not only to Greenock, but also to Ardrossan, Troon, Ayr, Port Glasgow, Dumbarton and Bowling: that is, the other Clyde ports which were visited by Irish ships on their way to Glasgow.[30]

For most immigrants to Scotland, Glasgow was an immediate goal and from there many hoped to travel onwards to North America; but that was unrealistic in many cases as fares were considerably more expensive than the cost of a comparatively short trip across the Irish Sea. In the years between 1846 and 1853, 47,000 Irish 'paupers' were repatriated.[31] A high proportion of these were destitute, ill and unable to work. Doubtless, some who were fit enough made their way back to Scotland on the cheap and frequent steamers which serviced the city. Of course, not all immigrants ended up in Glasgow. Clyde ports like Dumbarton, Greenock, Port Glasgow and even Bowling, offered the possibility of industrial work, and those who alighted at these ports, did not stray far if they could find employment. The Clyde was an important focal point for the Irish in Scotland and when they arrived there, they found labouring jobs on the docks, in the shipyards and factories, either in Glasgow or in one of its growing satellite towns. This encouraged the Irish to settle close to the Clyde rather than move far inland, although mining towns and villages in Central Scotland also attracted Irish labour.[32]

By 1861, the number of Irish in England and Wales reached its peak at 602,000 or 3% of the total population.[33] In Scotland the peak was not reached until 1881 when there were just under 219,000 Irish born - 5.8% of the population. Even so, the Irish had comprised of 7.2 % of an albeit smaller Scottish population in 1851. The flow of migrants to Scotland was more continuous throughout the second half of the nineteenth century than it was to England and Wales where it declined steadily.

in Scotland in 1901 there were 205,000 Irish born similar to the 207,000 half a century earlier…[this] implies that the stream of Irish migrants continued for each generation (apart from a slight downturn in the 1880s)…This suggests a minimum of an average of around 8000 new Irish immigrants arrived in Scotland each year in the 1850s and 60s [34]

The following chapter will focus predominantly on the movement of the Irish to the Vale of Leven and Dumbarton in the 1861 to 1891 period.

NOTES

[1] See however, T.M. Devine, *The Scottish Clearances. A History of the Dispossessed* (2018)

[2] *Cebs* for Dumbarton and the Vale of Leven 1861-91.

[3] Regular reports of accidents in the printworks, shipyards, foundries and railways of West Dunbartonshire are found in the *Dumbarton and Lennox Heralds* throughout the 2nd half of the 19th Century. See Chapter 5

[4] Devine, *The Scottish Nation* p. 461

[5] Griffiths, *'Work, Leisure and Time'* p. 172

[6] Ibid.

[7] Available in the 'Local Collection' in Dumbarton Public Library

[8] Griffiths, *'Work, Leisure and Time'* p. 189

[9] The census enumerators recorded a 'G' or 'G&E' beside the names of, Gaelic only, or Gaelic with English, speakers respectively.

[10] Numbers from Skye, the rest of 'Inverness-shire', Ross and Cromarty, Sutherland and Caithness always made up less than 2% of the sample population in the Vale and Dumbarton at all four censuses.

[11] *LH* 11 September 1875

[12] Devine, *The Scottish Nation* pp. 418-9

[13] T.M. Devine, *The Great Highland Famine. Hunger, Emigration and the Scottish Highlands in the Nineteenth Century* (1988) p. 198

[14] J.H. Johnson, 'Harvest Labour Migration from Nineteenth Century Ireland' *Transactions of the Institute of British Geographers* No 41 (1967) pp. 97-112

[15] J.E. Handley, *The Irish in Modern Scotland* (1947) p. 38

[16] G. Davis, 'Little Irelands' in R. Swift and S. Gilley (eds) *The Irish in Britain 1815-1939* (1989) pp. 105-6

[17] D. Fitzpatrick, 'A Curious Middle Place: the Irish in Britain, 1871-1921', in Ibid. p. 18

[18] See R.F. Foster, *Modern Ireland 1600-1972* (1988) Ch14 pp. 318-344, for a brief discussion on the causes and consequences of 'The Famine'

[19] Davis, 'Little Irelands' p. 105-6. cites C. O'Grada, 'A Note on 19th Century Irish Emigration Statistics' *Population Studies* Vol. 29:1 (1975) pp. 143-9

[20] B.Collins, 'The Origins of Irish Immigration to Scotland in the nineteenth and twentieth centuries' in T.M .Devine (ed) *Irish Immigrants and Scottish Society in the Nineteenth and Twentieth Centuries* (1991) p. 10

[21] T.M. Devine, 'The Great Irish Famine and Scottish History' in Mitchell (ed) *New Perspectives* p. 20

[22] The Great Irish Famine BBC Radio 4, from the *'In Our Time'* series, 4 April 2019, available on BBC Sounds.

The government borrowed the money, which 'amounted to a massive 40 per cent of the treasury's annual income' to pay the slave owners. That debt was finally 'paid off' by taxpayers in 2015 according to taxjustice.net

[23] M.A.G O'Tuathaigh, 'The Irish in Nineteenth Century Britain: Problems of Integration' *Royal Historical Society Transactions* 31, (1981) pp. 149-73

[24] Estimates vary on the ratio of Protestant to Catholic immigrants that arrived in Scotland during the second half of the nineteenth century from between 1 in 3 to 1 in 4. See Mitchell, *New Perspectives*. Preface.

[25] F. Neal, *Black '47: Britain and the Irish Famine* (1998) p. 56

[26] C. Kinealy, Food Exports from Ireland (1997) *https://www.historyireland.com/18th-19th-century-history/food-exports-from-ireland-1846-47/*

[27] Neal, *Black '47: Britain and the Irish Famine* p. 108

[28] Ibid. p. 159

[29] Ibid. p. 161

[30] Ibid. p. 68

[31] Ibid. p. 237

[32] C. Pooley, 'Segregation or Integration. The residential experience of the Irish in mid-Victorian Britain' in R.Swift and S. Gilley (eds) *The Irish in Britain* p. 67

[33] O'Grada 'A Note on 19th Century Irish Emigration Statistics' contends that Irish emigration to the UK in the nineteenth and early twentieth centuries has been significantly under-estimated.

[34] B Collins, 'The Origins of Irish Immigration to Scotland' in T.M .Devine, (ed) *Irish Immigrants and Scottish Society.* Collins factored in notional death rates to produce estimate figures for Irish immigration to Scotland.

8 The Irish in Scotland: Dumbarton and the Vale of Leven in Context

'Thousands are sailing'[1]

The large numbers of poor and destitute Irish who arrived in Britain during and immediately after An Gorta Mor were not welcomed. Generally, reactions were hostile and antagonistic. The Irish were blamed for most of society's ills. Disease, overcrowding, squalor, poverty and lawlessness, hardly absent in Victorian Britain, would now be blamed on them. As the vast majority of immigrants were impoverished, their arrival exacerbated the social problems already present in towns and cities.

Animosity was greatest in the areas where the Irish settled in largest numbers, and where there was an understandable fear among the natives of being 'swamped' by the influx. Overcrowded cities like Liverpool and Manchester were breeding grounds of discontent, but the deepest and most enduring ire was to greet those who made the short journey across the Irish Sea to Scotland. The intensity of that response had its roots in the geography and demography of Irish immigration, and on social, cultural, religious and political differences both within the Irish 'community' and between the Irish and the Scots.

The Irish resided, to a great degree, in Glasgow and West Central Scotland. Within that area, particular locations were favoured. They were drawn to certain towns, distinct neighbourhoods within those towns, and particular industries. Beyond Glasgow and the West, the major Irish outlier was Dundee, and there were also small communities of Irish in and around Edinburgh, but no sizeable accumulations elsewhere. The reception which they received was rarely encouraging.

The vast majority of migrants arrived from the province of Ulster, already accustomed to sectarian bitterness. There is little doubt that the Ulster Protestant immigrant, very often bearing a Scottish surname, found it easier to integrate than the Catholic, and aggressively asserted his Orange and anti papistical sentiments as a way of allying himself to the native Scots and disassociating himself from his fellow Irishmen. The Catholic Irish were thereby driven even more firmly into a ghetto mentality, and clung to the bosom of mother church to find some kind of comfort and support in a totally unwelcoming environment. [2]

Undoubtedly intra Irish sectarianism did little to help assimilation of the Catholic Irish in particular, but Ian Wood, writing in 1978, suggested that the Scots themselves harboured:

A layer of xenophobia which has for long co-existed with the real or imagined facts of the Irish presence in Scotland.[3]

The official report on the 1871 Scottish Census reflects attitudes which were prevalent at that time, as this excerpt demonstrates:

The immigration of such a number of people from the lowest class and with no education will have a bad effect on the population. So far, living among the Scots does not seem to have improved the Irish, but the native Scots who live among the Irish have got worse. It is difficult to imagine the effect the Irish immigrants will have upon the morals and the habits of Scottish people.[4]

National and local examples of contemporary attitudes to the Irish in Scotland and their Catholic faith, which appeared in the press, helped to form or confirm native prejudices.[5]

Newspapers which served Dumbarton and the Vale of Leven were not that different and, as was the practice at the time, carried national and international stories from a variety of sources, as well as local news.

In 1851, the newly founded *Dumbarton Herald* printed a disputatious series of letters regarding the alleged ill treatment of Catholic children attending Dumbarton Academy.[6] The labels 'Irish' and 'Catholic' were used interchangeably at this time.[7]

The *Dumbarton Herald* also reported that '*The Belfast Telegraph* is greatly scandalised' by the attitude of the 'bigoted Prelate' Archbishop (later Cardinal) Cullen 'Head of the Catholic Church in Ireland'.[8] The outspoken Cullen sought to reassert Catholic liturgical practice and responded to the fundamental changes in Ireland's circumstances which saw the 'destruction of traditional peasant society' and the growing influence of the English language.[9]

In contrast, the 'anti-Catholic demagogue [and] former priest'[10] Alessandro Gavazzi who gave inflammatory talks in the Vale of Leven and elsewhere, is lauded as 'a distinguished Italian patriot and orator',[11] although the *Dumbarton Herald* was less kind to his fellow rabble rouser J. S. Orr, AKA 'The Angel Gabriel'. The newspaper questioned Orr's sanity, and, on the occasion of his 'flying visit' to Dumbarton in 1855, detailed numerous prior arrests for encouraging public unrest.[12] The most serious of these 'anti-Catholic and anti-Irish disorders' occurred in Greenock in 1851 and 1852 when Orr encouraged armed Scots to attack and loot the homes of Irish Catholics.[13]

In October 1855, a week after his visit to Dumbarton, Orr's incendiary language had the desired effect. Skirmishes between 'shipwrights' and 'Irish navvies' escalated into a much greater and potentially serious disturbance. The *Dumbarton Herald* reported that

there have been symptoms in the town of the revival of an old Dumbarton custom, of keeping up a breach between the shipwrights and the Irish labourers employed in the town and neighbourhood. Up till Saturday last these symptoms were generally confined to a street brawl or two on pay-night.[14]

The 'Angel Gabriel', who 'summoned his audiences with a trumpet', had inflamed the situation to the extent that:

…the shipwrights ran amok. They seized two Irish labourers employed in the yard of Denny and Rankine and only just failed to throw one of them into a furnace, the unfortunate men escaping with severe burns. They went on to systematic smashing of the windows of Catholics' houses in College Street.[15]

The *Dumbarton Herald* reported that at least 200 shipwrights gathered in the High Street close to the entrance to College Street, where many of the Irish lived, and which was 'densely packed' with 'navvies'. Improvised weapons were brandished by both sides. The 'navvies' and their families barricaded the street at either end and dug up cobble stones to be used as weapons against the shipwrights. The shipwrights gathered reinforcements, as did the 'navvies', with a large Irish contingent marching from Duntocher, intent on supporting their countrymen. Fortunately, 'magistrates' were able to calm the situation before extensive fighting broke out: but bad feeling remained, and for a time, Irish workers, that is, the 'navvies' and not the shipwrights, were banned from working in Denny and Rankine's yard.[16]

Contemporary historian Donald Macleod described the situation thus:

The shipwrights endeavoured to hunt the poor labourers, firstly out of their domiciles; secondly out of the town, and thirdly out of their senses…special constables, the county constabulary and the more influential of the residenters (sic) were brought to bear upon the rival forces and sweet persuasion, coupled with a goodly display of physical repressive force, happily prevented open hostilities…The navvies [from Duntocher] did come, not knowing but what their services might be required; but finding all things quiet they marched peaceably through the burgh, and a fine body of powerful men …would have done desperate execution in a scrimmage.[17]

It is to the credit of the local newspapers that they reported this event fairly and objectively. In the following year when they covered an extensive strike in the shipyards which culminated in what they called a 'riot' they were sued for their troubles.[18]

However, in 1864, the *Lennox Herald* reported that Irish illiteracy was the reason why houses had to be given numbers in Renton, the village with the heaviest concentration of Irish in the Vale of Leven.

These improvements are much needed as from the number of Irish now resident here who keep up correspondence with their friends across the channel, it is often no easy task for the postman to find the real Pat or Mike for whom the sometimes not very legibly addressed epistles are intended.[19]

A trivial example perhaps, but such attitudes were supported by widely held beliefs about the inferiority of the Irish Race, while cartoons in publications such as *Punch* magazine depicted the Irish as sly, untrustworthy, and ape-like. Tom Gallagher cites James Handley who provided a few stereotypical examples from the *North British Daily Mail:*

an ape-faced small-headed Irishman…

a middle-aged malicious looking Irishman…

Pat O'Shannon, a startled-looking Irish tailor, with a cruel Tipperary visage…

Ann Brady or Brogan, a wicked-looking daughter of the Green Isle...[20]

Neither the *Lennox Herald,* nor its sister paper the *Dumbarton Herald,* were guilty of stooping so low. And while it is true that the Irish were the subject of much discrimination, it would be a disservice to caricature them as poor, ignorant, passive, ghetto dwelling beings, universally hated and living on the margins of society - and, as the above quote from the *Lennox* proves, they were communicating with those at home who would be well apprised of the opportunities and pitfalls of coming to Scotland.[21]

Irish immigrants who settled in Scotland often lived in close proximity to each other but it would be difficult to argue that they inhabited 'ghettos'. A 'ghetto' being defined as 'part of a city especially a slum area, occupied by a minority group or groups' or 'an isolated or segregated group or area'.[22]

Such definitions are open to wide interpretation. One commentator has examined the degree of segregation of immigrant communities in Liverpool and described a spectrum between, on the one hand, the free choice of ethnic groups staying together and, on the other, cases where ethnicity, combined with a lack of social mobility, leads to the ghetto. He concludes that when an immigrant group has a similar socio-demographic and cultural background to the host community, then integration will be total and rapid. Where these factors are markedly different from those of the hosts, and when migrant socio-economic status is significantly lower, a ghetto forms.[23] The raw census data for Dumbarton and the Vale analysed in the succeeding chapters, supports the view that while the Irish often lived in close proximity to one another, they did not inhabit ghettos. Indeed, it has been suggested that:

Irish ghettos developed virtually nowhere in Britain, [but] the settlers were clustered in the most congested and decaying sectors of most British towns.[24]

Graham Davis cites Lynn Lees' study of the Irish in Victorian London, where:

poor Irish migrants were not… locked in to urban ghettos but were mostly relegated to side streets and back alleys of their neighbourhoods.[25]

The notion of a 'ghetto' can lead to the assumption that it is where people 'end up' when all other options have been exhausted. Given the characteristic mobility of Irish immigrants in nineteenth century Britain, the turnover of people in an 'Irish area' could be substantial.

Thus the composition of so called 'Irish' districts was constantly changing.[26]

In the Vale and Dumbarton, the locations where the Irish were concentrated changed over time (see Chapter 11).

Nor did all of the Irish who settled in Scotland fit the familiar stereotype. 'Irish society was not homogenous and neither was its emigration'.[27] During the Famine years the destitute Irish fleeing the country lived and worked where they could, but in the Famine's aftermath many were 'reluctant migrants'.[28]

In the nineteenth century, Irish migration to Scotland involved:

- more men than women, but this was not an even distribution. For example Dundee and the Vale of Leven received more female than male Irish immigrants. Young, single Irish women were not as reticent about emigration as their European counterparts

- more Catholics than Protestants. Catholics are estimated to have comprised more than two thirds of all Irish immigrants to Scotland, but in some mill towns, mining towns and relatively poor parts of Glasgow, especially in the pre-Famine years, Protestants outnumbered Catholics. Towards the end of the nineteenth and into the twentieth century many Protestant migrants from Belfast and the north east of Ulster were attracted to the Clyde by jobs in shipbuilding and engineering

- the poor, but not exclusively so. Many Irish brought appropriate skills with them. Irish Protestants often came with industrial experience and skills. Catholics were mainly, but not entirely, confined to less skilled occupations

- immigrants from the nine counties of Ulster. The majority of Irish immigrants to Scotland at this time were from Ulster. The others were mainly from the west coast. Mayo and Galway, for example, were listed often as places of birth in the Dumbarton and Vale of Leven *census enumerators'books*, although immigrants from the far south and east were less prevalent.

The immigrants arrived in Scotland during a period of tremendous economic growth and social flux. They were not 'invading' settled communities but joining with an even bigger stream of Scots migrants from villages and rural parishes moving to rapidly industrialising towns where they sought work. There were identifiable areas of Irish settlement in Scottish towns and cities. Many of these persisted as, or were perceived to be, Irish enclaves. The locations and extent of Irish areas would change and eventually dwindle through time.

After they had arrived in Scotland, Irish immigrants remained highly mobile and less inclined to settle at one address. The Scots were also extremely mobile, and they too were apt to desert one location for another in search of better living and working conditions, but the Irish were on average poorer, more likely to be in temporary, sporadic and low paid work and less able to afford a place to stay. With few possessions, they would be prepared to move for the slightest advantage.

Thomas McCann and his family from Ballynease, County Antrim, are a case in point. Following an altercation with the police, Thomas and his brothers arrived on the Clyde in the 1880s. As farm hands they were comfortable dealing with horses and were initially employed as draymen in the Bowling distillery. Thomas was aged 31 when he married Annie Connolly at St Patrick's Church Dumbarton in 1888. After their marriage they lived in High Street. By April 1891, they had two children and were living at 72 Church Street. By June of that year they had moved to 143 High Street where they lived until 1894.[29] Three children were born there, two of whom died in infancy. They had moved back to Church Street by 1895 and had another child there who also died. In 1896 they lived at 55 College Street, where three more children were born - all died before the age of five, and by 1900 they had moved to 1 Back Street, Renton where yet another child was born. Two more boys were born in Glasgow, one in a maternity hospital and the other in 'Dalmarnock Street' in 1903. In 1905, Annie died in childbirth along with her thirteenth child at her home in London Road, Glasgow. Of the six children who survived into adulthood, three returned with their father to live out their lives in Dumbarton, one remained in Glasgow, one emigrated to South Africa and the other to the USA.

As for Thomas's brothers, James remained in Dumbarton and worked in Dalreoch Quarry where he lived. The others returned to Ireland. Thomas's youngest brother Hugh who had not come to Scotland, emigrated to New Zealand early in the twentieth century.[30]

These were not exceptional circumstances. Thomas was a 'semi-skilled hammerman' employed in heavy industry, and while this was no guarantee that he would have a job in the days or weeks to come, he was of sufficient status to be recorded as a householder in the Dumbarton Directory and Almanac of 1892.[31] The McCanns' situation serves to illustrate the frenetic mobility, upheaval and routine hardship endured by countless individuals, both native and immigrant, at this turbulent time.

For itinerant labourers and their families, life was even more precarious than this. With no reliable source of income, they could ill afford to rent a room or two. Overcrowding and illegal lodging were rife. Landlords turned a blind eye to tenants who took casual lodgers into their cramped homes.

Evidence suggests that in mid-nineteenth century Glasgow, Irish workers, both Catholic and Protestant, occupied the lowest strata in society, in some places doing similar unskilled and labouring jobs.[32] Both groups were discriminated against by the native Scots.[33] Sporadic sectarian clashes did occur among the Irish, and when the Protestant and Catholic Irish worked in close proximity and did jobs of similar status, they often elected to live in separate streets.[34] There were streets or groups of streets which were overwhelmingly occupied by one religion or the other, but there was no large scale segregation of Irish Protestants from Irish Catholics in Glasgow. There was a strong socio-economic imperative to their distribution. In Liverpool and Leeds, for example, it is suggested that the residential location of Irish migrants 'owed more to socio-economic position than it did to ethnicity'.[35] Poor people don't get to choose from a wide variety of properties - but for the Irish, where there was an element of choice, most elected to stay with their own kind.

By the end of the Famine, the Irish population of Glasgow comprised around one fifth of the total, unevenly spread across the poorest districts of the city.[36] For destitute new arrivals it was a hand to mouth existence. Faith and community were secondary considerations. Large numbers drifted from the Church, and later in the century, Mass attendance in Glasgow was most likely lower than in the industrial towns around the city.[37]

For the Protestant Irish, Calton and Mile End were favoured destinations, being weaving districts which employed a large number of their kin in the 1830s, they subsequently became districts to which many Protestant poor were drawn, whereas Briggait, Saltmarket, Tradeston and Hutchesontown were already established as poor, predominantly Irish Catholic, enclaves.[38]

In the industrial towns of West Central Scotland such as Dumbarton, Greenock, Airdrie and Coatbridge where substantial numbers of Irish lived, experiences differed in some respects from those in the city. There were no large exclusively Irish areas in these towns, but according to Tom Gallagher, the greater degrees of residential segregation along ethnic lines, caused by 'a much sharper economic rivalry that occurred in earlier decades' resulted in more sectarian incidents than in Glasgow.[39] Gallagher believes that Glasgow was less prone to anti-Irish riots than Liverpool for example, because it was less segregated.[40] Large scale segregation may have been be more conducive to larger disturbances. Incidents in Glasgow might have been on a smaller scale, but given the size of the city, along with the extreme poverty and overcrowding which occurred there, it was less likely that many 'minor' incidents would come to the attention of the press: but that does not mean that they did not occur.[41] In towns with identifiable 'Irish areas', reportage in local newspapers ensured that there was much attention paid to disputes between the Irish and the Scots and amongst the Irish themselves. Whereas evidence of cooperation, particularly amongst industrial labourers who worked and lived beside each other, was not newsworthy. The Scots and Irish were not in constant conflict with each other, even if some newspapers gave the impression otherwise.

The Catholic Church played a prominent role among the immigrants, but it was initially overwhelmed by the sheer scale of immigration.[42] It became the focus for many who, faced with prejudice and discrimination, looked to it as a 'source of self-esteem and group solidarity'.[43] In the towns, church attendance was generally higher than in Glasgow, but many who were not churchgoers identified with the Church as a cultural and social link with home and as a source of succour, material aid and charity.

The *New Statistical Account,* lists the religious affiliations of Dumbarton Parish for 1837. The Established Church (the Church of Scotland) had 2311 adherents. The 'two dissenting places of worship' were the Catholic Church with 284 members and the United Secessionist Church with 113,[44] which suggests that few Irish Catholics lived in this area. But seven years before this the Irish Catholic community had built a 'chapel' in Church Street near the present site of the railway bridge, and in 1832 the Irish from far and near swelled the congregation to around 3,000 who attended a sung Mass and Benediction.[45] By the 1840s this was one of only five 'Catholic chapels or churches throughout western Scotland (but) by 1854 the number of churches had increased to forty nine, with priests numbering sixty three'.[46] A Religious Census of Scotland taken in 1851, reported that Dumbarton and Paisley had the highest rates of Catholic observance in Scotland.[47]

The Irish, at all census dates from 1861 to 1891, made up a substantial proportion of the population of Dunbartonshire, but within the 'shire there were significant contrasts. In the Vale of Leven the Irish born population was between 9% and 13% at the four census dates, whereas in Dumbarton it was between 15% and 21%. But these crude statistics hide several distinctive details:

- Over the thirty year period Dumbarton's population was lower than the Vale of Leven's so that at each census point the *numerical* difference was between 500 to 1000 more Irish in Dumbarton than the Vale of Leven.

- After 1861, there were more Irish women than Irish men living in the Vale, as the printworks were hiring more female labour.

- In 1881, the number of Irish women living in the Vale outnumbered those living in Dumbarton after an influx of Irish women in the preceding decade.

In 1871, Dumbarton had the highest percentage of Irish born residents of any town or city in Britain[48] (17.7%). The children of Irish parentage who were born in Dumbarton were not included in this figure, so that the 'Irish community' was considerably larger than this suggests. It is difficult to argue with James Handley's assertion that, given the numbers of children born to Irish parents registered as Scottish, the true impact of Irish immigration is underestimated.[49] Indeed, it has been suggested that nineteenth century Irish migration to Britain as a whole has been under enumerated.[50]

The Irish who continued to migrate to Scotland long after the Famine had subsided were more aware of available opportunities and were not as desperate as their forerunners who had fled starvation. Nonetheless, they were still relatively poor when compared to the rest of the population.

When the Chairman of the Dumbarton Parochial Board was reporting on poverty in the late 1860s, he declared that more than half of all paupers in 1867, 1868 and 1869 were Irish; although the figures showed otherwise.[51] When challenged, he indicated that the Irish population made up fully one third of the burgh's total, and that 'almost all of the labourers in the shipyards are Irish'. It was conceded that while the Irish population was '17.6%' of the total, 'if those of Irish descent are included, the Chairman's estimate may be correct'.[52]

The population statistics for those living at 137 High Street in 1871, an address which came to the court's attention for illegal lodging in that year, help to illustrate the difficulties of categorisation.[53] There were 98 people registered as living there: 53 were Irish; but of the

Scots born living there, 27 were children of Irish parentage - 25 born locally and two born in Neilston.[54] So, for this address, the number who were Irish or who had Irish parents, is 80 out of 98 inhabitants, compared to the census count of 53 Irish born. Furthermore, the total of 98 residents is an under enumeration as many people other than those recorded were living 'illegally' at this and other addresses throughout the burgh. The Irish were heavily involved in 'illegal' lodging as we see in Chapter 11.

There were fewer Irish in the Vale than in Dumbarton. However, the Vale attracted more female than male migrants of working age, and this was particularly true of the Irish. Bremner noted the large number of Irish females employed at Renton's Dalquhurn and Cordale works.[55] There was a 'Wumman Hoose' near the Dillichip works in Bonhill, built by Archibald Orr Ewing in the 1870s to accommodate migrant female workers.[56] The situation was similar to that found in Dundee where large numbers of Irish women worked in the city's textile factories, outnumbering their male counterparts by two to one in 1871.[57] By 1881, Dundee had five Irish women for every three Irish men resident, whereas in the Vale the ratio it was approximately four to three. In that year there were around nine Irish males for every five Irish females in Dumbarton.[58]

The Irish contributed to the growth and industrial development of Dumbarton and the Vale of Leven, but were over-represented amongst the most disadvantaged in society, did the least secure and worst paid jobs, and lived mainly in the poorest areas.

NOTES

[1] *'Thousands are Sailing'* by the Pogues (1988). The song was about emigration to North America, but its sentiments also applied to those emigrants who rather than sail 'across the western ocean' sailed eastwards across the Irish Sea.

[2] T.C. Smout, *A Century of the Scottish People 1830-1950.* (1986) pp. 22-3

[3] I. Wood, 'Irish Immigrants and Scottish Radicalism 1880-1906' pp. 65-8 in I. MacDougall, (ed) *Essays in Scottish Labour History.* (1978) p. 65

[4] Quoted in Immigrants and Exiles - *Irish in Scotland - Official Documents. bbc.co.uk*

[5] Handley, *The Irish in Modern Scotland* See for example pp. 239-53, and p. 352

[6] *DH* 16 October 1851

[7] Handley, *The Irish in Modern Scotland* p. 309. Even in the 1920s, the Church of Scotland 'Church and Nation Committee' used the terms in this way when it was describing 'the menace of the Irish race to our Scottish nationality'.

[8] *DH* 29 October 1851. For further information on Cullen see R.F. Foster, *Modern Ireland 1600-1972*, p. 338, and R.Hattersley, *The Catholics* (2017) Chapters 23 and 25

[9] MacRaild, *Irish Migrants in Modern Britain* Ch 3

[10] Devine 'The Great Irish Famine and Scottish History' in Mitchell (ed) *New Perspectives* p. 29

[11] *DH* 13 November 1851

[12] *DH* 22 March 1855. Orr's efforts in Dumbarton certainly bore fruit. See later in this chapter.

[13] R. Swift, citing Handley, *The Irish in Modern Scotland.* pp. 95-6 in Swift and Gilley (eds) *The Irish in Britain* p. 17

[14] *DH* 22 October 1855

[15] MacPhail, *Dumbarton Through the Centuries* pp. 81-3

[16] Handley, *The Irish in Modern Scotland* p. 147

[17] D. Macleod, *History of the Castle and Town of Dumbarton* (1877) pp. 97-8

[18] *DH* September - November 1856. See also cuttings from its editor Samuel Bennett in Dumbarton Library archives.

[19] *LH* 27 August 1864

[20] T. Gallagher, *Glasgow. The Uneasy Peace* (1987) p. 30 cites Handley, *The Irish in Modern Scotland*

[21] See examples given by M. Mitchell in 'Irish Catholics in the West of Scotland in the Nineteenth Century' pp. 1-19 in M. Mitchell, (ed) *New Perspectives*

[22] *Oxford English Dictionary.*

[23] C. Pooley, 'The Residential Segregation of Migrant Communities in Mid Victorian Liverpool' *The Institute of British Geographers* NS 2 (3) (1977) pp. 364-81

[24] Fitzpatrick, 'A Curious Middle Place' p.10. in Swift and Gilley *The Irish in Britain*

[25] Davis, 'Little Irelands' in Swift and Gilley *The Irish in Britain*, p. 112 citing L.H. Lees 'Mid-Victorian Migration and the Irish Family Economy' *Victorian Studies XX* (1976) pp. 25-43

[26] Ibid. p. 114

[27] Ibid. p. 105 citing D.Fitzgerald, 'Irish Emigration in the late Nineteenth Century' *Irish Historical Studies* 22 (1980) p. 134.

[28] *Fitzpatrick*, 'A Curious Middle Place p.10. in Swift and Gilley *The Irish in Britain*

[29] As a 'semi-skilled' or 'skilled' householder, Thomas was recorded at this address in the Dumbarton Directory 1891-92. He was not regarded as an itinerant 'general labourer'.

[30] I am grateful to Harry Scullin for this information. Harry researches and edits the extended Scullin family tree at *tribalpages.com*

[31] *Dumbarton Directory and Almanac* (1892) Copy held in the Local Collection, Dumbarton Public Library

.

[32] See J. Foster et al, 'Sectarianism, Segregation and Politics in Clydeside in the later Nineteenth Century' pp. 65-96 in Mitchell, (ed) *New Perspectives*

[33] Ibid. p. 95

[34] Ibid. p. 79

[35] Pooley, 'Segregation or Integration. The residential experience of the Irish in mid-Victorian Britain' in Swift and Gilley (eds) *The Irish in Britain* p. 78

[36] Devine, 'The Great Irish Famine and Scottish History' in Mitchell (ed) *New Perspectives* p. 22

[37] W. Sloan, 'Religious Affiliation and the Immigrant Experience: Catholic Irish and Protestant Highlanders in Glasgow 1830-1850' in Devine *Irish Immigrants and Scottish society* p. 70

[38] I. Meredith, 'Irish Migrants in the Scottish Episcopal Church in the 19th Century' pp. 50-1 in Mitchell (ed). *New Perspectives*

[39] T. Gallagher, 'The Catholic Irish in Scotland: In Search of Identity' in Devine *Irish Immigrants and Scottish society*. p. 23

[40] *Thesis,* p. 225

[41] From Catholics being verbally abused on their way to church, (W. Sloan, 'Religious Affiliation and the Immigrant Experience' p. 74 in Mitchell (ed) *New Perspectives,* to anti Catholic speakers inciting violence.

[42] Devine, 'The Great Irish Famine and Scottish History' in Mitchell (ed) *New Perspectives* pp.23-4

[43] Sloan, 'Religious Affiliation and the Immigrant Experience' in Mitchell (ed) *New Perspectives* pp. 85-6

[44] *NSA.* (1845) Vol VIII Dumbarton Parish p. 13

[45] B Aspinwall, 'Catholic Devotion in Victorian Scotland' in Mitchell (ed) *New Perspectives* p. 32

[46] MacRaild, *Irish Migrants in Modern Britain.* p. 83

[47] Cited by Aspinwall, 'Catholic Devotion in Victorian Scotland' in Mitchell (ed) *New Perspectives* p. 32

48 Pooley, 'Segregation or Integration. The residential experience of the Irish in mid-Victorian Britain' in Swift and Gilley (eds) *The Irish in Britain* p. 67

49 Handley, *The Irish in Modern Scotland.* p. 46

50 O'Grada, 'A Note on 19th Century Irish Emigration Statistics'

51 In 1867, 173 paupers were Irish out of a total of 552. In 1868 it was 198 from 631 and in 1869 it was 187 from 484. Ibid. p. 255

52 Ibid. p. 255

53 *LH* 8 June 1871

54 From cebs Dumbarton 1871. 30 of the 96 people living there were designated as 'lodgers'. It is certain that more lived there illegally and had evaded the count.

55 Bremner, *The Industries of Scotland* p. 301

56 Jones and Hopner. *On Leven's Banks* p. 28

57 Collins, *'The Origins of Irish Immigration to Scotland'* p. 11

58 B. Braber, 'The influence of immigration on the growth, urban concentration and composition of the Scottish population 1841-1911'. *Journal of Scottish Historical Studies* 32 (2) (2012) p. 196 and *Thesis,* Ch 14

9 Ebb and Flow: Migration Trends

As described in the previous chapter, the Irish made up a significantly larger sector of the population in Dumbarton than they did in the Vale. This marked contrast in settlements only a few miles apart was fundamentally about job opportunities. In the Vale, as in textile towns such as Paisley and Dundee, known job opportunities influenced both the size and gender balance of the migrant stream, and to an extent, where the migrants came from.[1] By 1861, opportunities in industry were becoming more readily available in Dumbarton than the Vale. Crucially, these opportunities were much more plentiful for males than for females. The opposite was true in the Vale. The result was the imbalance in the ratios of women to men among the working population described earlier.

Irish migration in the second half of the nineteenth century and the first half of the twentieth century deviated from the typical European model where migration comprised of, in the main, a stream of young, usually unattached, males: a familiar pattern in the early, pioneering stages of many mass migrations. In contrast, the Irish migration at this time involved almost as many females as males.[2] In America, they were in demand as domestic servants, a path not largely open to them in Scotland until the twentieth century. In Scotland they often gravitated to places where they found work independent of their male counterparts. They were welcomed in textile mills and printworks.[3]

Dumbarton's industrial success made it strongly attractive to migrants, at a time when the Irish were leaving home in ever increasing numbers.[4] In contrast, the Vale's longer established industries, did draw both Scots and Irish migrants, but over the period not to the same extent, because there were fewer jobs for males. In addition, immigrants coming directly from Ireland and arriving on the Clyde, were more likely to pass through Dumbarton. As was common, intervening opportunities could have put paid to any planned onward journey to the Vale. Not all arrived with a plan in mind and went where circumstances took them.

Streams of Scots and Irish migration gathered momentum. Many migrants had connections with their compatriots in Dumbarton and the Vale of Leven and migrated on that strength. The phenomenon of lodging or boarding with friends or relatives was commonplace (and is discussed in Chapter 12). Once links were established and potential employment opportunities were identified, then movement was more likely. As both individuals and families migrated, the web of contacts widened. This 'chain migration' became commonplace among both Irish and Scots, where individuals who had migrated from specific places encouraged neighbours, friends and relatives to join them, and small communities of people from such places proliferated in locations that were often far from home. One example closer to home, was the movement of people from Killearn, the home of the Orr Ewings, to the Vale where the family had their factories. There will certainly have been other distinct parishes, towns and villages in both Scotland and Ireland that sent significant numbers of people to the Vale and Dumbarton.[5]

There was a net surge in Irish immigration to Scotland in the 1871 to 1881 decade, which was not replicated across England and Wales. There, Irish immigration had been stronger in the 1850s, 1860s and 1880s than in the 1870s.[6] It is no coincidence that Irish emigration statistics show that of the four provinces (Ulster, Munster, Leinster and Connacht) Ulster, the province closest to Scotland, and where most of the emigrants to Scotland originated, recorded the greatest loss of population in the 1870s.[7] It was also in this decade that the proportion of Irish in the Vale of Leven came close to the Dunbartonshire county average, and although Dumbarton burgh remained the most enduring focal point for Irish migrants, Clydebank was at the beginning of a period of phenomenal population growth, with both Scots and Irish migrants arriving there in great numbers.

In this decade too, there had been a resurgence of overall net in-migration to the Vale, where the population had risen by over 4,600. In Dumbarton, population growth had slowed, but was still substantial, with around 2,600 more people in the burgh over the same period, but while the Irish population grew significantly in both places, the growth was, for once, greater in the Vale than in Dumbarton. The number of Irish in the Vale had barely changed over the 1861-71 decade, and there was a net loss of around 400 in 1881-91. In contrast, by 1881, there were over a 1,000 more Irish in the Vale than ten years earlier, but the Scottish arrivals were even more numerous and outnumbered the Irish by a few hundred. In Dumbarton there were around 700 more Irish over the same decade and this was slightly more than double the number of Scots net arrivals (see Figures 6:1 and 6:2, Chapter 6 and Appendix 3:Tables 10:1 and 10:2.)

The 1870s was a decade when the Scots were more likely to move to towns and cities within the country rather than to emigrate beyond it, and it is as if emigration from Ulster to Scotland had become a part of that pattern of internal circulation.

The Irish influx was a trend unmatched in the rest of Britain. There was a net total of 11,000 more Irish in Scotland in 1881 than in 1871. The Irish population of Scotland reached its numeric peak in 1881, whereas in England and Wales the Irish born population had declined by a few thousand over this decade.[8]

Sample figures suggest that by 1881, the number of Irish in the Vale and Dumbarton alone, accounted for more than a tenth of the net increase for the whole of Scotland in the preceding decade. But not all of these new residents would have come directly from Ireland. Some would have been living in other towns in Scotland prior to this.

In both Dumbarton and the Vale of Leven, the biggest group of incomers had been born in the 'contiguous counties'; the rest of Dunbartonshire; and nearby Ayrshire in the West Central Scotland region. These Scots accounted for roughly a third of all the people living in the Vale and a quarter of those living in Dumbarton during the 1861 to 1891 era.[9] As the populations of both Dumbarton and the Vale had grown substantially, by over 8,500 in each location over the period, the consistent proportions of 'neighbouring Scots' represents a strong and continuing net inflow of people. Those from the 'other' counties of Scotland according to the sample, comprised between 3%

to 6% of the Vale's population, but a slightly larger proportion of between 7% and 9% in Dumbarton.

 Approximately one in three of the 'neighbouring Scots' living in the Vale was from Lanarkshire which includes Glasgow, whereas in Dumbarton the figure was around one in two. As for the other counties, with the exception of Renfrew in 1861, no other county provided more than 5% of Dumbarton's population over the period, whereas in the Vale at several census years the sample records show that Renfrew, Argyll, and Stirling all contributed more than this. Stirling especially provided a higher percentage of the Vale's population than Dumbarton's: the Stirling parishes of Drymen and Buchanan are contiguous to the Vale, and as described above, Orr Ewing family connections with Killearn saw a transfer of workers from there (See Appendix 3 Tables 10:1 and 10:2.). Not all migration was inward and there were high outflows from Dunbartonshire to other counties and abroad.

Summary of Main In-Migratory Trends by decade 1861-1891

The census data allows for a summary of net decennial change in the numbers of 'non-natives', that is those born in places other than Bonhill, Cardross and Dumbarton parishes, who were living in the Vale and Dumbarton at each of the four census dates within the period.

1861-1871

- The Vale's population grew by around 650 in this decade. Much of this was due to natural increase as there was little change in the numbers of both 'neighbouring Scots' and Irish, as in-migration was only just replacing those who had died or moved away. Natural increase would have been greater had more people present in 1861 stayed and raised families. Those from the 'other' Scottish counties may have made a small but significant contribution to the Vale's population growth, proportionally their largest in the period.

- In 1861, around one in five of Dumbarton's population was Irish, the highest proportion of Irish people in the burgh over this period, when the ratio of Irish males to Irish females was about 10:7. Around a quarter of the population were Scots, born in 'neighbouring' counties and parishes. There was very little difference in the number of 'neighbouring Scots' males to females resident in the burgh.

- In Dumbarton between 1861 and 1871 there were around 1,200 net arrivals from within Scotland. Two-thirds of those came from the 'neighbouring' Scottish counties. However, in both the Vale and Dumbarton, this period was likely to have seen the largest proportional contribution from the 'other' counties over the three decades. The Irish tide had subsided somewhat, with around 200 more Irish in Dumbarton at the end of the decade.

1871-1881

- This was a better decade for the Vale of Leven, if in-migration is seen as an indicator of industrial health. Of the in-migrants, there were about 1,500 more non-locally born Scots living in the Vale at the end of the decade, the vast majority coming from the 'neighbouring' parishes and counties. It was in this decade that both Scots and Irish females would arrive in greater numbers than their male counterparts.

- The Vale's Irish population grew by 1,000: their only significant influx in the three decades under consideration here, when the net growth in female 'arrivals' would outnumber male 'arrivals' by about three to two.

- For the 'neighbouring Scots' there was slight balance in favour of female to male net 'arrivals'. By 1881, one third of the total sample population in the Vale were in the 15-29 age group, where most recent migrants are usually found.

- In Dumbarton, in-migration in this decade was less robust than in the Vale. A distinctive feature of the Irish migration figures for the burgh was the male to female imbalance, with a ratio of around 6:1 in favour of male 'net arrivals'. Clearly, the majority of Irish immigrants were young men intent in securing jobs in the shipyards or in heavy industry. And yet, from the sample, the figures suggest that the net growth in the numbers of 'neighbouring Scots' over this decade was only around 300, with an approximate ratio of 2:1 in favour of females among the incomers. Perhaps some of these women would find work in the Vale, rather than Dumbarton.

1881-1891

- There were around 1,000 additional Scots from the 'neighbouring' parishes and counties in the Vale by the end of this decade. In contrast, the Irish population had declined by around 400.

- Dumbarton had also gained around 1,000 Scots in-migrants, mostly from the 'neighbouring counties', but including a small number from the rest of Scotland. There had been a slightly smaller decline in the number of Irish residents in Dumbarton than in the Vale.

- In both the Vale and Dumbarton, the ageing Irish population was not being fully replaced by new immigrants. This was part of a national trend, as the numbers of Irish in Scotland dropped from 218,745 in 1881 to 194,807 in 1891. There had been a brief resurgence by 1901, when 205,054 Irish were recorded as resident in Scotland, but thereafter, their numbers declined rapidly in the early decades of the twentieth century.

Out-Migration

While there was a sizeable migration to Dumbarton and the Vale during this period, it was not all one way. Again, the ten year gap in the gathering of census data means that inter-censal trends cannot be determined using this data alone. However, the net movement of locally born people out of the area can be estimated using 'census survival' techniques, where the number of 'locals' in an age cohort can be compared to the number in that same group ten years on. For example, the numbers of 'locally born' in the 15-44 age group in 1861 can be compared to their numbers (as members of the 25-54 age group) ten years later. The shortfall at the later census can be attributed to either death or net out-migration. When estimated age-specific death rates are factored in, the 'expected survival' numbers can be calculated and compared to the actual number present in any cohort at the next census.[10]

The movement of 'non locals' can also be examined using the 'census survival' method. The difference in their numbers, census upon census, is the result of death and net-migration, but that gives no indication of the numbers of migrants who were recorded at one census and had left before the next one. The net total number of migrants in a cohort at one census compared to the same group at the succeeding census, reveals nothing about the ebb and flow of migrants who may have come and gone within those ten years. If, as is likely, migrants would be less inclined to remain than the locally born, then there would have been an even greater turnover of migrants than locals.

For the Vale, over the three decades considered, it appears that around 30% to 40% of all locally born people in the 15-44 age group at one census date had left by the time the subsequent one was taken. There was little appreciable difference in the numbers of females and males who moved away, but most leavers were at the younger end of this broad age group. There may have been a slightly larger number of males than females leaving in the 1880s when the 'sample' records that 32% of females had gone, compared to 37% of males. Those at the older end of the age continuum, with comparatively secure jobs and family ties, were more likely to stay put: but there were losses through out-migration recorded for the three 10 year age cohorts (15-24; 25-34 and 35-44) at each subsequent census. The greatest losses were always among the youngest of the three cohorts. The highest losses for both females and males came in the 1861-71 decade when in-migration had also slowed.

The losses recorded for males in the same 'mobile' age group in Dumbarton were between 25% to 30% in the first two decades, 1861-71 and 1871-81, and slightly more, at 35% in the 1881-91 decade, when there had also been an upturn in the number of 'locally born' males leaving the Vale. This was a decade of major emigration from Scotland, and it is safe to assume that many, mainly young, men departed these shores headed principally for North America or Australia and New Zealand.[11] Again, the general rule applied: losses were greatest from the youngest cohort, the 15-24 year olds, and that applied to females as well as males in both Dumbarton and the Vale (see figures 11.3 and 4 and 12.3 and 4).

Comparing locally born females leaving Dumbarton and the Vale, the percentage was notably lower from the burgh. Dumbarton born females were also less migratory than males born in either Dumbarton or the Vale.

The sample figures show that around 10% to 15% of Dumbarton born females in the 'mobile' age range had left over the 1861-71 decade, increasing to 20% and then 25% over the next two decades.

In Dumbarton, the contrast between the loss of locally born females and males is clear. Females were less migratory earlier in this period.

With fewer jobs available to women in Dumbarton, it might have been expected that many would leave in search of work. Indeed, the Vale's printworks were the biggest employers of female labour in Dumbarton over the last quarter of the century. In the Vale, it would appear that many locally born females followed the example of their mobile, enterprising and unmarried counterparts who had been attracted to the area for work and who, when the situation became less favourable, sought opportunities elsewhere. It was a feature of the textile industry that when conditions became less attractive in one location, workers would leave in pursuit of similar jobs in other towns. Perhaps female printworkers from Dumbarton, working in increasing numbers in the Vale, also followed this path.

Across Scotland young, unattached women were disposed to migration, but this tended to involve movement within the country rather than emigration. It has been suggested that factors encouraging their migration included: lack of employment opportunities in rural areas; urban demand for domestic servants; and the fact that women were more likely to move upon marriage than men.[12] This did not exclude emigration, and as in the 1881-91 decade which was one of heavy emigration, many young women left the country for England and overseas.[13]

162

NOTES

[1] B. Collins, 'Irish emigration to Dundee and Paisley during the first half of the 19th century' in J. M. Goldstrom and L A Clarkson (eds) *Irish Population, Economy & Society: Essays in honour of the late K H Connell* (1981) pp. 195-212

[2] S. Connolly, *On Every Tide: The making and remaking of the Irish World* (2022) p. 65

[3] Nenadic and Tuckett, *The Turkey Red Printed Cotton Industry* p. 5 quote a letter written on 19 September 1873, held in University of Glasgow Archives UGD 13/1/8/229.

[4] See Chapter 6. Adult male migrants outnumbered locally born adult males by 4:1 in 1861

[5] Further study of unprinted *census enumerators books,* could reveal information on this.

Eileen Kane who worked in Donegal in the 1960s, spoke to locals about immigration...

when they go to America they go to Butte Montana ... some to Mauch Chunk, Pennsylvania and to Illinois and ...

What about Northern Donegal, say in Gweedore?
We don't know said one man:

They think they've got a little paradise on earth up there, they don't leave it except to work in Scotland

E. Kane, *Sightlines. Beyond the Beyond in Ireland* (2022) p. 140
The South side of Glasgow has remained their favoured destination in Scotland

[6] O'Grada, 'A Note on 19th Century Irish Emigration Statistics' p. 146

[7] Statistics taken from Census of Ireland, 1881-1911; Emigration returns 1911-20, quoted in MacRaild, *Irish Migrants in Modern Britain,* Table 1.4 p. 39

[8] The proportion of Irish in the Scottish population was however at its greatest in 1851 when it comprised 7.2% of the total, as the result of the net in-migration of 81,000 people in the preceding decade.

[9] The figures used here are derived mainly from the data contained in sample of families taken from each census in the years 1861,1871, 1881 and 1891. Where proportions, percentages or ratios are quoted, these are from the sample. The sample data are shown in Appendix 3 Figures 10:1 and 10:2. Some figures have been extrapolated by applying percentages from the sample to the published total population present in Dumbarton and the Vale of Leven at each census point. This sample data used for this is principally contained in Figures 9:1, 9:2, 14:1 and 14:2 of the *Thesis,*. There is a danger in inflating the importance of small numeric differences in the sample by applying them to the total number of people recorded in the printed census records. Figures derived thus are only referred to in broad terms, and only where there appear to be wide margins worthy of comment.

[10] *Thesis,* Ch 7 pp. 110-15 describes how the census survivorship method is used to calculate net outflows of those who were born locally. This is used in *Thesis,* Ch12 and 13 to examine net-migration. Three sets of survivorship figures were calculated for each of the mobile cohorts, based on (1) average death rates, (2) age specific death rates and (3) no death rate. The age specific death rates are derived from the Register Generals Reports' on the censuses to provide the best estimates of 'survivorship' and thus the most accurate estimation of locally born net out-migration between the censuses. The 'average death rate' and 'no death rate' figures provide the most pessimistic and optimistic limits respectively, of survivorship within the mobile age groups. These tables are not reproduced here, but are found in *Thesis,* Ch 11 and 12.

[11] Anderson, *Scotland's Populations* p. 131

[12] D.B. Grigg, 'E.G. Ravenstein and the Laws of Migration' *Journal of Historical Geography* Vol 3 (1) (1977) pp. 41-54

[13] Anderson, *Scotland's Populations* p. 115

10 Social Status

Contrasts in Social Status of Males in the Vale of Leven and Dumbarton

Broad occupational groupings such as 'shipbuilding' or 'printworking' encompass managers, journeymen, apprentices and casual labourers, and as such, reveal little of the *social status* of workers. Social status is largely based on a person's occupation.[1] The scheme shown below, based with minor alterations on one by M Anderson (1972), reflects Victorian employment characteristics, and helps to describe social status in this and succeeding chapters.[2]

    I Professional and Managerial

    II Clerical

    III Trade

    IV Higher Factory (Skilled work)

    V Artisan

    VI Lower Factory (Unskilled Work)

    VII Labourer

    VIII Clothing Worker -
           dressmaker, milliner etc.

    IX Unclassified

    X Not employed

In most cases the terms above are self explanatory, but it can be difficult to distinguish between for example, those who were in 'Trade' and those who were 'Artisans'. Those in 'Trade' included shopkeepers, dealers in commodities such as coal or wine and spirits and those running small businesses, such as joiners and builders. 'Artisans' were craftsmen: those who made a broad range of goods or commodities such as furniture, household items, jewellery, food items, tools and watches. Bakers and blacksmiths for example, could be considered as both traders and artisans. Under this scheme they are regarded as artisans.

Fortunately, it is easier to assign status to those employed in the major manufacturing industries. The occupations recorded in the *census enumerators' books* largely enable individuals to be classified as either 'higher factory' (skilled workers) or 'lower factory' (semi-skilled or unskilled workers). This is an important distinction as 'skilled male workers' wages were between two and three times more than those of 'semi-skilled and unskilled men'.[3]

However, just as there was an appreciable gap between 'skilled' and 'unskilled' factory workers, there is a distinction to be drawn between those who were working as 'unskilled' labourers in factories and shipyards, category VI, and those who were in the 'labourer' category VII. The latter were unskilled men, but *not* employed in industry. This included agricultural workers, builders' labourers, quarrymen and those working on the roads or railways. Also within this category were an even less privileged group whose *occupation* was recorded as *'general labourer'* in the *census enumerators books'*. 'General labourers' were those whose situation was even more precarious than those in named occupations such as construction or railway labouring. When a man was recorded as a 'general labourer' it was often an indication that he had no fixed means of employment. Working when and where he could, a 'general labourer' was at the extreme end of the social spectrum, a poorly paid casual worker in irregular or erratic employment, hired on a short term or daily basis and doing a variety of menial tasks such as scavenging, road sweeping and sewage disposal. They were engaged in a wide variety of work, often amidst uncertainty, as they moved from job to job as the need arose. As a whole they were of conspicuously lower status than industrial workers. They suffered not only from lower pay, but from intermittent working, which was less prevalent, but certainly not unheard of, among 'unskilled' industrial workers. Most 'labourers' aspired to factory work and had to enlist the help of their wives and children to augment household incomes and 'make ends meet'.[4]

The banks of the River Leven from north of Alexandria to Dumbarton and the Clyde were heavily industrialised, but there were striking contrasts between the status of workers in the printwork dependent villages and those who worked in Dumbarton's heavy industries.

Using the above classification,[5] few males in the sample were in the 'Professional and Managerial' category - slightly more in Dumbarton than the Vale, as would be expected of the administrative centre of the County

- Between 1.5% to 2% of employed males in the Vale were in the 'Professional and Managerial' cohort over the 1861-91 period, compared to 2.5% to 3.5% in Dumbarton.

- In the Vale those who were in the 'higher factory' category were almost all skilled printworkers, and the percentage of workers in this group over the period, and was remarkably consistent, hovering around 20% to 23.5%, in spite of the large increase in population which occurred over these thirty years.

- This is in contrast to the number of 'unskilled or 'semi-skilled' printworkers (that is 'lower factory' workers). In 1861, 1881 and 1891, they accounted for between 41.5% and 45% of the male workforce. As with so many statistics for the Vale, the 1871 figure is anomalous, and significantly lower, at 36.5%.

- The overwhelming evidence is that over the period, the Vale had a very large pool of unskilled labour, employed both in and out of factories. Taken together, this accounted for between 55.5% and 58.5 % of the male workforce in 1861, 1881 and 1891 and 53% in 1871.

(See Appendix 2 Table 10:1 Social classification of employed males in the Vale of Leven 1861-1891)

In the Vale over the 1861-71 decade, when population growth slowed, the number of unskilled factory workers declined. More men were earning a living as 'artisans', in 'trade' or in non-factory labouring. Over this decade the printworks largely retained 'skilled' workers while hiring fewer 'unskilled' ones.

The bleach, print and dye works would recover, but the Vale was still chronically dependent on them, and this was to have serious repercussions for its inhabitants, as the the works began to fail in the 1890s and into the twentieth century.

Dumbarton in 1861 still retained vestiges of its pre-industrial craft and commercial functions, with a bigger proportion of people in 'trade', working as 'artisans', or in non-factory, 'unskilled' work than in the Vale of Leven. It also had a larger proportion of skilled factory ('higher industrial') workers than the Vale. These included tradesmen working in shipyards, foundries and machine shops.[6] Shipbuilding was a more diverse operation than printworking, necessitating many stages of production, a wide array of components and a broad range of skills. Ships required castings, mouldings, propellors, metal plates and engine parts which had to be put together. 'Fitting out' a ship involved cabinet making, joinery, painting and metal working. This is not to belittle the skill and technical expertise invested in the printworks where, for example, engravers, printers, engineers and chemists were valued and well paid, and where printing processes became even more sophisticated as time progressed. Shipbuilding and its attendant industries demanded many more skilled tradesmen, and they comprised 28% of the male workforce in 1861, but 38% in 1891. As with the Vale, this was achieved against a background of rapid population growth.

- At the same time, the number of 'lower factory' or 'unskilled' men working in factories or shipyards, grew from 14% of the workforce in 1861 to 23% of a much larger workforce in 1891, demonstrating the increasing domination of heavy industry in the burgh.

- Consequently the percentage of 'non-factory' labourers decreased decade on decade from 23.5% to around 12%.

- Unskilled labour, both in and out of the factories and shipyards, thus amounted to between 35% and 40% of the total male workforce across the period, much less than in the Vale where more than half of all employed men were in these categories.

- By 1861, the impact of heavy industry was certainly being felt in Dumbarton, with around 45% of the workforce engaged in it, but by 1891 it had risen to 62.5%, dwarfing all other modes of employment.

(See Appendix 2 Table 10:2 Social classification of employed males in Dumbarton 1861-91)

Dumbarton was primarily a shipbuilding town and most other branches of its heavy industry were ancillary in support of that activity. Fortunately for Dumbarton, the years of industrial decline were still many decades away, but like the Vale, rapid population growth in response to employment opportunities across a narrow industrial base would result in unemployment and hardship in the twentieth century. Many families were impelled to leave Dumbarton and the Vale, making new lives elsewhere in Scotland, the UK and abroad.

Female Employment and Status

During this period in the Vale and Dumbarton, the vast majority of women in employment outside of the home were poorly paid compared to men. Consequently, irrespective of the skills which they may have needed to pursue their work, their wages would suggest that they were of lower social status. Most of those who were married and part of a household were automatically assumed to be of the same social status as their husbands who were designated 'Heads of Household' by census enumerators and others.

- A higher proportion of females in the Vale were in 'formal' employment than in Dumbarton, with the vast majority of these working in the printworks where their pay rates were lower than those of 'unskilled' male factory workers, and where they were rarely accorded skilled status (see Chapter 5).

- Dumbarton offered no equivalent employment for females, and by 1881 the Vale's printworks were the biggest employer of Dumbarton's female labour.

- In both areas small numbers of women worked as clerks and as 'teachers', many of the latter being untrained and poorly paid.

- Women rarely developed careers. Most left work upon marriage, which 'was virtually synonymous with withdrawal from the labour force'.[7] Some had to chose between marriage and employment. Female teachers were commonly expected to remain unmarried should they wish to continue with their careers.

- Married women supplemented household incomes by taking in washing and sewing, as well as catering for those who lodged with their family.

- It was necessary for widowed women to seek employment in support of themselves and their families. Domestic service was a favoured occupation, and more women in the Vale and Dumbarton worked in that sector than in any other with the exception of the overwhelmingly dominant bleach, print and dye works. Other occupations included dressmaking, shirt-making and work as seamstresses, cleaners, charwomen and laundry workers. The work was often part-time or casual and among clothing workers, 'piece work' was prevalent.

Textile workers were known to seek familiar employment when they chose to move on. Those single Scots women, who like their Irish counterparts, had experience working in textiles, were attracted by growing opportunities in the Vale, as the works' owners sought to employ cheaper female labour at the expense of unskilled men.

Scots and Irish Social Status Compared

Here, the focus is on the contrast between the Scots and Irish incomers who moved to the Vale and Dumbarton, both in relation to the work they did and their social standing. Locally born people are not included in this comparison, albeit very many of them were the children of migrants. Some of these first generation 'locals' enhanced their status by securing better jobs than their parents, but they had to contend with prevailing occupational conservatism and lack of social mobility. In Scotland, whether it was into the mill, the shipyard or down the pit, children followed in their parents' footsteps. The sons of 'skilled' workers were often apprenticed to the same trades as their fathers', whereas 'industrialists' sons' either followed their fathers into the family business or trained for the professions. In rare cases they even took factory apprenticeships as part of their wider education. Sir Archibald Denny, son of Peter Denny, began his apprenticeship in a shipyard joiners' shop in 1876.[8] His career as a joiner was, of course, merely temporary, but the experience would have provided him with some insight into working conditions in the yard and was yet another example of Denny's innovative ethos.

The Dennys were among the 'business and professional' elite. Throughout Scotland, the gulf between this group and the rest was so vast that it was almost unbridgeable. 'Professionals' represented a very small percentage of the population, and were to a great degree, male. But most employed males in the Vale and Dumbarton were manual workers.[9]

Irish and Scots Males in the Vale of Leven.

As described earlier, the Vale of Leven was initially host to factory colonies dependent on a very narrow industrial base. The bleach, print and dye works continued to dominate the industrial landscape throughout the second half of the century, providing work for most of the Vale's families, but there were distinct contrasts in the social status of male Scots and Irish workers.

Irish males were always 'under-represented' among skilled printworkers.[10] During the slump of the 1860s, many of the Irish who remained in the Vale, were forced to diversify their activities and found themselves in the unfortunate position of being grossly 'over-represented' in the 'labouring' category: that is in non-factory work which was often casual, erratic and unreliable.[11]

'General labourers' accounted for around 5% to 7% of the total male workforce in 1871, but more than 20% of employed Irish males were in this category. The situation did not change drastically over the next twenty years. A 'general labourer' was a person who did not have a 'named' job and whose employment was even more precarious than that of the non-factory labourer, who worked in the building trades or on the roads, for example. There were small groups of Irish labourers working in agriculture and on the railways.

- Three-quarters or more of all employed Irish males in the Vale were either of semi-skilled / unskilled ('lower factory') or 'labourer' status at each census year, with a peak of around 85% being reached in 1881, after an increase in Irish immigration in the preceding decade.

- Only in 1891, did more than 10% of Irish males achieve skilled ('higher factory') status.

- In contrast, the 'neighbouring Scots' had between 21% to 26% of their number in the 'higher factory' category at each census year in the 1861 to 1891 period.

- Nevertheless, the 'lower factory' category, contained the largest percentages of *both* Scots and Irish workers at all four census years. The Irish were far from being alone on the lower rungs of the status ladder.

- The notable contrast between Irish and Scots was among the non-factory labourers. The highest proportion of the Scots workforce in this group was 14% in 1861, whereas it was never less than double that for the Irish, and in 1881, 42% of all male Irish workers were labourers who were not employed in the printworks. Comparing percentages of Scots and Irish in this way disguises the fact that numerically, there were slightly more Scots than Irish employed as non-factory labourers in 1861, 1871 and 1891 because the Scots labourers made up a small percentage of a large pool of Scots workers. 1881 saw the highest proportion of Irish men in 'non-factory' labouring work recorded over the period and suggests that many Irish males who had arrived over the previous decade had little or no experience of printworking, and unlike their compatriots in Dumbarton, had few skilled workers in their ranks (see Appendix 4, Table 10:3).

- It is possible that some of these Irish men migrated along with their womenfolk who were more likely to secure immediate employment.

With such a heavy bias towards low status employment among the Irish, it is axiomatic that while the Scots in-migrants were generally 'over-represented' among the small number of public and professional employees, the Irish were rarely found there.

5% to 6% of employed male Scots in-migrants were in the top two echelons of the social status ladder: the 'professional, managerial' and 'clerical' categories. The Irish were at the lower end of the status continuum: a position that can be explained by the nature of their migration; a perceived lack of appropriate skills; discrimination; and the willingness to take jobs which many Scots would eschew. Their lowly status and the work that they did, counter the argument that they were taking jobs from the Scots. In fact, they were doing work which most Scots were able to avoid.

In the aftermath of the Famine, the impelled nature of Irish immigration to Scotland gradually subsided and Irish arrivals were, like the Scots, drawn to the industrialising towns of Central Scotland by the prospect of work. Many were very likely to have left home as young, single individuals. The Irish were generally poorer than the Scots and much more willing to take a chance, to suffer low wages in poor status jobs and endure inadequate accommodation, as long as this situation was perceived to be temporary. Lack of close family ties in the Vale, with no sense of attachment, combined with insecure low status employment, led to a turbulent ebb and flow of Irish people in the Vale of Leven.

The Scots may have travelled shorter distances than the Irish, but they were far from sedentary and most were far from affluent.[12] They too had to find work and accommodation in new surroundings. Nonetheless, the stark fact remains that within the migratory population, Irishmen were much less likely to find work of modest social status, compared to those born in Scotland.

Irish and Scots Males in Dumbarton

In Dumbarton, Irish representation in the major employment categories of shipbuilding, engineering and iron and steel trades grew stronger towards the end of the nineteenth century. An increase in Irish immigration to Dumbarton in the 1871-81 decade was based on known possibilities of work, rather than on desperation or mere speculation.

There is no data on how many of Dumbarton's Irish shipyard workers were Protestant and how many were Catholic, but one study suggests that Irish Catholics were known to favour Dumbarton and Clydebank, whereas Irish Protestants favoured Govan and Partick.[13] The Irish in Dumbarton were, like their countrymen in the Vale, very mobile, but they were not alone in this, as circulation of labour was a common feature of the Clyde shipyards.[14] This movement increasingly involved the Northern Irish shipyards which were not renowned for employing Catholics. Towards the end of the nineteenth century into the early twentieth century, the number of Northern Irish, Protestant shipyard workers on the Clyde increased, and this had an impact on the overall status of the Irish workforce as many of them were employed in skilled jobs.[15]

The Irish in Scotland were to be found in disproportionately high numbers among 'general labourers'. In the burgh, the proportion of workers in this category declined dramatically over the period, but, as in the Vale, the Irish were always greatly 'over- represented' here. In 1861, the Irish were among a small group of agricultural labourers, and throughout this period, they found employment as quarrymen. Irishmen worked and lived in Dalreoch quarry into the twentieth century. James McCann, brother of Thomas, lived with his family in a house in the quarry, where he died in 1931.[16]

The construction industry in Britain has always been associated with Irish labour. Many Irish 'navvies' worked on large scale projects. They dug canals and later they helped to build the railroads which saw lines extended through Dunbarton county in the 1840s and 1850s. In contrast, during the second half of the nineteenth century, the majority of Dumbarton's building firms were small scale, family businesses, and like those in retail, tended to avoid hiring Irish labour. Understandably perhaps, they preferred to employ family and friends. Yet, Scots who were not born locally were 'over-represented' in both retailing and building. Some had set up businesses in the burgh, but others worked for local firms, where they were preferred to the Irish.

There were employers who expressly refused to hire Irish Catholics, a situation that persisted well into the twentieth century. In the nineteenth century, few Irish were employed as domestic servants.[17] The Scots preferred to employ Scots workers.

The Irish supported their fellow countrymen and women as best they could, but having neither financial nor political muscle, this was limited to providing lodgings, identifying potential employment opportunities and, 'speaking up for' or endorsing individuals seeking employment.

There was more to it than simple preferment. 'Looking after your own' is a natural impulse but it is far removed from the structural discrimination which was rife in places where the Irish settled in appreciable numbers. The Irish were deliberately excluded from civic life and concerted efforts were made to prevent their progress and participation in the economic and social life of the community, although the mere fact of poverty among both Irish and Scots ensured exclusion.

On the other hand, the village of Duntocher had sufficient numbers of settled Irish and their offspring to elect John Torley in 1890. He was one of the first Irish Catholic county councillors in Scotland.[18]

In the Vale five years later, the Irish were thwarted in their attempt to gain representation on the first Bonhill parish council. This election 'created considerable excitement' and was the first 'by popular ballot'. Two of the elected members of the council 'were from the artisan class', but 'all the Irish candidates' were defeated.[19]

Two years after that, the council struggled with the thorny issue of a Catholic request to buy a thousand lairs 'to be used exclusively for Catholic burial'. This did not sit lightly with

'those who can afford grandeur after death' and who 'might not wish to lie so close to the poor despised Irishman. At all events, rampant bigotry was shown and the demand would in all probability have been refused had not the Catholics offered to buy the choice ground as well.'[20]

As David Fitzpatrick points out, 'towards the end of the century' progress of sorts was being made... 'sectarian and ethnic animosities were more often expressed through political struggle or local councils rather than rioting or window smashing' and the purchase of 'some corner of a foreign cemetery serves as a fit, if ambiguous symbol of immigrant upward mobility in Scotland.'[21]

The Irish community in Scotland has been portrayed as 'inward looking' and unwilling to engage with native Scots.[22] Discrimination would foster that. Certainly, priests encouraged Irish Catholics to attend their religious 'duties'. They promoted Catholic clubs and societies, and were keen to ensure that Catholics married partners of their own faith. On the other hand, 'mixed marriages' were no more popular among the Protestant clergy than they were among their Catholic peers.

There were a handful of Irish businesses in Dumbarton. The Burgh Directory for 1877 lists among the following who had Irish surnames: John Tierney, of 26 West Bridgend, a partner in Tierney and Holmes, cabinet makers, upholsterers and turners based in 'West Bridgend House'; Mrs McBride a grocer whose business was at 177 High Street had a house at 180 High Street; J McBride, grocer and potato dealer who lived at the same address; Mrs M Killea, a wine and spirit merchant who lived at 49 High Street and whose business was next door at number 47; D Cullen, fish merchant at 56 High Street and P Gallacher, a grocer whose business was at 7 College Street and whose house was next door at 9 College Street. John Kellie was a barber based at 175 High Street and James Kellie, a brewer, lived at the same address; P Donnelly, chimney sweep at 47 College Street; and A Mauchan who had a butcher's shop at 4 Bridge Street, lived in Rosebank place. There were a few others, mainly among the grocers and provision merchants, but none among the joiners, slaters and plumbers. Some of the Irish businesses were conducted from home. They were all located in College Street, West Bridgend, and High Street (or very close to it).

These surnames above are not definitive proof of Irish nationality. Some could be second or third generation Irish, others with no real sense of an Irish identity at all. But it is telling that no Irish surnames are found elsewhere in the 1877 directory.

The Irish who arrived in Scotland after the post Famine rush, had their sights set on the opportunities afforded by heavy industry. Those drawn to Dumbarton were more intent on working with the larger firms such as Dennys or the Dennystown Forge, and it was in those firms that they were employed in ever increasing numbers. Similarly, throughout Scotland, firms involved in large projects such as canal and railway construction, and in the twentieth century, hydro electric dam building, were more likely to employ Irish labour than were the local, intimate and insular small scale businesses which proliferated in sectors such as building and retailing.

Only five 'builders' firms are listed in the Directory. They are: W Barclay of Levengrove; J and D Gourlay of Strathleven Place; A Mair of 7 Church Street; A Watson of Quay Street and H Williamson of

Risk Street.[23] These were not big firms and did not employ many of workers. With the exception of Watson's on Quay Street, they were located on the periphery of the burgh's overcrowded core.

- The Irish in Dumbarton were found mainly at the lower end of the status spectrum. Between between two thirds and three quarters of employed Irish males were in either 'lower factory' or 'labouring' categories.

- There was however, a definite improvement in the standing of male Irish workers over the period, with a drift away from the non-factory 'labourer' status which encompassed a mass of underpaid, irregular and often casual or part-time work.

- In 1861, just under half of all Irish workers in Dumbarton were labourers who were not employed in the the yards, foundries or engine works (perhaps a testament to their relatively recent in-migration). The jobs that the surge of immigrants in the 1871-81 decade could expect to secure were a marked improvement on that.

- In 1861, an Irishman was almost twice as likely to be of 'labourer' status than 'lower factory' status. Whereas by 1881, an Irishman was two and a half times more likely to find himself in unskilled or semi-skilled industrial employment than in 'non-factory' labouring.

- The proportion of Irish in skilled industrial trades also increased. It was around 17% in 1861, but by 1891 25% of all employed Irishmen were in a skilled trade. There is no doubt that many of these had learned their skills in Northern Ireland.

- Scots were far less likely than the Irish to be in 'non-factory' labouring and, with the exception of 1891 when the gap had narrowed, were twice as likely to be in skilled work than the Irish.

- Scots workers were always well represented among the skilled trades, with around 37% to 43% of their number in this category over the period.

- Scots workers were 'over-represented' in the building trades and grossly 'under-represented' among 'labourers'.

- Comprising the bulk of in-migrants, the Scots were often to be found outside the major areas of employment, in minor categories such as public and professional services and transport.

- In marked contrast to the Vale, there was not a large proportion of Scots in the semi-skilled/unskilled industrial workforce, (10% and under in 1861 and 1871, and about 15% in 1881 and 1891).

Consequently, the employment pattern for the Scots was more evenly balanced, spread over a range of sectors, whereas the Irish aimed for labouring work in Dumbarton's shipyards, forges and machine shops. If that was unavailable, they would move on, or do unskilled or casual work wherever it was to be found.

When industry experienced a slump, the Irish were usually among the first to leave. This occurred for a number of reasons: firstly, they were often employed in unskilled work, where workers were shed in greatest numbers; secondly, they were less well favoured by the management who generally preferred local or lowland Scots workers; and thirdly, they left when conditions deteriorated as they had the least to lose.

For the Irish, the importance of the shift from 'non-factory' towards 'factory' labouring cannot be underestimated. It meant the chance of a regular income on which longer term planning could be based, particularly with respect to housing. It did not secure a stable and settled existence for all, but it may have marked a decline in hand to mouth living.

General or casual labouring per se, was becoming less prevalent: shipyards, foundries and engine works were, over the period, thriving, buoyant and labour intensive industries. The Irish were enjoying greater acceptance, perhaps because of their sheer force of numbers and the fact that their locally born children made up a large segment of the burgh's population. As in Glasgow and Dundee, the Irish had come to work, and were actively involved in shaping the identity of the growing burgh. For Dumbarton's industries to flourish, they needed a steady supply of both Scots and Irish in-migrants.[24]

The second half of the nineteenth century saw Dumbarton's occupational and social structure transformed from that of a small, county burgh to a middle sized, busy, industrial town. In-migrants, the Scots born outside the burgh, and the Irish, were an integral part of that transformation.

Dumbarton may well have been favoured by Irish Catholics, but Irish Protestant shipyard workers were far from absent. Wages for unskilled men on the Clyde were significantly higher than in Belfast where there was a glut of labourers, and this would have encouraged Protestants as well as Catholics to cross the Irish Sea.[25] That said, Catholics were excluded from the Belfast yards at all levels, and the need to find work elsewhere was a strong incentive to emigration.

There were both Catholic and Protestant Irishmen in the burgh throughout the second half of the nineteenth century, and those of Irish birth did find that social patterns were slowly beginning to change for the good. Gains may have been modest, but there was a greater chance of factory or shipyard employment by the later decades of the nineteenth century.

Some migrants brought useful skills or experience of working in factories or shipyards, and they were not fleeing from a famine but being drawn towards Dumbarton by an improving web of contacts and by the burgh's vibrant and successful industries. The Irish knew about opportunities in the shipyards from friends and relatives already in the burgh, many of whom were prepared to offer lodgings, legally or otherwise. They were not leaving behind difficulties at home in the vague hope of securing work in Scotland. Many were not coming directly from Ireland at all; having worked elsewhere upon arrival in the country, they had already joined the ranks of the highly mobile West Central Scottish workforce.

The 'neighbouring' Scots were two and a half to four times more likely to be in skilled factory employment than in unskilled factory employment, and while they were very much 'under-represented' among the 'general labouring' classes compared to Irish incomers, there remained a sizeable group, within the order of eight percent of their employed male population in this category. The Irish were definitely the least favoured ethnic group, but the corollary is not that all Scots enjoyed enhanced status: many lived a precarious existence, in poverty and uncertainty.

In both Dumbarton and the Vale, the percentage of Scots born in counties beyond the West Central Region, Stirling and Argyll, was small and never reached double figures. But although these small percentages, derived from the sample of households, are more prone to statistical error, they do appear to indicate that those from further afield were prepared to move for 'professional' and 'artisanal' employment.[26] Certainly, unskilled industrial work could be found closer to home (see Appendix 4 Table 10:4).

Summary: A Comparison of Status - Male Workers in the Vale of Leven and Dumbarton

The industrial profiles of the Vale and Dumbarton were markedly different, but with a few exceptions, the status of the Scots and the Irish in both places followed similar trends.

- The Irish were to be found in disproportionate numbers in the lower strata of society. In the data drawn from the 1881 and 1891 censuses, this had become more pronounced in the Vale with significantly more non-factory labourers present there than in Dumbarton.

- The Scots who made up the largest proportion of 'migrant' labour were slightly 'over-represented' in the upper echelons of society in both locations.

- There were significant differences between the percentages of 'neighbouring Scots' males in the skilled industrial category when the Vale compared to Dumbarton. In the Vale it was about 21% to

26% over the period, whereas in Dumbarton it was much higher at 37% to 43% .

• This variation was reflected in the proportion of 'neighbouring Scots' in the semi-skilled/unskilled category. The figures were between 30% to 44% in the Vale compared to around 7% to 15% in Dumbarton. It appears that skilled work was more prevalent in heavy industry than in printworking.

• While the Irish were significantly 'under-represented' among the skilled workforce at all four censuses, there was a distinct contrast between the Vale and Dumbarton in the number of skilled, male, Irish workers employed. [27]

• In the Vale, the highest percentage of skilled, male, Irish industrial workers was recorded in 1891, at 17.5% of the total male Irish workforce. It had been 6% in 1881 after the Irish influx in the preceding decade, which suggests that, in contrast to Dumbarton, many unskilled men had arrived in the Vale.

• In Dumbarton, the highest proportion of Irish males in skilled industrial work was 26.5%, also recorded in 1891. Furthermore, the percentage had hovered between 17% to 20% at the earlier three census dates.

There is a clear indication that the number of skilled, Irish shipyard workers coming to Dumbarton was on the rise, and many of these were coming from the industrialised north east of the country.[28] However, it is important to acknowledge that there was also a rise in the number of Irish among the semi-skilled/unskilled industrial workforce, with a commensurate decrease in the proportion who were employed in non-industrial and general labouring, so that over the thirty year period there was a definite improvement in the social status of Irish workers in Dumbarton. In the Vale, over the same period, around 40% to 50% of male Irish workers were in semi-skilled or unskilled employment in the printworks, and their numbers among non-factory labourers remained relatively high throughout. In 1891 when 16.5% of male Irish workers in Dumbarton were non-industrial labourers, the corresponding figure was 28.5% for the Vale (see Appendix 4, Tables 10:3 and 10:4).[29]

NOTES

1 Here 'social status' and 'social class' are taken as one and the same. Many social scientists would argue that 'social status' is an objective measure, i.e. based on employment and wealth, whereas 'social class' is subjective and is largely determined by a person's own perceptions and attitudes. However, a worker's status is largely determined by the job they do.

2 M Anderson 'Standard tabulation procedures for the Census Enumerators' Books 1851-1891' in E.A .Wrigley (ed) *Nineteenth Century Society. Essays in the use of quantitative methods for the study of social data* (1972) Pp 47-81. In this scheme category VIII was designated 'hand loom weaver'. There were few, if any, handloom weavers in the Vale of Leven or Dumbarton, but those of similar status were to be found in dressmaking and millinery trades where 'piece' and 'casual' work was commonplace. Category VIII here has been renamed 'Clothing Worker'.

A word of caution on the use of occupational categories is required, as the data lifted from the census enumerators books' reflects an individual's description of his/her work as interpreted by the census enumerator. There may be a tendency for individuals to inflate their occupational status, e.g. a semi-skilled printworker could refer to himself/herself as a (skilled) 'printer'. Thus there could be some over-estimation of the number of skilled factory workers, and those in other occupations where those were 'semi-skilled' or 'unskilled' would state that they were in a 'skilled' job. For example, a blacksmith's labourer, may describe himself as a 'blacksmith' and be enumerated as such.

3 Hutchison, *Industry, Reform and Empire* p. 82

4 Ibid. p. 83

5 *Thesis*, Chapter 8. Figures quoted are expressed as a percentage of employed males at each location.

6 Shipbuilding trades, such as 'hammerman' and 'riveter' could be regarded as 'skilled' trades, but some would consider them to be 'semi-skilled' and therefore in the 'Lower Factory' category. Here 'riveters' have been included in the skilled workforce whereas 'hammermen' are designated as semi-skilled.

7 Rodger, 'Employment, Wages and Poverty' p. 33

8 Lyon, *Jubilee Souvenir of Dumbarton Building Society*. Forward.

⁹ See Chapter 5.

¹⁰ Whether an ethnic group is 'under-represented' or 'over-represented' in an occupational or social status category, is determined by a comparison of the percentage of that group's members in a particular category, against the total percentage of the workforce from that ethnic group. One way of quantifying this is by determining a simple 'Location Quotient' (or LQ) for a group i.e .the percentage of workers from ethnic group A in a category, divided by the total percentage of workers from ethnic group A. So, for example if 50% of the Scots workforce are working in Shipbuilding, and the Scots make up 50% of the total workforce, then 50/50 = 1. A number less than one signifies 'under-representation' and a number more than one represents 'over-representation'.

¹¹ In this case, the term 'labourer' refers to an individual's social status. Common occupations which fall into that category include 'general labourers', 'agricultural labourers,' hawkers and pedlars.

¹² See Chapter 5. Also, Devine, *The Scottish Clearances* Ch 6 refers to long established high levels of labour mobility in Lowland Scotland and to the low status of many internal migrants. pp. 119-21

¹³ See J. Foster, et al Sectarianism, Segregation and Politics p. 68

¹⁴ MacRaild, *Irish Migrants in Modern Britain* p. 108

¹⁵ G. Walker, *Intimate Strangers. Political and cultural interaction between Scotland and Ulster in modern times* (1995) p. 9 cites E. McFarland, *Protestants First! Orangeism in 19th Century Scotland.* (1991) Ch 5

¹⁶ See Chapter 9

¹⁷ Fitzpatrick, 'A Curious Middle Place', states that female immigrants found that in 'many towns' ... 'even domestic service was largely reserved to the natives of the country' p. 10
G. Vaughan. *The 'Local' Irish in the West of Scotland. 1831-1921* (2013) found that there were few Irish servants among the workforce of Greenock in 1851. p. 24

[18] B. Braber, *in* T. Devine and J. Wormald (eds) *The Oxford Handbook of Modern Scottish History.* (2012) Ch 26 p. 499. Torley was a well regarded councillor, but he had also been a prominent member of the Irish Republican Brotherhood and was a supporter of Irish land rights campaigner Michael Davitt who lent his support to the Scottish crofters. See F. Boyle 'John Torley - The Forgotten Rebel' published by the '1916 Rising Centenary Committee' (2016) available on-line.

[19] Jones and Hopner, *On Leven's Banks* p. 73

[20] Fitzpatrick, 'A Curious Middle Place' p. 24 cites *The Glasgow Observer* 26 March 1898

[21] Ibid. p. 24

[22] Griffiths and Morton (eds), *A History of Everyday Life in Scotland* Ch 4 p. 133

[23] *Dumbartonshire Directory* (published by Bennett Brothers. George Langlands Post Office. Dumbarton) (1877)

[24] Collins, 'Irish emigration to Dundee and Paisley during the first half of the 19th century'

[25] Foster, et al 'Sectarianism, Segregation and Politics' p. 67. Here the authors also assert that as the wages for skilled shipyard workers were 'slightly higher in Belfast throughout the later nineteenth century' there would be less of an incentive for them to move to the Clyde.

[26] Appendix 3. Table 10:1 and 10:2

[27] *Thesis*, Figure 15:10 p. 279

[28] Appendix 4. Table 10:3 and 10:4

[29] *Thesis*, Figures 15:1 and 15:6 p.259 and p. 269, show location quotients for Scots and Irish workers in the 'general labouring' category at each census year 1861-91.

11 Residence: Persistence and Change

During the second half of the nineteenth century the inexorable separation of the 'middle class' from the 'working class' was becoming evident in most large towns and cities throughout Scotland and the UK.[1] The professional and managerial classes were moving from locations close to town and city centres towards the periphery, leaving behind disease, overcrowding and the poor. It was a movement which was aided by transport improvements, as train, and later, in the twentieth century, tram and bus services, enabled people to travel longer distances to their workplaces, in and out of town or city centres. This separation was less evident in villages and smaller towns, but the urban landscapes of both the Vale and Dumbarton changed greatly over the second half of the nineteenth century as they encroached into the surrounding countryside and were redeveloped at the centre.

The Vale of Leven

By 1861, only 5% of the Vale's male working population could be considered 'middle class'[2] and four in ten of those lived in two distinct areas of the Vale. One was in Alexandria, around Bank Street, close to the old core of the village and also close to the printworks, and the other was a small grouping in the newly extended village of Jamestown.

As Alexandria became the Vale's prime service and retail centre, the number of professional and managerial workers resident there increased. Jamestown quickly lost its lustre and thereafter, almost exclusively housed manual factory workers. Renton was always the most predominantly 'working class' village along the Leven. There were few professional/managerial workers recorded living in Renton until 1891. By then, several large houses had been constructed on high ground at the south-western edge of the village where the land begins to rise steeply towards Carman Hill.

The population of the Vale rose steeply in the 1871-91 period, with a growth of around 8,000 people. The latter part of this period saw a substantial increase in house building, especially on the fringes of the villages. These dwellings were largely occupied by the more affluent. In general, housing was better here than in neighbouring Dumbarton, but conditions were far from ideal. There were overcrowded streets and slum properties, but they were not pervasive.

In the Vale of Leven, the large print and dye works were strung out along both sides of the River Leven from north of Alexandria to the south of Renton, at Dalquhurn, beyond which point the river becomes tidal and increasingly brackish, thus unusable for dyeing cloth. Workers did not necessarily live closest to the factory which employed them. A fluidity in the housing and jobs markets meant there was a good deal of circulation between the villages, which were not so far apart as to exclude the daily movement of workers. Disputes over the toll exacted on the 'Bawbee Bridge' between Alexandria and Bonhill, illustrate that daily commuting on foot was commonplace.[3] Walking from Renton to Alexandria's northernmost print works (Levenbank) was a journey of no more than two miles, but it was an added inconvenience after a long shift at the factory. The preference for living close to the workplace was a feature of many Victorian towns and was especially important if there was a practice of daily or short term hiring.[4] There was a commute for the female print workers who lived in Dumbarton and the male shipyard workers who lived in the Vale. The Renton Road witnessed this daily procession in either direction at the beginning and end of a long working day. Even so, while living close to one's place of work was desirable, many workers in the Victorian era had to make longer journeys than this.

The Irish in the Vale of Leven

The Irish presence in the Vale of Leven was smaller than in Dumbarton just a few miles to the south, but as in Dumbarton, the Irish tended to congregate in specific areas in each of the villages on

187

the Leven's banks. Their distribution is, not surprisingly, similar to that of non-factory labourers, who were always a more segregated group than factory workers, and among whom Irish workers were found in large numbers.

Renton and Bonhill had the strongest and most persistent Irish communities, whereas the Irish presence in Alexandria and Jamestown was subject to greater fluctuation and was, particularly in the latter, less enduring. The Irish established, few if any, core areas in either village.

Over the period, Alexandria had a sizeable, but declining, share of the Irish population scattered throughout the town. Large numbers of those born 'locally' or in 'neighbouring' counties predominated. Only around 1861 was their a concentration of Irish in one area, when half of the Irish population in Alexandria, (14% of the Vale's total Irish population), was grouped together in one enumeration district, close to the river and just north of the Ferryfield works.

Jamestown, recently developed by 1861, was host to very few of the Vale's Irish except around 1881 with the surge of Irish in-migration prior to that. By 1891, as the Irish population of Jamestown both proportionally and numerically declined, the Irish retreated to their core areas in Bonhill and Renton, leaving Jamestown with much the same ethnic profile as it had in 1861 and 1871 when small numbers of Irish were greatly outnumbered by Scots.

Renton and Bonhill were the only villages in which the Irish were present in substantial concentrations throughout the period, their presence centring on the core of each village. In Bonhill that was around Burn Street and adjoining Main Street. In Renton, with an Irish population of similar proportions to Dumbarton, they were really only excluded from the newer developments at the southern end of the village built between 1881 and 1891.

These Irish agglomerations had much in common over the 1861-91 period. They persisted in specific areas of the Vale - in the older and poorer parts, which tended towards overcrowding and unhygienic conditions. Renton, as a whole, and Burn Street in Bonhill, gained reputations for poor health, 'fever' cases and high death rates. The heavily polluted stream which gave Burn Street its name, ran down the middle of the street, with houses built on either side. As well as being a main conduit for carrying raw sewage to the Leven, it was an invitation to dump garbage and was identified as an obvious source of disease.

Printwork owners were keen to employ Irish females, and consequently, they were to be found in considerable numbers throughout the Vale. They lodged with friends and relatives or lived in lodging houses or hostels like the 'woman only' one near Dillichip in Bonhill (see Chapters 7 and 8). As in Dundee, which had a large population of Irish women working in the textile industry, an awareness of job opportunities was apparent. There, the Irish female textile workers tended to be drawn from the mill towns and villages of North Central Ireland, rather than from areas nearest Scotland. In the Vale, like Dundee, women sought out work that was familiar to them.[5]

The migration of Irish women to the Vale was different from that undertaken during, or immediately after, the Famine, when thousands of immigrants, in effect refugees, were set down at large British ports, most notably Glasgow and Liverpool. Then, people were desperate: they survived and worked where and when they could. Many had intended their stay in Britain to be a temporary one - with America the ultimate goal - but realistically their options were extremely limited.

The Irish in the Vale of Leven were constrained by low status and a relative inability to compete in the jobs or housing market, and like their compatriots in Dumbarton, they were part of a community that gradually got smaller and, particularly noticeable by 1891, older. As the settlements in which they lived began to grow outwards, the Irish were left behind in their core neighbourhoods within Bonhill and Renton.

Dumbarton

Dumbarton's townscape was dominated by its oldest street: High Street. As late as 1891, just under a quarter of Dumbarton's population (approximately 4,200 people) were registered as living there, but there were likely to have been many more than that. According to census returns, in 1861 High Street housed nearly 4 in 10 of Dumbarton's population (approximately 3,300 people). So in spite of housing a smaller proportion of the population in 1891, such was Dumbarton's growth that it contained around 1,000 more inhabitants than it did thirty years earlier. High Street and the streets running off it: Brewery Lane, Bridge Street, Quay Street, Church Street and College Street formed the old core of the burgh and became more densely populated as the century progressed. There was a broad assortment of housing types, ages and styles, in close proximity to each other, although sandstone tenements predominated later in the nineteenth and into the twentieth century.

Certain addresses recur in newspaper reports of overcrowding and illegal lodger keeping. In 1871 the *Lennox Herald* reported on cases of the latter coming before the court, highlighting 'closes' at 137, 171 and 178 High Street as having the greatest problems.[6]

Taking another look at 137 High Street in 1871, which featured in Chapter 8: it had eighteen 'families', with ninety eight people in total registered. In common with many High Street tenements, the people recorded first in the *census enumerators' books* were of the highest status, probably occupying the first houses that the enumerator visited at an address, usually on the ground floor facing the street. In this case, locally born Mary Thomson, a commercial lodging keeper and her brother Robert Lang, a coal merchant, shared two rooms (with windows). Mary, may have owned the tenement or part of it, or administered the lodgings for a third party. It is likely that some, if not all of the other residents were her 'lodgers'. Of the 98 recorded residents, 65 were males and 33 were females: indicative of a prevalence of male lodgers in a tenement that was notorious for overcrowding.

The next 'family' to be recorded consisted of an English 'actor' and his Scottish wife and daughter. They had three windowed rooms in their apartment. They housed two Scots lodgers - a 'riveter' and a 'reporter/printer', who each had a windowed room. A 'retired blacksmith' who had a 'live-in' domestic servant had four windowed rooms; and, two retired domestic servants lived together in accommodation with two windowed rooms.

Four 'families' in total consisting of eleven people, who, with the exception of the actor, were all Scots born.

Of the remaining fourteen 'families', with an average of over six people per household, - it is safe to assume that they inhabited the poorer dwellings in the 'close'. Their houses had either one or two rooms with windows. There was a family from Argyllshire a sister and brother, who accommodated one Argyll born and two local born lodgers. The rest were Irish households: fifty-three people are recorded as being born there, and of these twenty-eight were male lodgers. Almost all Irish adult males here were 'labourers'. In 1871, the census enumerator of this district often recorded Irish residents' county of birth and in this 'close' most came from Galway or Sligo. The majority were living in 'family' groups where heads of households had taken in young lodgers from their own locale. But the 'close' also contained people from 'Down, Antrim, Belfast, Londonderry, Donegal, Tyrone, Cavan, and Leitrim'. [7]

Those born 'locally', included people from Renton, Cardross and Bonhill, as well as Dumbarton, but other Scots birthplaces: Roxburghshire, Dundee, Glasgow, Edinburgh, Neilston, 'Row' (Rhu), Kilmartin and Sadell, were recorded at this address.

One man was designated as 'a visitor for the night'. 'Visitor' was a common description given to someone who was really a lodger. In a tenement where illicit lodger keeping was a problem, there were many other temporary residents or casual visitors undeclared, probably not to the landlady and certainly not to the census enumerator or local officials.

Number 171 was also mainly, but not exclusively, an Irish 'close'. It housed a dense web of networks and relationships. Of the 86 people registered as living there in 1871, 38 were Irish born and 19 of the others were born to Irish parents. There were seven lodgers recorded: five Irish lodgers and one born in Dundee, lodged in Irish households; the other lodger was a locally born 'fitter in a shipyard' who stayed with a Dumbarton born railway porter and his family. With the exception of one semi-skilled man, the Irish heads of households and their lodgers were all industrial labourers, working in the shipyards or foundries.

This tenement was at the far end of the High Street near the corner of Bridge Street, and immediately north of the bridge. It backed on to the Leven and a few yards away there was a slipway which allowed access to the water. John McLeod and his wife Christina, both from Rosshire also lived at 171. John worked on a river dredger. His oldest son Angus was twelve years old and he was a shipyard labourer. There were three families of fishermen named McNaught living at this address: Dumbarton born William, his Fort William born wife Catherine and their three children who occupied one apartment; James, born in Glasgow, lived with his Paisley born wife Agnes and two young Dumbarton born children; he shared his home with Peter McNaught, a Luss born widower and his Dumbarton born son John who was an apprentice house painter. But James also shared his rooms with two other 'families'. Firstly, that of John Downie, a 'forge furnaceman', his daughter Rose and son Alexander who was a hammerman in an engine works - all three were born in Ireland; and secondly, that of John Galloway and his family. John worked in a foundry. He and his wife Mary Ann were born in Ireland as were four of their six children, who worked as 'rope spinners'. The two youngest children aged six and two were born in Dumbarton. They were most likely related to another family named Galloway living in this tenement where two of the children were also employed as rope spinners.

But these are the only people we know about from census records.

In the spring of 1871, householders accused of 'unregistered lodging' had been summoned to the Police Court. At 171 High Street, James Fallon's house had been visited by the police,

'it was found to contain Fallon, 3 of his family, and 6 lodgers, the one garret room in it being about ten feet square, with a ceiling at the centre of little more than six feet in height... the whole floor was covered with beds, and the smell was very bad'[8]

Fallon said that it cost him '£5 10s a year for it to Mr Fleming, the landlord' and asked, 'what can a man with 13s a week do if he is not to keep lodgers?'

The humane and sympathetic 'Baile' Ure who was hearing the case, stated:

It is most lamentable that poor people have to pay such rents, and most disgraceful to landlords to charge them for such places as this. Ten people in one small room, however, could not be but detrimental to health, and was not to be allowed.

With regret he imposed 'a mitigated penalty of 7s 6d'.

Others from 171 High Street were fined: Patrick Lacey, who had nine occupants in one room; Fistie Cannon, who also had nine in one room; and Patrick Corbet, who housed eight in his two apartment house.

At 137 High Street, Patrick Connolly 'a newly married man, living with his wife and two lodgers in one apartment' where his annual rent was £5 10s, came before 'Baile' Ure, who said 'you should stand out against paying such a rent as that for one small apartment'. The charge was deserted.

The cases of two householders at 179 High Street were also heard: Michael Sullivan who housed 'eleven men and women in two apartments' and Margaret Connolly who housed seven in a 'garret-room in which the (police) officers could not stand upright'. She paid £4 a year for this dwelling and was fined 1s 6d for her transgression.

Michael Murray who housed eight people in one room at 171, failed to appear in court along with three others from number 137 (one of whom had twelve in one room) and another from 126 High Street. Warrants were issued for their arrest. Whether this was enough to persuade them to leave the burgh or stay and face the consequences is not known.

This was from just one sitting of the court, among many others which could have been considered, but several themes emerge: the householders were Irish or of Irish parentage and many, if not all of their illegal lodgers would have been too; the householders and not the landlords were held responsible for the overcrowding and punished accordingly; and, the cases all involved addresses at the northern end of the High Street.

Close by, on the other side of the street, 144 High Street, was a 'close' noted for containing 150 residents living in thirty households at the 1871 census, ten more residents than it had in 1861. In spite of the obvious overcrowding, it housed people with a wider variety of occupations than Number 137. Many residents were well qualified: ships carpenters, cabinet makers and engine fitters were to be found here, as were labourers. This was a grossly overcrowded 'close' and yet it housed many skilled workers and their families forced to live in extremely disagreeable conditions and unable to find adequate housing in elsewhere in Dumbarton. As well as an array of Scots (not only from the 'neighbouring counties' but from a variety of locations such as Perth, Aberdeen, Mull, Morayshire, Caithness and Wigtownshire) Protestant and Catholic Irish lived here.[9] Not all of the Protestant Irish had moved to better houses, and not all were in skilled occupations.

Just a short distance away, at '51 & 53' High Street, closer to Church Street than the bridge, affluent families like that of John Robertson, a 'physician/surgeon' from Kilwinning, lived with his Glasgow born wife, two Dumbarton born infant daughters and two young female, domestic servants born in Stirling and Perth respectively. It was an address they shared with the Forfar born owner of a small painting firm, an Irish 'engineer/fitter and his wife, and a locally born 'ships blacksmith' and his English wife who was employed as a 'dressmaker'. Nearby in the 'back houses' at '59 High Street' there were 27 people living in nine family groups whose birthplaces were Dumbarton, Bonhill, Glasgow, Greenock, Barrhead, Stewarton, Islay, Inverness and Ireland. One of these families employed a 'live-in' domestic servant.

There was a remarkable heterogeneity in the High Street. This was not so much about the types of buildings constructed there, but in the households that inhabited them: in the number of families resident at each address; in variations in the size and composition of each family - it was not uncommon for three generations to comprise a household -

parents, children, grandparents and other relatives, sometimes along with lodgers; keeping lodgers was commonplace; whereas other families employed 'live in' domestic servants; birthplaces of residents ranged from across the whole of Scotland and parts of Ireland, to small numbers from England and elsewhere; industrial occupations may have dominated, but people were engaged in a wide range of occupations and therefore came from a broad spectrum of social classes.

While the old core of the burgh remained overcrowded, Dumbarton was growing along new streets, especially in the 'Newtown' to the east. Improvements in housing and sanitation were slowly beginning to alleviate overcrowding and ill health, although they were still stubbornly present into the twentieth century.

Meanwhile, towards the end of 1871, a few months after the court was busy addressing the issue of dangerous overcrowding in the burgh, the *Dumbarton Herald* was able to proclaim that 'in the year now about to close the trade of this town has had a course of uninterrupted and unexampled prosperity'.[10]

The professional and managerial classes had always been present in the centre of town, but as early as 1861 they were fleeing the insanitary and overcrowded conditions found there. At that date there were areas of middle class housing adjacent to the High Street in Church Street and Strathleven Place. By 1871, this extended to Bonhill Road and, eventually over the next twenty years to Boghead Road and Round Riding Road. Kirktonhill an exclusive suburb, was set on rising ground above the burgh. It contained the grandest houses and the wealthiest families. In common with many of the highest class housing developments in British towns and cities, it was built on the western edge of the built up area where the prevailing wind protected it from the smoke and the smells emanating from the houses and factories below.

There was a noticeable trend in the growing separation of the professional / managerial and working class residences. At each of the four census years from 1861 to 1891, the disassociation became more marked, but it was far from complete by 1891, when around 15% of 'professional and managerial' males still lived in the High Street. This group, which included people such as John Robertson mentioned above, had a definite preference for the southern end of the High Street adjacent to Church Street. In 1860, there were two banks located there, and, as the century progressed it became more associated with churches, banks and offices. Prominent among the latter was the grand office of MacMillan and Sons Shipyard, which in the 1930s became the office of Hiram Walker, owners of the adjacent Ballantine's Distillery. Thereafter it housed the Procurator Fiscal's office. After a vacant period, The Clipper bar and restaurant occupied the building, before closing down prior to the Covid pandemic in 2020.

Those of highest social status, were least likely to be found, not in the decaying, medieval heart of the burgh, but in Dennystown, built specifically by William Denny for his employees. It had initially attracted 'skilled factory' workers, and at the 1861 census the enumerator, departing from the usual practice of providing a simple description of his district, noted that this area was 'all inhabited by the working classes'. By 1871, many of those skilled factory workers had deserted it, and it became very much the preserve of foundry workers employed at nearby Dennystown Forge. Between 1861 and 1871, Dennystown had undergone a process similar to that of Jamestown in the Vale, which had initially attracted some middle class households. When Dennystown was first built it had been popular with skilled workers, but it quickly became the home of unskilled or semi-skilled factory labourers.[11]

In Dumbarton, there was a fluidity in the jobs and housing markets, but what was emerging here was a gradual separation of the skilled industrial worker from their semi-skilled or unskilled colleagues, and indeed a separation of non-factory 'labourers' from those who worked the yards or factories. The 'lower factory' workers were housed in parts of the High Street, but more particularly along College Street in the old core of the town, and from 1871 onwards they were numerous in Dennystown. Many of these workers were Irish. Initially College Street and later Dennystown, came to be regarded as Irish enclaves.

In the 1850s, Dennystown was a new development of workers' housing: by contemporary standards it was far superior to the accommodation being endured by many 'over the bridge' in the old burgh. Initially, it attracted many skilled industrial workers. Even so, the problems of intense overcrowding afflicting the High Street and its immediate surroundings, could not be kept at bay and, in spite of determined efforts by the Dennys, lodging and sub-letting became commonplace. The result was that the difficulties being experienced in the old core of Dumbarton soon infected the new suburb. As early as 1864, there was an average of three persons per room in Dennystown, with some two apartment dwellings containing as many as ten or fifteen people.[12] This tended to repel those skilled workers who were turning their attentions towards housing developments elsewhere. From 1861 to 1871, Dennystown slowly began to lose its status as a residence for skilled workers, becoming very much the preserve of the 'lower factory' worker.[13] The joiners strike of 1865, which saw an exodus of skilled workers and their families, not only from Dennystown but from Dumbarton, may have accelerated this process.

The main areas favoured by the the skilled workforce shifted from Dennystown to areas being developed in the east of the burgh as it spread along the Glasgow Road, to include Clyde Street and Leven Street, described as 'new streets in 1861'.[14] Once again, skilled workers were moving into new housing developments as soon as they were built, thus freeing up Dennystown for semi-skilled and unskilled industrial workers.

The consequence of building in 'Dumbarton East' was to cream off skilled shipyard workers who were moving, eastwards, along with the shipyards, where there was space for both industrial and residential expansion. Dennys shipyard was moved in 1867 from Woodyard on the west bank to its final and largest site: the Leven Shipyard near the confluence of that river with the Clyde. Shipyard and foundry workers who had once lived side by side were now significantly separated. Foundry workers, with proportionally fewer skilled men in their ranks, gravitated towards Dennystown near the eponymous forge, which endured for more than another hundred years. 37% of the burgh's foundry workers lived there in 1861. This percentage spiked at 65% in 1871. In 1881 and 1891 just over half of all foundry workers in Dumbarton lived in the comparatively small area of Dennystown which had become a foundry man's enclave, but it had become an Irish enclave too.

Shipyard workers gravitated towards the east of the burgh, whereas foundry men were more inclined to live in the west. Those who were deemed to have 'labourer' status were less segregated. They were a large and disparate group scattered throughout the oldest parts of the burgh and included almost all of the unskilled and non-factory workers, builders' labourers, quarrymen, farm workers, artisans' labourers and 'general labourers'. Many were intimately tied to the workplace, living above the shop or in the back shop or workshop, in a farm cottage or close to the busy High Street where casual work could be pursued. As factory and shipyard workers began to move away from the centre of the burgh, it became a location where there was a preponderance of non-factory labourers. Even so, the High Street and College Street area remained intensely overcrowded and continued to house people varied social classes and a wide array of occupations. Rapid population growth continued to outstrip house building and ensured that the High Street, even as late as 1891, was not the preserve of the lowest status groups, but had skilled and unskilled workers of all varieties as residents.

The Irish in Dumbarton

In Dumbarton, the contrast between the locations of the Irish and the Scots was somewhat similar in pattern to that of foundry and shipyard workers, with the former clearly located in distinct areas and the latter spread more evenly. In the 1860s, the Irish population was mainly found in the centre of the burgh, particularly in College Street, and on the High Street running north from there. The southern end of the High Street, adjacent to Church Street, part of which was referred to as 'Church Place', came to be associated with banks, offices and churches.

The 1871 to 1881 decade was one of change. The Irish were settling in Dennystown, firstly in 'Levenhaugh' and then in 'Henryshott'. The nickname 'Wee Dublin', later applied to Dennystown as a whole, referred initially to Henryshott. For the Irish, Dennystown was becoming a favoured destination. College Street or 'The Vennel'[15] as it was known, would always be regarded as the Irish heartland in Dumbarton because of the enduring nature of its Irish connections, but it was not inhabited exclusively by them. The Irish, in the 1861 to 1881 period, were to be found in almost equal numbers in the north eastern segment of the High Street, 'round the corner' from College Street. It was persistence, not exclusivity, which made College Street an Irish street. It had many second and third generation 'Irish Scots' residents and their presence through time, along with an upsurge in immigration in the 1870s, lent credence to the view that the street had a unique identity: the place where the Irish first settled, put down roots and faced up to native antagonism.[16]

By 1891, the Irish had also gravitated towards the north west or 'river' side of the High Street close to the bridge and a short walk to Dennystown. The number of Irish in the north eastern segment of the High Street was showing signs of decline. The overall population of that side of the street had dropped by about 400 to just over half of its 1881 total, as slum clearance and piecemeal redevelopment took place. The Irish were still over-represented here and in other, older properties, which were being vacated by those who were moving to better accommodation elsewhere.

Although many College Street residents born locally were of Irish descent, it is highly unlikely that the majority of the 'neighbouring Scots' living there had Irish parents.[17] These Scots, may have been 'under-represented' in College Street, but were far from absent. At no time was College Street an Irish ghetto. Neither the varied social status, nor the ethnic origins of its inhabitants would allow such a conclusion.

By 1891, there was a definite social dichotomy in the main areas of Irish settlement. Those in the High Street were less likely to be found grouped together and tended to be 'labourers'. They were most probably 'general' labourers, scavengers and odd job men, whereas those in College Street and in Dennystown tended to be unskilled or semi-skilled foundry or shipyard workers.

The Irish invasion of Dennystown contrasted with the movement of the skilled lowland Scots who were concentrating evermore in the growing suburbs of the Newtown. However, as with the in-migrant Scots in Dennystown, the Irish were not excluded from the east end, merely 'under-represented'. In 1891, around 57% of Dumbarton's Irish population, was to be found in four enumeration districts covering College Street, the High Street north of its junction with College Street and Dennystown, the other 43% being spread, unevenly, over the remaining fourteen enumeration districts. Of course, some of the skilled Irish workers living in the east end were Ulster Protestants, while many of the 'locals' living in College Street and Dennystown were of Irish Catholic descent. The areas with the strongest Irish presence were peopled mainly by Irish Catholic families, where their distinct religious, occupational and social status contributed to this separation. There were fewer Ulster Protestants, but with many in skilled jobs, they had a wider selection of houses available to them. In contrast, this distinction was blurred in the poorest tenements in the heart of the burgh, as Scots along with Irish on both sides of the religious 'divide' lived in close proximity.

The prime reason for the growing segregation of the Irish in the last two decades of the nineteenth century, was a declining and ageing population. Apart from a substantial drift to Dennystown by the Irish after 1861, they were largely staying put. Skilled workers, including many 'neighbouring Scots', were leaving the centre of Dumbarton at a greater rate than the ageing, Irish labouring classes. This desertion of the core was aided by an ability to buy or rent superior accommodation in the burgh's newer housing developments. The better off Scots people were distancing themselves not only from the Irish, but from a town centre that was dirty and disease ridden.

During the 1880s and 1890s, Irish immigration to Dumbarton slackened. The Irish population aged as a consequence, and their number in 1891 was slightly less than it had been in 1881, so those dying or leaving the burgh were hardly being replaced by new arrivals. Dennystown remained the principal reception area for new immigrants, as it had been in the 1871-81 decade when there had been a surge in Irish immigration. In the old core of the burgh around High Street and College Street the ageing Irish population was less mobile, less able, and in many cases, less inclined, to move on, although paradoxically, there had been a proportional increase in the number of skilled Irish industrial workers in Dumbarton. Many of these more recent arrivals may have been able to secure better accommodation away from the most overcrowded tenements, but there was no guarantee of that.

Those who had the most to gain by staying, were those in regular and skilled employment, but the old and unskilled, who had little choice, were merely left behind. Along with social status, a combination of life cycle stage and ethnic cohesiveness, influenced location. A similar process was happening in the Vale of Leven around the same time and was repeated across many Irish communities in nineteenth century Scotland.[18]

What cannot be ignored, is that many of the Irish settled with their own people by choice and were neither destitute nor unskilled. This was especially true later in the century. Some learned skills or brought skills with them, and when they reached Dumbarton they were likely to gravitate towards their countrymen. Here, they would feel safe, establish or widen contacts and look for lodgings if these had not been prearranged. Letters home to Ireland certainly encouraged young adults to emigrate. In the second half of the nineteenth century they joined the Scots who were moving in great numbers to the industrial towns of the Central Belt. Along with the Scots, they played a full part in forging the character of the West of Scotland. Theirs was not an incursion into a settled and sedentary land.[19]

Connections

One theme of this book has been that the Vale of Leven and Dumbarton, while geographically close, grew and 'prospered' as a result of two dominant, but very different industries. There has been an emphasis on the contrasts between the settlements rather than their links. Yet, there is ample evidence of people living in one part of the Leven Valley while working in another. It was a time of tremendous population churn, so there were people who were born in the Vale but were resident in Dumbarton and vice-versa. It is easy to overlook that relocation was not confined to movement between counties, but occurred within counties too.

Of the four factory villages in the Vale of Leven, connections between Renton and the burgh of Dumbarton were possibly the strongest. Renton itself is often considered as a highly distinctive entity within the Vale of Leven, not least by its own residents.[20]

Renton, unlike the other three Vale settlements, was not in Bonhill Parish but in Cardross Parish, which once extended to the western edge of the Leven at Dumbarton. It was the nearest village to Dumbarton and had a lot in common with it. It was overcrowded, housing was poorer and disease was more prevalent than in the rest of the Vale. Both had large Irish communities. In the latter part of the nineteenth century Dennystown, the district of Dumbarton closest to Renton, was a centre of Irish in-migration, and women living there and in adjoining Westbridgend, were regularly employed at Cordale and Dalquhurn.

The connection between Renton and the burgh predated the arrival of the Irish. In the 1790s the demand for housing in the Renton area had been so great that 'a number of houses' were built on the west bank of the Leven opposite Dumbarton (at that time this land was still part of Cardross Parish).

upon feus from Mr Denniston of Colgrain; and a village is just now begun upon the property of Mr G Graham of Gartmore, which it is probable, when the present stagnation of business is over, will fast increase in population.[21]

The most substantial increase in population at this location did not occur until the building of Dennystown in the 1850s. Named, it is assumed for the Dennys, but maybe with a nod to the original feu holder too.

Renton has a long history of religious dissent, and there were two dissenting churches serving Renton in 1796. These dissenters 'consist chiefly of people connected with the printfields. The farmers, in general, are attached to the establishment'.[22] In 1875, Orr Ewing, in his testimony to The Royal Commission enquiry into the operation of the Factory and Workshop Act, mentions that forty years ago he had employed 'an immense number of Highlanders'.[23] Renton's distinctive Free Gaelic Church founded by Highlanders, moved to Latta Street, Dumbarton, early in the twentieth century.[24]

The sample of *census enumerators' books* used here produces evidence of males living in Renton but working in the shipyards. This was less prevalent among residents of Alexandria, Jamestown or Bonhill. It was not uncommon for someone born in Renton to have children born in Dumbarton and vice-versa. Many families recorded here had children born in two or more of the local settlements, demonstrating the footloose nature of life for many and the connections between the Vale and Dumbarton. However, similarities in social and ethnic status, and the proximity of Renton to Dumbarton, were factors which encouraged a close relationship.

NOTES

1 *Thesis,* Ch 2. pp. 24-8

2 That is, working in professional, managerial, clerical or 'trade' but not including skilled factory workers.

3 A bawbee was the name given to a Scottish halfpenny.

4 Foster, et al 'Sectarianism, Segregation and Politics' p. 86

5 Collins, 'Irish emigration to Dundee and Paisley '

6 *LH* 8 June 1871

7 There were no instructions given to the enumerator to record the towns or counties of birth of those born beyond Scotland, although some did.

8 *LH* 13 May 1871

9 Foster, et al in 'Sectarianism, Segregation and Politics' p. 66 used a large sample from the 1901 Irish Census and lists of Irish prisoners at Barlinnie Prison where religious affiliation was recorded. They found that there were a number of almost exclusively Protestant and Catholic first names. For example, Albert, Andrew, David and Samuel were among those strongly associated with Protestantism and Patrick, Bernard and Michael associated with Catholicism. This method has been informally applied here.

10 *DH* 14 December 1871

11 *Thesis,* Ch. 16 pp. 299-312

12 *L H* 17 September 1864

13 *Thesis,* p. 301, Figure 16:4 shows Location Quotients for Higher Factory workers to be 1.2 in 1861 and 0.9 in 1871. For Lower Factory workers there was distinct difference over the decade from 0.5 in 1861 to 2.1 in 1871.

14 Unpublished *'Census Enumerators Books'* for 1871

15 The Vennel, pronounced as ' Vinnil' by the locals. The name harks back to a time when the street was known as Cross Vennel. Cross Vennel, along with High Street and Quay Street formed Dumbarton Cross: the centre point of the burgh.

16 See Chapter 8

[17] The Scots who were not locally born came from a wide variety of counties, towns and villages, many of which were not settled in any numbers by the Irish.

[18] This process is known as 'residualisation', where, just as today in the poorer parts of communities it is the older, poorer, less mobile and least healthy people who are 'left behind' as younger, mobile, more prosperous and healthy people move to better areas.

[19] See Collins, 'Irish emigration to Dundee and Paisley'

[20] Vale of Leven History Project, *www.valeofleven.org.uk/renton.html*

[21] *OSA* Vol XVII, Cardross pp. 216-7

[22] Ibid. p. 219

[23] *LH* 11 September 1875

[24] Jones and Hopner, *On Leven's Banks* p. 71

12 Lodgers and Servants

In Victorian Britain, lodging and servant keeping were common practice, illustrative of the gulf between rich and poor in a very unequal society. Lodging and boarding were borne out of necessity in a rapidly industrialising age.[1] Large scale migration to towns, low wages and an inadequate housing stock, which being unable to keep pace with demand, led to higher rents and a symbiotic relationship between householders and boarders. The 'boarder' or 'lodger', often a new arrival, could not afford adequate and separate accommodation and the householder was often glad of the extra revenue which the hiring of a room, or a mere space to bunk down, could bring. It was common for recent migrants to lodge with people they knew. Incomers who had established themselves in Dumbarton and the Vale encouraged others to join them. This mutually beneficial arrangement, made with or without the consent of the landlord, led to gross overcrowding and squalor. Police Acts provided powers to tackle the problem, but they could never really attack its nub: inadequate and insubstantial housing.

The statistics used here and taken from the unpublished census records, undoubtedly underestimate the number of boarders and lodgers present. Householders often concealed the presence of lodgers from landlords and government officials. In numerous instances where lodgers were present they were designated as 'friends' or 'visitors' in the *census enumerators' books*.[2] The local press regularly reported on cases coming before the 'Police Court' where in the most overcrowded tenements many lodgers went unrecorded (see Chapter 11).

Here, most lodgers worked in the same industry, belonged to the same ethnic group or enjoyed similar social status to the household head with whom they lodged. If there was a difference then the lodger was often younger and of slightly lower status. Many were young adults and teenagers, recently arrived and with little experience of industrial work.

Servant keeping was much more prevalent than it is today.[3] The rich, with large families in large houses, could afford to hire servants on low wages which were augmented by food and board. James Denny living with his wife, her sister and his three children at Levenford House in 1861, employed four female servants aged between twenty and twenty-seven, all were Scottish, two were Dumbarton born. By 1881 when the house was owned by prominent engineer Walter Brock, he lived there with his wife and three children along with a 'housekeeper', a 'tablemaid', a 'laundrymaid' and a 'nursemaid' as well as a 'gardener' and his wife and daughter.[4] Relative security of employment with accommodation and meals, was seen by some to be a better option than searching for a higher wage in hard, manual factory work, and it attracted very young women who were sought out by affluent householders, along with widows and older women who did not have young, dependent children. Not all servants 'lived in' and in this era women were employed, even by lower middle class households, as day servants, housekeepers and cleaners. It is impossible to quantify, but this work was often casual and went unrecorded, unless women declared it as an occupation to the census enumerator.

Vale of Leven: Lodging

Quite clearly, lodging increased during times of greatest industrial prosperity when the demand for accommodation was at its highest. The percentage of the total male and female population in lodgings was, by present day standards, substantial, but the census reports suggest that instances of 'multiple occupancy', where one family shared a home with another, or had more than one or two lodgers, were low. It is a recurring theme here, that housing conditions were more favourable in the Vale than in Dumbarton and lower levels of overcrowding, especially true of Alexandria, were in part attributable to the availability of 'superior' housing stock. This is not to suggest that Alexandria was slum free, nor that Bonhill and Renton were unaffected by severe overcrowding, but this was neither as widespread nor as dire as in Dumbarton.

The sample shows that male levels of lodging ran slightly ahead of the female levels in 1861 and 1871, with female levels being higher in 1881 and parity being achieved in 1891. Between 4.5% and 8.5% of all males were lodgers over the period. For female lodgers the figures were between 3.5% and 10%. The lowest rate for both sexes was recorded in 1871 and the highest in 1881.[5] The link between population growth and lodging is clear. The period leading up to 1871 was one of low in-migration, whereas the next decade saw the highest levels of in-migration across the thirty year period.[6]

Over the period, more Scots men than Scots women were in lodgings, whereas for the Irish, the opposite was the case, with the exception of 1871. This anomaly was due to the economic slump in the preceding decade which saw the number of Irish females in the 15 - 54 age group drop.[7] A decline in the Irish male population occurred too, but because Scots males left in even greater numbers, Irish males were 'over-represented' amongst lodgers at this date.

By 1881, after a strong resurgence in Scots and Irish migration, around 40% of the lodging population consisted of 'neighbouring' Scots, with similar numbers of both males and females in lodgings. The Irish accounted for 32% of male lodgers and 43% of female lodgers, but from a much smaller population.[8]

Over the period, 22% to 47% of all female lodgers were Irish in spite of the fact that they made up only 9.5% to 14.5% of the female population. Thus with the exception of 1871, Irish females were more likely to be in lodgings than Irish males, Scots males or Scots females.

Locational aspects of lodging in the Vale of Leven

The incidence of lodging in both the Vale and Dumbarton was directly correlated to relative industrial success and a concomitant increase in both Scots and Irish in-migration. In the Vale, Renton was almost always the core area for lodging and this is associated especially with the large Irish presence in the village. Around the centre of the village, along Main Street and Back Street were favoured destinations, but other than the extreme south of the village, lodgers both male and female, were to be found throughout. Bonhill Village in contrast, experienced a decline in population over the 1861 to 1871 decade and had no lodgers living in two of its four enumeration districts at the later date The old core of Alexandria, between Bank Street and Bridge Street, along with some of its oldest streets, North Street, Alexander Street and Susannah Street, had high instances of lodging. The attractiveness of Jamestown's terraced rows waned rapidly as they became overcrowded and a popular location for both male and female lodgers, in the last quarter of the century.

There was an ebb and flow of lodgers around these core locations with seepage into adjacent areas. Few lodgers were to be found at the southern end of Alexandria, and the northern end of Bonhill, where the villages became more rural in character, contained fewer terraced rows and had more individual cottages. The western flank of Alexandria, where the houses were newer and bigger, contained fewer lodgers than the older parts of the town.

Dumbarton: Lodging

Dumbarton was host to higher levels of male lodging than the Vale of Leven, with between 8% and 15.5% of the male population in lodgings: a reflection of the dire housing situation which also meant that some shipyard workers had to live outside Dumbarton, most often in Renton and Bonhill.[9] This was an inevitable consequence of the rapid growth and success of Dumbarton's heavy industrial sector. Only in 1891 did the proportion of lodgers drop to levels akin to those in the Vale, not because of a slackening in population growth, but due largely to the extension of housing. The differential between male and female lodgers was much greater than in the Vale simply because the lack of job opportunities for females deterred the in-migration of young unattached women. The proportion of the female population in lodging was very small, 2.3% at its highest point in 1861.[10] With a larger Irish population than the Vale, Irish male immigrants made up a bigger proportion of the lodging population than those from neighbouring counties. By 1881, six in every ten recorded lodgers in Dumbarton were Irish. Again, this was linked to the net influx of immigrants in the preceding decade.

In 1891, when Dumbarton had the lowest percentage of adult males recorded in lodgings over the 1861-91 period, the Vale of Leven, recorded its second lowest total (after 1871). It appears that as jobs became more secure, and the population became less migratory, access to housing improved and lodging waned. An older and more sedentary Irish population combined with a reduction in Irish immigration, contributed to this decline.

This was far from the end of significant levels of lodging, nor of overcrowding, erratic employment cycles or high rates of disease. The spectre of disease encouraged by overcrowding and insanitary conditions was ever present in the industrial West of Scotland well into the twentieth century. Diseases such as typhus, caused by dirt and poor sanitation may have been dwindling as the nineteenth century came to a close, but infectious diseases such as diphtheria and whooping cough still targeted the young, and tuberculosis was a potentially lethal disease which struck the urban poor well into the twentieth century.

Locational aspects of lodging in Dumbarton

The highest incidences of lodgers were to be found throughout the old core of the burgh. A stretch of less than 200 yards on the western side of the High Street which backs on to the river, between Quay Street and Bridge Street, housed some of the highest population densities in the burgh, and never had fewer than 10% of the burgh's lodgers living there from 1861 to 1891.[11] The west side of College Street was area which was persistently 'favoured', particularly by Irish lodgers. It had over 17% of all lodgers in 1881 and two thirds of these were Irish.

As the Irish population of College Street had declined by 1891, it was no longer a conspicuously 'over-represented' address among male lodgers. Dennystown, in contrast, had assumed the main role as the

Irish reception area, containing over 16% of all lodgers, with nine out of ten being Irish. No major agglomeration of lodgers existed elsewhere, although there was a small group at Burnside, a terraced row on the eastern edge of the burgh, which housed Scottish semi-skilled and unskilled industrial labourers. Overall, lodging was on the wane by 1891. The proportion of lodgers in the male population was just under half of that recorded ten years earlier.

However, lodging had begun to drift eastwards as lodgers were marginally 'over-represented' on the western fringe of the 'Newtown' along Castle Street, Bruce Street and Clyde Street. When Dennystown was a new development in the 1850s, it had contained few lodgers. As the housing stock aged and was subject to population pressure, the numbers of lodgers increased dramatically. This process was beginning to affect the streets of Dumbarton East closest to the centre of the burgh in the same way, although the problem would never be as severe as it had become in Dennystown.

Lodging did not die out, and, wherever employment was available and accommodation for new arrivals was inadequate, it thrived.

Servant Keeping

As might be expected in predominantly industrial settlements, there were few servants 'living in', that is residing with their employers. Fewer than 1% of the Vale's total population were in this category. In Dumbarton the number was always higher, but declined proportionally from around 2.5% of the population in 1861 to around 1.7% in 1891.[12] Small percentages, admittedly, but they accounted for around 75-150 individuals in the Vale and 200-300 in Dumbarton; far higher than modern rates. At the earlier date, around a quarter of all Dumbarton's residential servants were to be found in the High Street, with the majority living in its eastern end. It is clear evidence that high status households were still living in the centre of the burgh at that time.

In Dumbarton, of all occupational groups considered here, 'live-in' servants were the most 'segregated', with small numbers found in highly specific areas. In 1861, the main areas of servant keeping were the west side of Westbridgend, Church Street, and the adjoining Strathleven Place. In 1871, Westbridgend retained its status as an established location for servants in residence, but as the burgh expanded, Church Street had become became less important in this regard. The principal servant keeping areas were now Strathleven Place and the area which had been developed north east of it - Bonhill Road and the beginnings of Round Riding Road.

The major change in the last quarter of the century, was the development of grand houses at Kirktonhill which unsurprisingly became an area with relatively large numbers of servants.[13]

There were comparatively few 'live in' servants in the Vale. They were not to be found in any particular locations, but in some of the printwork owners' houses adjacent to the factories and in the larger houses which fringed the villages.

The vast majority of 'live-in' servants were female. Young girls from poor but 'respectable' families were favoured. However, the greater number of those employed as 'servants' lived in their own homes and commuted to their employers' residences. In addition, many women worked as housekeepers, cooks and cleaners. It is difficult to quantify the numbers in such occupational groups, given that they included casual and part time employees. We can only assume that they would not necessarily disclose their employment status to a census enumerator.[14] Therefore their numbers will have been under-recorded. That said, from the sample used here, the percentage of those in the adult female population whose occupation was recorded as 'servant' was between 2.3% to 4.6% in the Vale but higher in Dumbarton, at 6.5% to 10%. In both cases, lower percentages were recorded in the second half of the period, at the 1881 and 1891 censuses, signalling a decline in servant keeping, which was replicated across Scotland.[15] In the 1901 census, when employment figures for all females over the age of 10 in Dumbarton were made available, 7.6% of them were in 'domestic occupations'.

There were higher numbers of professional, managerial workers, tradespeople and artisans in Dumbarton who were able to afford servants, than in the Vale. Household heads with relatively modest incomes aspired to servant keeping and would, in turn, offer modest wages.

Lack of alternative female employment in Dumbarton also encouraged more women to enter service, and servants were the largest female occupational group in the Dumbarton sample at the 1861 and 1871 censuses until being overtaken by printworkers at the 1881 census.

NOTES

[1] In Scotland most people regarded as lodgers were in fact boarders, i.e. they were part of a 'family' or 'co-residing group' which was not their immediate family. If they were true lodgers, with their own rooms and fending for themselves then in Scotland they would usually be accorded separate status, and deemed to belong to a separate household. The census enumerators used the terms lodger and boarder interchangeably. So here the more commonly used term 'lodger' is preferred.

[2] 'Friend' or 'visitor' were also terms used in the census enumerators books to describe children born out of wedlock. Typically, a family with a grown up daughter in residence will have a young child, who shares the family surname, but is described as a 'friend' or 'visitor'.

[3] In this instance only servants resident in their employers' households are considered.

[4] Census returns quoted in Levenford Factsheet. (Local History factsheet) published by West Dunbartonshire Libraries Local Studies Departments at *www.wdcweb.info/library*

[5] It was equally high, at around 8.5%, for males in 1861.

[6] *Thesis*, Ch 17 Figs 17:8 and 17:9 p. 337

[7] Ibid. There were fewer Irish than 'neighbouring Scots' in the Vale, but location quotients demonstrate that they were always 'over-represented' among lodgers. (See below)

[8] Location Quotients in the 1881 sample for 'neighbouring Scots' males and females were respectively 1.4 and 1.3. For the Irish it was 2.7 and 2.9.

[9] *Thesis*, Ch. 17 Fig 17:10. p. 340

[10] Ibid. Fig 17:11. p. 340

[11] Ibid. Ch. 17 Figure 17:14. p. 347

[12] This does not include those whose occupation is recorded as 'servant' but who do not 'live in'.

[13] *Thesis*, maps pp. 353-4

[14] Under-recording of both servants, and lodgers is a likely source of inaccuracy in the nineteenth century census enumerators' books.

[15] Rodger, 'Employment, Wages and Poverty' p. 32

13 Epilogue: into the twentieth century, the Vale and Dumbarton in the Scottish Context

Decline and Closure

For the printworks of the Vale, problems of amalgamation and closure dragged on into the twentieth century. The Great War (1914-18) and its aftermath, along with the 'Great Depression' in the late twenties and early thirties killed off most of the factories. The Ferryfield and Dalmonach factories owned by the Manchester Calico Printers group, closed in 1915 and 1929 respectively, thus ending that company's association with the Vale. Of the United Turkey Red factories, Milton closed just after the war in 1919, Dillichip closed in 1936, Levenbank and Cordale both in the 1940s, at which point the extensive Alexandria Works became the main factory of the United Turkey Red company whose operations ended in 1960. Dalquhurn, which had been a part of that company moved unsteadily onwards for another two years after that, but only as the home of the Lennox Knitwear Factory, which employed 300 people, and of C & F Taylor, 'worsted spinners of Shipley, Yorkshire' who employ(ed) about 200, mainly women'.[1] Dalquhurn had ceased to be a recognisable printworks before this.[2]

The textile tradition persisted until 1980 when the British Silk Dyeing Company went out of business. Operational from 1929, it had failed after a few months, reopening under Swiss management three years later. It was acquired by an American company in 1960, and at one time employed around 500 people. Cheaper foreign textiles were a major cause of its demise.[3]

The Argyll Works, housed a car manufacturing company, whose lasting legacy is the grand facade at the north end of Main Street Alexandria. In its brief but glorious existence - it opened in 1906, reorganised in 1908 and was liquidated in 1914 - it employed 1,500 people at its zenith. Thereafter it became a munitions factory and later the Admiralty's 'torpedo factory'. Plessey's electronics firm was its last industrial owner. Now only the facade and the structures immediately behind it remain. It serves as a centre for retail outlets.[4]

In Dumbarton, Dennys would benefit from orders during two world wars. Regular overtime was to be had during both conflicts, but not so much in the interim.[5] Post 1945, the firm would profit from constructing vessels to replace those lost in the preceding war, but it would suffer, like the much of the British shipbuilding industry, from a decline in orders and 'both shipyard and engine-works closed suddenly in 1963'.[6]

MacMillan's yard had closed three decades before Dennys, and its site had been bought by Canadian company Hiram Walker in 1937. There they would construct the massive Ballantine's Distillery. Whisky making, storing and bottling would become vital to the burgh's economy in the second half of the century as shipbuilding and heavy industry declined.

Population

The population of Dunbartonshire continued to grow strongly in the first decade of the twentieth century. Dumbarton burgh had 20,600 inhabitants by 1911. In Clydebank the trajectory of growth was much steeper than Dumbarton's with some 37,500 people living in a town which had been a greenfield site just forty years earlier. By 1931, the population of Clydebank had grown by another 9,500, while Dumbarton's had grown by just under 1,000. Both burghs suffered a small decline in population during the thirties, so that by 1951 Dumbarton's population had only grown by a few thousand since 1931, but Clydebank had recorded a net loss of 2,500 over the same period.[7] What these figures hide is that both burghs had an excess of births over deaths, which masked the extent of out-migration, estimated to be 1,100 for Dumbarton and 9,000 for Clydebank.[8]

The situation was slightly different in the Vale. Going into the twentieth century, growth was not so strong. The parish of Bonhill which included the settlements of Bonhill village, Alexandria and

Jamestown had a population of 14,581 in 1901, by 1911 it had risen by 1,388, reaching a peak of 16,622 by 1921. It would decline by over a thousand in the next decade, and in 1951 the population was 16,339, slightly smaller than it was in 1921. The situation in Renton was predictably similar, 5,170 people lived there in 1951, 'which is practically the same population as at the end of the nineteenth century'.[9]

Immigration, In-migration and Emigration

The scale of continuous Irish immigration to Scotland began to ebb in the first decade of the twentieth century. While 'overall numbers remained fairly constant through to 1901, the Irish share of the population fell back and continued to do so...'.[10] For Dunbartonshire

'this declining percentage does not at first indicate a decreasing total: in 1901 there were nearly one and a half times as many Irish coming into the county as in 1861, and a slight increase was recorded in 1911, but thereafter a total decline set in. In 1951 there were only 5,393 Irish-born, and for the first time English born (8,576) were greater in number'.[11]

Table 13:1 Percentage of Irish born, 1901-1951

Year	Scotland	Dunbartonshire
1901	4.6	8.7
1911	3.7	7.2
1931	2.6	5.1
1951	1.7	3.3

From accounting for 7.1% of Scotland's population in 1851, the Irish proportion was 4.6% in 1901, but that was just over 2,000 fewer people than at the earlier date, due to the overall growth in the Scottish population. The Irish losses after 1901 were substantial: there were around 29,500 fewer Irish in Scotland by 1911; a further 50,000 were lost in the 1911-31 period and a further drop of just under 40,000 occurred between 1931 and 1951.[12] In contrast to the nineteenth century, those who were dying were not being replaced by new immigrants. In 1901, there were over 200,000 Irish born people resident in Scotland. By 1951, that figure had shrunk to just over 86,500. Doubtless some of the Irish returned home, and certainly others moved overseas, but overall 'Irish emigrants had one of the lowest return rates to the homeland of any other nationality in Europe'.[13] As the Australian joke has it 'the Irish have invented a boomerang - it doesn't come back, it only sings about it'.

It was not as if the Irish had ceased to emigrate, it was merely that they had stopped coming to Scotland. Population loss in Ireland was phenomenal. In the 1950s immigration had reached 'levels not seen since the late nineteenth century'.[14] By 1961, 'a scarcely imaginable 45 per cent of all those born in Ireland between 1931 and 1936 and 40 per cent of those born between 1936 and 1941 had left'.[15] Restrictions and quotas had greatly reduced Irish emigration to the USA in the 1920s, so that 'after 1930 the overwhelming majority of emigrants went to Britain and not the United States.'[16]

Most of those who went to Britain settled in London, the South of England and the Midlands, areas where construction workers, female servants and factory workers were in demand. Traditional destinations such as Scotland, Lancashire, and the North East (of England) were in recession, and unemployment in these regions remained well in excess of the National Average even after the end of World War II.[17]

Proximity to Britain and the ease of getting to and from there, meant that emigration did not have to be permanent, but the lack of opportunities in Ireland and the better rates of pay to be had across the Irish Sea, acted as disincentives to those contemplating a permanent return home. Irish women were now in demand as domestic servants which they had not been for much of the nineteenth century. Part of their popularity lay in the low wages and poor conditions that they would tolerate.[18]

In Dunbartonshire where the Irish had once settled in large numbers, they accounted for 8.7% of the the county's total population in 1901, compared to the national share of 4.6% (see Table 13:1 above). Across four census points - 1901, 1911, 1931, and 1951, the county figures followed the national trend of decline. So that over those fifty years, the county had just under twice the national average of a dwindling Irish population. By 1851, 3.3% of the county's population was Irish born, whereas the national figure was 1.7%. Over the 1931-1951 period, there was a drop of 2,109 in the Irish population of Dunbartonshire.[19]

In 1951, half of Dunbartonshire's population had been born in the county, which was about the same as the proportion for Dumbarton burgh in 1891. The Vale had a slightly higher percentage of 'locals' living there in 1891 (~ 55%).

The Scots continued moving to, and within, the West Central region, which had been the focus for growth in the second half of the nineteenth century. By 1951, the County of Dunbartonshire had 31.3% of its population born in the 'neighbouring counties'. This was slightly higher than the figures for the Vale and Dumbarton in 1891.[20] Clearly, the Scots were still highly mobile, and for those who chose to stay in Scotland, most of that movement was conducted within the West Central area dominated by the Clydeside conurbation.

One striking feature of the in-migrant stream in Dunbartonshire at the 1951 census, is the number of Glasgow born residents, whose citizens made up nearly two-thirds of the 'neighbouring Scots' in the county (19.1%, of the total county population). This is indicative of the dominance of Glasgow. In 1891, the Vale of Leven and Dumbarton had around 10%-11% of their population born in Lanarkshire, including Glasgow, but after a large boundary extension in 1912, Glasgow encompassed not only parts of Lanarkshire, but 'populous industrial burghs' such as Pollokshaws, which was formerly part of Renfrewshire. This extension added around 224,000 people to the city, taking its total population to over a million.[21] Additionally, in 1937, part of New Kilpatrick parish was also transferred to 'the county of Lanark (city of Glasgow)' and it contained upwards of 1000 people who would have been resident in Dunbartonshire in 1951 had the boundary not changed.[22] It is likely that the location of the Glasgow born population of Dunbartonshire was skewed towards the eastern part of the county, where Clydebank abuts Glasgow and where Bearsden, Milngavie, and Lenzie were becoming ever more important dormitory settlements, housing many of the city's 'professional and managerial' workers.

The county had long been an area of strong in-migration. It was the only county in Scotland that recorded a substantial mean net in-migration over the 'emigration' decade of the 1880s (7%), when the biggest losses were recorded in the rural counties both north and south of the Central Belt.[23]

The Scots were susceptible to migration. In Western Europe from 1855 until 1913, overseas emigration of Scots 'per head of population exceeded those of any country other than Ireland and probably Norway, in this period (and the Scottish rate was actually the highest of any Western European country in the 1920s)'.[24]

'Some evidence suggests that from the later nineteenth century the volume of emigration varied inversely with internal migration'.[25] This was certainly true for Dunbartonshire in the 1871-81 decade when its population rose by 28%. In that period, the Vale's population growth was well above the county average at 41%. It had certainly rebounded after the travails of the previous decade. And whereas Dumbarton's growth was below the county average at 18%, it maintained a strong and steady growth begun in the 1850s.[26] In the years 1871 to 1881, the indigenous population was joined by the Northern Irish in the movement to towns and cities in Scotland's Central Belt. This decade coincided with a slump in emigration from Scotland.[27] Between 1901 and 1911, which was a period of strong emigration, only the counties of Dunbarton, Fife and Renfrew 'all areas where mining and heavy industry were prospering at this time, show net inflow'.[28] High levels of emigration continued until the beginning of the Great War when it all but disappeared, recovering quickly into the early twenties. 'After 1930, gross overseas emigration collapsed with the onset of worldwide depression'.[29] From 1900 until 1930 the rate of Scots emigration was, per head of population, much greater than that of England and Wales.[30] Indeed, it had been higher since the 1860s, and 'from 1881 to 1931, Wales lost an average of 17 inhabitants per thousand; England 14; but the Scottish figure was 35 per thousand'.[31] Scotland lost many people to England and beyond, but this internal UK movement was not reciprocated.[32]

After the Second World War, emigration resumed. 'Between 1951 and 1981, 753,000 Scots left the country, around 45% of them for England and the rest for new lives overseas'.[33]

In the immediate post war decades, few Scottish families were unaffected by the loss of friends, relatives, acquaintances or neighbours who left for Canada, the USA, Australia, New Zealand or South Africa, as well as England.

NOTES

1 *TSA* Vol 6 p. 204

2 Jones and Hopner, *On Leven's Banks.* pp. 39-48

3 Vale of Leven History Project, *www.valeofleven.org.uk/valeindustry4.*

4 Jones and Hopner, *On Leven's Banks.* pp. 49-51

5 MacPhail. *Dumbarton Through the Centuries.* p. 96

6 Ibid. p. 97

7 Anderson, *Scotland's Populations* Table 7.4 p. 106

8 *TSA.* Vol 6 p. 55

9 *TSA.* Vol 6 pp. 52-9, pp. 190-1, pp. 202

10 Anderson, *Scotland's Populations* p. 144

11 *TSA.* Vol 6 p. 55. Although there was a 'slight increase' in the numbers of Irish in Dunbartonshire by 1911, the overall population of the county was growing faster relative to its Irish population, hence the percentage decline between 1901 and 1911 shown in table 13:1.

12 *Source:* Anderson, *Scotland's Populations* Table 8.1 p. 115 and Table 9.2 p. 143

13 Devine, *To the Ends of the Earth.* p.128 cites T. Guinnane, *The Vanishing Irish: Households, Migration and the Rural Economy in Ireland 1850-1914.* (1997) p. 107; and J. Bodner, *The Transplanted: A History of Immigrants in Urban America.* (1985) p. 53

14 M. Daly, *The Slow Failure. Population Decline and Independent Ireland 1920-1973* (2006) p.184

15 F. O'Toole, *We Don't Know Ourselves. A Personal History of Ireland Since 1958* (2021) p. 14. citing Daly, Ibid.

16 Daly, The Slow Failure p. 140

17 Ibid. p. 141

18 *See for example* L. Dulap. *'Yes ma'am: domestic workers and employment rights'* historyandpolicy.org (2012)

[19] *TSA* Vol 6 pp. 55-6

[20] *Thesis,* Table 14:1 p. 238 and Table 14:2 p. 246

[21] A. Gibb, *Glasgow. The Making of a city* (1983) pp. 124-5 Table 6.ii. Glasgow's population in 1911 was 784,496. Its boundaries were considerably extended by the Glasgow Boundaries Act Annexation and this brought the population of the city to over a million. So that Glasgow in 1912 contained one in five of the total population of Scotland.

[22] *TSA* Vol 6 p. 55

[23] Anderson, *Scotland's Populations* Table 8.5 p. 130. Bute, with a growth of 0.3% was the only other county to show any increase.

[24] Ibid. p. 143

[25] Devine, *To the Ends of the Earth* pp. 100-1

[26] *TSA.* Vol 6 p. 52. See also Chapter 10.

[27] Anderson, *Scotland's Populations* Figure 9:3 p. 141

[28] Ibid. p. 132

[29] Ibid. p. 143

[30] Ibid. Figure 9:3 p. 141

[31] Devine, *To the Ends of the Earth* p. 88

[32] Anderson, *Scotland's Populations* p. 119

[33] Devine, *To the Ends of the Earth* p. 270

Afterword

Them and Us? Cooperation and Conflict into the Twenty-First Century

Manoeuvrings to find out name and school…
with hardly an exception to the rule…[1]

Irish immigration to Scotland declined greatly in the first half of the twentieth century, but the descendants of Irish immigrants make up a significant proportion of its population. Over the years there has been a gradual assimilation of this ethnic group within Scottish society. But the journey has not always been a smooth one. Discrimination has been rife as obstacles were placed in the way of progress, so that it was difficult for people to achieve parity.

The final chapter and conclusion of Tom Gallagher's 'Glasgow the Uneasy Peace' (1987), and the last essay in 'New Perspectives on the Irish in Scotland' (2008, editor, Martin Mitchell) by Tom Devine, provide concise overviews of the Irish experience in modern Scotland.[2]

Devine refers to the descendants of the Irish in Scotland as 'Irish Scots' and I have used that term here. This is consistent with the terminology used to describe ethnic groups such as 'Irish Americans':- those who identify as having Irish ancestry and who live in the USA, a country of immigrants where there is a very keen sense of lineage and family ties to the 'Old World'.

Terms such as 'Ulster Scots' and 'Scots (Scotch) Irish' are used, without question, to describe the descendants of Scots who moved to the North of Ireland.[3] Nevertheless, in Scotland, many would regard labelling of this sort to be unnecessary in the twenty-first century. And yet, unlike many cities worldwide affected by the Irish diaspora, Glasgow, the epicentre of Irish immigration to Scotland, appears reluctant to acknowledge, let alone celebrate, the impact that this transformational movement of people has had on Scottish society.

225

Among all of this, when considering communities and conflict, we must remember 'the essential lesson':

the past cannot be understood as a story of simple tribal allegiances. Human relationships complicate every historical narrative and get in the way of absolute conclusions. [4]

NOTES

[1] S. Heaney, 'Whatever You Say Say Nothing' from his collection *'North'* (1975)

[2] Devine, 'The End of Disadvantage? The descendants of Irish-Catholic immigrants in modern Scotland since 1945' and Gallagher, Glasgow. *The Uneasy Peace* Ch 7 and Conclusion.

[3] Walker, *Intimate Strangers* p. 2, pp. 29-32

[4] F. Keane, *Wounds. A Memoir of War and Love* (2017) p. 266

Appendices

Appendix 1. Major Occupational Groupings

OCCUPATIONAL GROUPING	Census Year			
	1861	1871	1881	1891
Bleaching, Printing & Dyeing	61	49	58.5	52
Shipbuilding	2.5	3.5	3	4
Iron & Steel Trades	2.5	3.5	2.5	2.5
Machinery	1	1.5	1.5	2
Other Manufacturing	2	2.5	2.5	2
Agriculture	1	2	1.5	1
Mining & Quarrying	1	1	0.5	0.5
General Labouring	4	7	6	5.5
Building Trades	6.5	8	8	8
Public & Professional	2.5	2	1.5	3
No Job (as a percentage of the total male population)	35.5	35	33	39

Table 5:1 Selected Male Occupational Groupings in the Vale of Leven; expressed as a percentage of the employed male population sampled for each census year.

	CENSUS YEAR			
OCCUPATIONAL GROUPING	1861	1871	1881	1891
Bleaching, Printing & Dyeing	24.5	26	30	26.5
Clothing, Tailoring, Dress and Shoemaking	2	1.5	2.5	2
Public & Professional	0	0	0.5	1
Domestic Servants	2	3	1.5	1.5
Food & Drink Dealing	0.5	1	1	1
No Job	68	66	62.5	66.5

Table 5:2 Selected Female Occupational groupings in the Vale of Leven; expressed as a percentage of the total female population sampled for each census year.

	CENSUS YEAR			
OCCUPATIONAL GROUPING	1861	1871	1881	1891
Shipbuilding	25.5	41	44.5	39.5
Iron & Steel Trades	12	13	11.5	15
Machinery	7.5	1	5	8
Other Manufacturing	4	5	3.5	3
Agriculture	3.5	1	2	0.5
Mining & Quarrying	3	0.5	0	0
General Labouring	12	9.5	4	3.5
Public & Professional	4.5	3.5	2.5	4.5
Bleaching, Printing & Dyeing	-	-	1.5	0.5
No Job (as a percentage of the total male population)	37	38	37.5	40

Table 5:3 Selected Male Occupational Groupings in Dumbarton, expressed as a percentage of the employed male population sampled for each census year.

	CENSUS YEAR			
OCCUPATIONAL GROUPING	1861	1871	1881	1891
Domestic Service	6.5	5.5	4	4
Bleaching, Printing & Dyeing	0.5	2	8	6.5
Clothing, Tailoring Dress	1.5	2	1.5	3
Public & Professional	-	0.5	0.5	1
Food & Drink Dealing	1	1	1.5	1.5
No Job	80	85	81	80

Table 5:4 Selected Female Occupational Groupings in Dumbarton, expressed as a percentage of the total female population sampled for each census year.

Appendix 2. Social Classification of Males.

	CENSUS YEAR			
SOCIAL CLASSIFICATION	1861	1871	1881	1891
I Professional & Managerial	2	1.5	1.5	1.5
II Clerical	3	3.5	3	2.5
III Trade	3.5	7	5	7.5
IV Higher Factory	22	20	21	23.5
V Artizan	12	15	10.5	9
VI Lower Factory	44.5	36.5	45	41.5
VII Labourer	12.5	16.5	13.5	14
VIII Clothing Worker		0		0
IX Unclassified	0.5	0	0	0.5
III + V	15.5	22	15.5	16.5

Table 6:1 Social Classification of Males in the Vale of Leven (categorisation after Anderson 1972) expressed as a percentage of employed male population sampled for each census year.

	CENSUS YEAR			
SOCIAL CLASSIFICATION	1861	1871	1881	1891
I Professional & Managerial	3.5	3	2.5	3
II Clerical	2.5	3	2.5	4.5
III Trade	9.5	5	5.5	7
IV Higher Factory	28	37	36.5	38
V Artizan	18	13.5	13.5	11.5
VI Lower Factory	14	17.5	25.5	23
VII Labourer	23.5	19	14	12
VIII Clothing Worker	0	-	0	0
IX Unclassified	0.5	1	0	0.5
III + V	27.5	18.5	19	18.5

Table 6:2 Social Classification of Males in Dumbarton (categorisation after Anderson 1972) expressed as a percentage of employed male population sampled for each census year.

Appendix 3. Birthplaces of Inhabitants

	1861				1871				1881				1891			
	M	F	T	R	M	F	T	R	M	F	T	R	M	F	T	R
LOCAL	51	51.5	50.5	-	54	51.5	52.5	-	53	48	50.5	-	58.5	53.5	55.5	-
IRELAND	9	11.5	10	1	9	9.5	9.5	1	12	14.5	13.5	1	7.5	10	10	2
RENFREW	5.5	4.5	5	5	5	5.5	5.5	4	4	4.5	4	4	4	5	5	4
ARGYLL	5.5	7	6	3	3	3.5	3	6	2.5	3.5	3	6	2	2	2	7
AYR	1.5	2	1.5	7	2	2.5	2.5	7	2.5	3	3	7	2	2.5	2	6
REST OF DUNBARTON	4.5	4.5	4.5	6	4	5	4.5	5	3	4	3.5	5	3.5	3	3	5
STIRLING	6	5.5	6	4	6	7.5	7	3	6.5	6	6	3	9.5	8.5	9	3
LANARK	9.5	9.5	9.5	2	9	7.5	8	2	10.5	10	10	2	8.5	11	10	1
LOTHIAN	1	0.5	1	11	0.5	1	0.5	11	1	1.5	1.5	9	1	0.5	0.5	11
FORFAR/ PERTH	2	1	1.5	9	2	2	2	8	2	2	2	8	2	1	1.5	8
NORTH	1	1	1	10	2	1.5	2	9	0.5	1	0.5	11	1	1	1	9
NORTH-EAST	-	-	-	14	0.5	0	0.5	13	0.5	0.5	0.5	12	0	0.5	0	14
SOUTH	0.5	0.5	0.5	12	0.5	1	0.5	11	0	0	0	14	0.5	0.5	0.5	12
ENGLAND & WALES	2	1.5	1.5	7	1.5	1.5	1.5	10	1.5	1	1	10	1	1	1	10
OTHER	0	0.5	0.5	13	0	0.5	0.5	13	0.5	0	0.5	12	0.5	0	0.5	13

Table 10:1. Birthplaces of the Inhabitants of the Vale of Leven 1861 - 1891.

*'Local' born are those born in Dumbarton, Cardross and Bonhill
Parishes.
Key:
Cells show percentage of population born in each of the areas listed. (From the sample to the nearest 0.5 %)
F= percentage of female population
M= percentage of the male population
T= percentage of the total population
R= Areas in Rank order 1-13

	1861				1871				1881				1891			
	M	F	T	R	M	F	T	R	M	F	T	R	M	F	T	R
LOCAL	40	44.5	42.5	-	44	46	45	-	45.5	49	47.5	-	46.5	50.5	48.5	-
IRELAND	23.5	19	21.5	1	19	15.5	17.5	1	22.5	15	19	1	17.5	13	15.5	1
RENFREW	7.5	6.5	7	3	4.5	5.5	5	3	4	5	4.5	3	4.5	4.5	4.5	3
ARGYLL	2.5	3	3	5	3	3	3	5	2	2.5	2	7	2.5	2.5	2.5	6
AYR	2.5	2.5	2.5	6	4	3	3.5	4	2.5	3.5	3	5	2.5	3	3	5
REST OF DUNBARTON	3.5	3.5	3.5	4	2.5	3	2.5	6	2	2.5	2	8	2	2	2	9
STIRLING	2	2.5	2	7	1.5	3	2.5	7	3.5	3.5	3.5	4	3.5	3.5	3.5	4
LANARK	8.5	9.5	9	2	9.5	10.5	10	2	7	10.5	8.5	2	10.5	11	11	2
LOTHIAN	1	1.5	1.5	11	2	2.5	2.5	8	1.5	2	1.5	10	2	1	1.5	10
FORFAR/PERTH	2	2	2	8	2.5	2	2	9	3	2	2.5	6	3	1.5	2.5	7
NORTH	1.5	1	1.5	11	1.5	1.5	1.5	11	2	1.5	1.5	10	1	1.5	1	12
NORTH-EAST	1	1	1	13	2.5	2	2	9	1	0.5	1	13	1	0.5	1	13
SOUTH	1.5	1.5	1.5	9	1.5	1.5	1.5	12	1.5	1	1	12	1.5	1	1.5	11
ENGLAND & WALES	2	1.5	1.5	9	1.5	1.5	1.5	12	2	1.5	2	9	2	2.5	2.5	7
OTHER	0.5	0	0	14	0	0	0	14	0.5	0.5	0.5	14	0.5	0.5	0.5	14

Table 10:2. Birthplaces of the Inhabitants of Dumbarton 1861 - 1891
Key as in 10:1 above.

Appendix 4. Social Status of Employed Males by Place of Birth

Dates		I	II	III	IV	V	VI	VII	VIII	IX
1861	Total	2	3	3.5	22	12	44.5	12.5	-	0.5
	Nearby Scots	2	3	4	23.5	12.5	40.5	14	-	-
	Irish	-	1.5	1.5	10.5	9	47.5	31	-	-
	Others	7	1.5	-	27.5	20.5	27.5	15.5	-	-
1871	Total	1.5	3.5	7	20	15	36.5	16.5	0	0
	Nearby Scots	2.5	4	9	21.5	19	30.5	13.5	-	-
	Irish	-	-	3.5	7.5	7.5	41.5	40	-	-
	Others	2.5	4	11	17.5	24.5	28.5	12	-	-
1881	Total	1.5	3	5	21	10.5	45	13.5	-	0
	Nearby Scots	3.5	2.5	5.5	22.5	12.5	44	9.5	-	0.5
	Irish	-	-	-	6	9	43.5	42	-	-
	Others	5	1.5	3.5	19.5	13	46	11.5	-	-
1891	Total	1.5	2.5	7.5	23.5	9	41.5	14	0	0.5
	Nearby Scots	3	2	7.5	26	11.5	39	11	-	-
	Irish	-	-	4	17.5	1	49	28.5	-	-
	Others	3.5	5.5	16	23	12.5	30.5	9	-	-

Figure 10:3 – The Social Status of Employed Males in the Vale of Leven (categorisation after Anderson 1972) : 'Neighbouring Scots', Irish and 'Others': expressed as a percentage for each group.

Dates		I	II	III	IV	V	VI	VII	VIII	IX
1861	Total	3.5	2.5	9.5	28	18	14	23.5	0	0.5
	Nearby Scots	2.5	1.5	12.5	39.5	24	7.5	11.5	-	1
	Irish	1		1	17	7	26	48	-	-
	Others	10	5	7.5	35.5	29	3.5	10	-	-
1871	Total	3	3	5	37	13.5	17.5	19	-	1
	Nearby Scots	4	3	6.5	43	19	10	14.5	-	-
	Irish	-	0.5	1.5	20.5	7.5	31.5	38.5	-	1
	Others	5.5	5	5	49	17.5	8.5	9.5	-	-
1881	Total	2.5	2.5	5.5	36.5	13.5	25.5	14	0	0
	Nearby Scots	3	3	6	43.5	16.5	14.5	13	0.5	-
	Irish	-	0.5	5	19.5	6	50.5	19	-	-
	Others	4	3	6.5	43	23.5				
1891	Total	3	4.5	7	38	11.5	23	12	0	0.5
	Nearby Scots	4	6.5	12.5	37	16.5	14.5	8.5	-	-
	Irish	1	-	4.5	26.5	3.5	48	16.5	-	-
	Others	3	4	6	42	17.5	11	14.5	-	2

Figure 10:4 – The Social Status of Employed Males in Dumbarton (categorisation after Anderson 1972): 'Neighbouring Scots', Irish and 'Others', expressed as a percentage for each group.

SOURCES and BIBLIOGRAPHY

Unpublished Census Enumerators' Books

A stratified random sample of 'households' (co-residing groups) from the 1861, 1871, 1881 and 1891 censuses was taken from each enumeration district in Alexandria, Bonhill Village, Renton, Jamestown and Dumbarton Burgh. Details of eight hundred households for the 1861 census and one thousand households for each of the 1871, 1881, and 1891 censuses, divided equally between the Vale and Dumbarton, were examined.

Printed Census Documents

Population tables II , Vol I England and Wales Divisions VII-XI. Scotland. Islands. 1851

Census: Population report Scotland. Vol I 1891

Population Scotland Vol I 1901

Statistical Accounts

Old Statistical Account of Scotland -Bonhill Vol III. (1792); Cardross Vol XVII. (1796); Dumbarton Vol IV. (1792)

New Statistical Account of Scotland -Volume VIII (1845)

M.S. Dilke and A.A.Templeton (eds), *The Third Statistical Account of Scotland,* Volume 6 The County of Dunbarton (1959)

Newspapers and Directories

Dumbarton Herald

Glasgow Herald

Lennox Herald

Dumbartonshire Directory (published by Bennett Brothers. George Langlands Post Office. Dumbarton) (1877)

The Dumbartonshire Directory 1885

Dumbarton Directory and Almanac 1892

Dumbarton Directory and Almanac 1892-3

Websites and on-line resources.
(In alphabetical order by web site address)

The Great Irish Famine. BBC Radio 4, from the *'In Our Time'* series, 4 April 2019,
Today programme BBC Radio 4, 4 March 2023 both available on BBC Sounds.

Immigrants and Exiles - *Irish in Scotland - Official Documents. bbc.co.uk*

encyclopedia-titanica.org

L. Dulap. *'Yes ma'am: domestic workers and employment rights' historyandpolicy.org* (2012)

C. Kinealy, Food Exports from Ireland (1997) *https:// www.historyireland.com/18th-19th-century-history/food-exports-from-ireland-1846-47/*

National Library of Scotland http://nls.uk

Oxford Reference at *oxfordreference.com*

Medical Officer of Health reports 1891 - Dunbartonshire. p.19
scotlandsplaces.gov.uk

scottish-places.info

'Shipping lines involved in New Zealand Immigration' *https://
sites.rootsweb.com/~nzbound/lines.htm*

taxjustice.net

tribalpages.com

Twitter - *@WDCHeritage*

Vale of Leven History Project.*www.valeofleven.org.uk/*

Levenford; Shipbuilding in Dumbarton; and, Textile Industry in the
Vale of Leven, Factsheets at *www.wdcweb.info/library*

Maps

Dumbarton Burgh Map (1832) published by the electoral boundaries
commission at a scale of six inches to one mile. (1: 10,560)

First addition of the Ordnance Survey Maps of Dumbarton and the
Vale of Leven (published 1864). Surveys for the maps were carried
out for Dumbarton in 1860 and the Vale of Leven in 1859-60.

An update of the first edition Ordnance Survey Map of the Vale of
Leven (dated 1879) in J. Irving, Book of Dumbartonshire Vol 1

Second addition of the Ordnance Survey Maps of Dumbarton and the Vale of Leven (published 1899)
Surveys for the maps were carried out in 1896-7.

Both first and second additions were published at a scales of 1:10,560 and 1:2,500 or approximately six inches to the mile and twenty five inches to the mile respectively.

Photographs

Some of the photographs here are unattributed as their provenance is unknown. Most are by courtesy of West Dunbartonshire Council Arts and Heritage Service and were digitised by William Henderson and Mary Frances McGlynn. I have used one photograph from from James Lyon's 'Dumbarton Building Society. !873 -1923, Fifty Years History' and two from John Hood's book 'Old Dumbarton' published by Stenlake Publishing in 1999. John acknowledges the photographs in his book as being from Dave Crocker's collection. I have been unable to contact either man to obtain permission to use them. I hope that an attribution will satisfy both.

Unpublished Sources

C.G. Docherty, *The Growth and Morphology of Dumbarton* (1975) Undergraduate dissertation, Department of Geography, University of Strathclyde.

_____ The growth of the Vale of Leven (1981) M.Litt Postgraduate Dissertation, Department of Geography and Topographic Science, University of Glasgow.

_____ Migration, Ethnicity and Residence in contrasting West of Scotland Settlements. The Case of Dumbarton and The

Vale of Leven 1861-1891(1988) Ph.D Thesis, Department of Geography and Topographic Science, University of Glasgow.

Articles and Selected Bibliography

I.H. Adams, *The Making of Urban Scotland* (1978)

J. Agnew, *The Story of the Vale of Leven* (1975)

L. Alcock, 'A multi-disciplinary chronology for Alt Clut, Castle Rock, Dumbarton' *Proceedings of the Society of Antiquaries, Scotland, 107* (1975-6) pp. 104-5

M. Anderson, 'Standard tabulation procedures for the Census Enumerators' Books 1851-1891' in E.A. Wrigley (ed) *Nineteenth Century Society. Essays in the Use of Quantitative Data. Methods for the Study of Social Data* (1972)

M. Anderson, *Scotland's Populations from the 1850s to today* (2018)

B. Aspinwall, 'Catholic Devotion in Victorian Scotland' in Mitchell (ed) *New Perspectives*

B. Braber, 'The influence of immigration on the growth, urban concentration and composition of the Scottish population 1841-1911' *Journal of Scottish Historical Studies* 32 (2) (2012)

_____, in T. Devine and J. Wormald (eds) *The Oxford Handbook of Modern Scottish History* (2012) Ch 26

D. Bremner, *The Industries of Scotland, their Rise Progress and Present Condition.* (1869 Reprinted in 1967)

J. Burrow, and co. (eds), *Denny 1844-1932* (1933)

J. Butt, 'Labour and Industrial Relations in the Scottish Cotton Industry during The Industrial Revolution' in J. Butt and K.G.Ponting, (eds) *Scottish Textile Industry.* (1987)

J. Butt and K.G.Ponting, (eds) *Scottish Textile Industry* (1987)

I.Brown (ed) *Changing Identities Ancient Roots the history of West Dunbartonshire from earliest times* (2006)

M. Brown, *The Wars of Scotland 1214-1371* (2004) online version (2012)

R.H. Campbell, *Scotland since 1707. The rise of an Industrial Society* (1971)

_____ , *The Rise and Fall of Scottish Industry* (1980)

E.A. Cameron, *Impaled Upon a Thistle. Scotland since 1880* (2010)

D. Cannadine, *Victorious Century. The United Kingdom 1800 - 1906* (2017)

T.J. Clarkson, *Strathclyde and the Anglo-Saxons in the Viking Age* (2014)

B. Collins, 'Irish emigration to Dundee and Paisley during the first half of the 19th century' in J.M. Goldstrom and L.A.

Clarkson (eds) *Irish Population, Economy & Society:Essays in honour of the late K. H. Connell* (1981)

_____ 'The Origins of Irish Immigration to Scotland' in Devine (ed) *Irish Immigrants and Scottish Society*

S. Connolly, *On Every Tide: The making and remaking of the Irish World* (2022)

A. Cooke, *The Rise and Fall of the Scottish Cotton Industry 1778-1914.* (2010)

J. Crowley, W.J. Smyth and M. Murphy (eds) *Atlas of the Great Irish Famine* (2012)

G. Davis, 'Little Irelands' in R. Swift and S. Gilley (eds) *The Irish in Britain 1815 - 1939* (1989)

T.M. Devine, *The Great Highland Famine. Hunger, Emigration and the Scottish Highlands in the Nineteenth Century* (1988)

_____(ed) *Irish Immigrants and Scottish Society in the Nineteenth and Twentieth Centuries* (1991)

_____ 'The Great Irish Famine and Scottish History' in Mitchell (ed) *New Perspectives* p. 20

_____ 'The End of Disadvantage? The descendants of Irish-Catholic immigrants in modern Scotland since 1945' in Mitchell, *New Perspectives*

_____ *To the Ends of the Earth. Scotland's Global Diaspora 1750-2010* (2011)

_____ *The Scottish Nation. A Modern History* (2012)

_____ *The Scottish Clearances. A History of the Dispossessed* (2018)

T. Devine and J. Wormald (eds) *The Oxford Handbook of Modern Scottish History* (2012)

T. Dickson, (ed) *Capital and Class in Scotland* (1982)

C.G.Docherty,'The Growth and Decline of the Bleaching, Printing and Dyeing Industry in the Vale of Leven', *Scottish Industrial History*. Vol 8:2 (1985), pp. 4-14

S.T. Driscoll, 'Celtic Britain in the Early Historical Period' in J. Hunter and I. Ralston (eds) *The Archaeology of Britain, An introduction from earliest times to the* i *Century*, 2nd Edition (2009)

R.J.Findlay, 'Urbanisation and Industrialisation: West Dunbartonshire since 1750', Ch 4 p. 71
In I. Brown, (ed) *Changing Identities Ancient Roots*

D. Fitzpatrick, 'A Curious Middle Place: the Irish in Britain, 1871 - 1921', in Swift and Gilley (eds) *The Irish in Britain*

M. Flinn, et al, *Scottish Population History from the Seventeenth Century to the Nineteen Thirties* (1977)

S. Forder, *The Romans in Scotland and the Battle of Mons Graupius* (2022)

J. Foster, et al, 'Sectarianism, Segregation and Politics in Clydeside in the later Nineteenth Century' in M. Mitchell, (ed) *New Perspectives on the Irish in Scotland* (2008)

R.F. Foster, *Modern Ireland 1600-1972* (1988)

J. Fraser, *From Caledonia to Pictland: Scotland to 795* (2009)

R. Gallacher, 'The Vale of Leven 1914-1975: Changes in Working Class Organisation and Action' in T. Dickson, (ed) *Capital and Class in Scotland* (1982)

T. Gallagher, *Glasgow. The Uneasy Peace* (1987)

T. Gallagher, The Catholic Irish in Scotland: In Search of Identity, in Devine *Irish Immigrants and Scottish Society*

T. Griffiths and G. Morton, *A History of Everyday life in Scotland 1800-1900* (2010)

T. Griffiths, 'Work, Leisure and Time' in *Ibid.*

F.H. Groome (ed) *Ordnance Gazeteer of Scotland: A study of Scottish Topography, Statistical, Biographical and Historical* (1882-85)

H. Hamilton, *The Industrial Revolution in Scotland.* Reprint (1966)

B. Harris and C. McKean, *The Scottish Town in the Age of the Enlightenment 1740-1820* (2014)

J.E. Handley, *The Irish in Modern Scotland* (1947)

R. Hattersley, *The Catholics* (2017)

S. Heaney, *North* (1975)

R. Hewitt, *Map of a Nation: A Biography of the Ordnance Survey* (2011)

J. Hood, *Old Dumbarton* (1999)

I.G.C. Hutchison, *Industry, Reform and Empire Scotland, 1790-1880* (2020)

J. Irving, *The History of Dumbartonshire: From the earliest period to the present time* (1857)

_____ *The Book of Dunbartonshire* (1860)

J. H. Johnson, 'Harvest Labour Migration from Nineteenth Century Ireland' *Transactions of the Institute of British Geographers* No 41 (1967)

J.H. Johnson and C. G. Pooley, *The Structure of Nineteenth Century Cities* (1982)

A.F. Jones and G.N. Hopner, *On Leven's Banks* (1980)

E. Kane, *Sightlines. Beyond the Beyond in Ireland* (2022)

F. Keane, *Wounds. A Memoir of War and Love* (2017)

L. Levi, 'On the Cotton Trade and Manufacture as Affected by the Civil War in America'. *Journal of the Royal Statistical Society* (1863) Vol 26 No1 pp 26-48

D.G. Lockhart, 'Patterns of Migration and Movement of Labour to the Planned Villages of North East Scotland' *Scottish Geographical Magazine* Vol 98 (1) (1982)

J. Lyon, *Jubilee Souvenir of Dumbarton Building Society. 1873 - 1923 Fifty Years History* (1923)

I.MacDougall, (ed) *Essays in Scottish Labour History* (1978)

I.M.M. MacPhail, *Dumbarton through the Centuries* (1972)

D.M. MacRaild, *Irish Migrants in Modern Britain 1750-1922* (1999)

D. Macleod, *History of the Castle and Town of Dumbarton.* (1877)

_____ *Dumbarton, Vale of Leven and Loch Lomond* (1884)

E. McFarland, *Protestants First! Orangeism in 19th Century Scotland* (1991)

J.D. Marwick, *The River Clyde and the Clyde Burghs* (1909)

J. Melling, 'Scottish Industrialists and the Changing Character of Class Relations in the Clyde Region c.1880-1918', in T. Dickson (ed) *Capital and Class in Scotland*

I. Meredith, 'Irish Migrants in the Scottish Episcopal Church in the 19th Century', in Mitchell (ed) *New Perspectives*

F. Neal, *Black '47: Britain and the Irish Famine* (1998)

S. Nenadic and S. Tuckett, *The Turkey Red Printed Cotton Industry in Scotland c 1840-1940* (2013)

C. O'Grada, 'A Note on 19th Century Irish Emigration Statistics' *Population Studies* Vol. 29 (1975)

R. Oram, *Domination and Lordship: Scotland 1070-1230* (2011)

_____, *Alexander II, King of Scots 1214-1249* (2012)

B.D. Osborne, 'Dumbarton shipbuilding and workers' housing 1850-1900' *Scottish Urban History* Vol 3 (1) (1980)

C. Pooley, 'The Residential Segregation of Migrant Communities in Mid Victorian Liverpool' *The Institute of British Geographers* NS 2 (3) (1977)

_____ 'Segregation or Integration. The residential experience of the Irish in mid-Victorian Britain', in Swift and Gilley (eds) *The Irish in Britain*

J.F. Riddell, *The Clyde. The Making of a River* (1979)

P. Robertson, 'Shipping and Shipbuilding. The Case of William Denny and Brothers', *Business History* Vol 16 Issue 1 (1974)

R. Rodger, 'Employment, Wages and Poverty in the Scottish Cities 1841-1914' in G.Gordon, (ed) *Perspectives of the Scottish City* (1985)

J.Schwerin, 'The evolution of the Clyde region's shipbuilding innovation system in the second half of the nineteenth century' in *Journal of Economic Geography* Vol 4 Issue 1 (2004)

J. Shields, *Clyde Built: A history of shipbuilding on the Clyde* (1949)

A. Slaven, *The Development of the West of Scotland 1750-1960* (1975)

W. Sloan, 'Religious Affiliation and the Immigrant Experience: Catholic Irish and Protestant Highlanders in Glasgow 1830-1850.' in Devine, *Irish Immigrants and Scottish society*

T.C. Smout, *A Century of the Scottish People 1830-1950* (1986)

D. Spaven, *The Railway Atlas of Scotland. Two Hundred Years of History* (2015)

R. Swift and S. Gilley (eds) *The Irish in Britain 1815-1939* (1989)

N. Tarrent, 'The Turkey Red Dyeing Industry in the Vale of Leven' in J. Butt and K.G. Ponting (eds) *Scottish Textile Industry*

M.A.G. O'Tuathaigh, 'The Irish in Nineteenth Century Britain: Problems of Integration' *Royal Historical Society Transactions* 31, (1981)

S. Taylor, 'The Early History and Languages of West Dunbartonshire' in I.Brown (ed) *Changing Identities Ancient Roots, the history of West Dunbartonshire from earliest times* (2006)

G. Vaughan, *The 'Local' Irish in the West of Scotland 1831-1921* (2013)

G. Walker, *Intimate Strangers. Political and cultural interaction between Scotland and Ulster in modern times* (1995)

K.L. Wallwork, 'The Calico Printing Industry of Lancastria in the 1840s' *Transactions of the Institute of British Geographers.* Vol 45 (1968)

J.T. Ward, 'Textile Trade Unionism in 19th century Scotland', in Butt and Ponting, *Scottish Textile Industry*

I. Wood, 'Irish Immigrants and Scottish Radicalism 1880-1906' in I. MacDougall, (ed) *Essays in Scottish Labour History*

E.A. Wrigley (ed) *Nineteenth Century Society. Essays in the use of quantitative methods for the study of social data* (1972)

Acknowledgements

This book has been long in the making and many people have made significant contributions. Kathleen has typed, proof read and provided insightful comments and criticism throughout. Both Theo, who transcribed the tables and graphs from their original state into their current form with absolute accuracy, and Shauna, who placed maps, diagrams, photographs and tables within the text, provided expertise without which the book would never have been completed. Ken reviewed the text and offered helpful suggestions which improved the end product.

Paul Murdoch has offered advice on preparing a manuscript for publication and priceless information on finding a publisher and the potential and pitfalls of self-publishing. Were it not for him, this book would have come to fruition very much later than it did. William Henderson and Mary Frances McGlynn of West Dunbartonshire Council's Heritage Department unselfishly helped locate sources and prepare photographs from their archive for publication. Those interested in local history would also do well to visit their web pages at *https://www.west- dunbarton.gov.uk/libraries/archives*

I thank all local historians who give generously of their time so that others benefit from their hard work and expertise. In particular, locals are very lucky to have the Vale of Leven History Project for reference. I didn't know Harry Summers, but the work that he and his fellow local historians have done to bring the history of the Vale to life is very special.

I want to use this opportunity to acknowledge the help given to me at the University of Glasgow many years ago when I submitted the PhD Thesis, on which a lot of the statistical data used here is based. Bunty Edgar, Jacqueline Wellington, Aileen Urquhart, Bette Gibb and John Buchanan provided technical advice and first rate administrative support. A special debt was due to Eddie Toole who used his own time, equipment and expertise to run programs from home while linked to a mainframe computer at the university. This saved me weeks of travel to the university in the days before WiFi, mobile phones and iPads made life a lot easier.

Finally, I would like to pay tribute to my research supervisor, the late Andy Gibb, formerly Senior Lecturer in the Department of Geography and Topographic Science at the University of Glasgow. Andy's constant help, encouragement, good humour, optimism and friendship were vital in steering me through my research. Andy often told me that there was 'a book in there' if only I'd write it.

Page numbers in italics indicate photographs. The page numbers of graphs and maps are listed in bold.
References to notes are shown by the use of 'n'.

256

Dumbarton High Street circa 1895

Alexandria at the Fountain circa 1904

Milton Keynes UK
Ingram Content Group UK Ltd.
UKHW031849170324
439575UK00014B/781